BLACK AMERICANS

Third Edition

ALPHONSO PINKNEY

Hunter College
The City University of New York

PRENTICE-HALL, INC., Englewood Cliffs, New Jersey 07632

Library of Congress Cataloging-in-Publication Data

Pinkney, Alphonso.
  Black Americans.

  (Ethnic groups in American life series)
  Includes bibliography and index.
  1. Afro-Americans—History I. Title. II. Series.
E185.P5 1987   973'.0496073   86-18680
ISBN 0-13-077488-X

For My People

Editorial/production supervision and
  interior design: Mary Bardoni
Manufacturing buyer: John B. Hall

Prentice-Hall Ethnic Groups in American Life Series

© **1987, 1975, 1969 by Prentice-Hall, Inc.**
A Division of Simon & Schuster
Englewood Cliffs, New Jersey 07632

Printed in the United States of America

10 9 8 7 6 5 4 3 2 1

ISBN   0-13-077488-X   01

Prentice-Hall International (UK) Limited, *London*
Prentice-Hall of Australia Pty. Limited, *Sydney*
Prentice-Hall Canada Inc., *Toronto*
Prentice-Hall Hispanoamericana, S.A., *Mexico*
Prentice-Hall of India Private Limited, *New Delhi*
Prentice-Hall of Japan, Inc., *Tokyo*
Prentice-Hall of Southeast Asia Pte. Ltd., *Singapore*
Editora Prentice-Hall do Brasil, Ltda., *Rio de Janeiro*

ETHNIC GROUPS
IN AMERICAN LIFE SERIES

ALBA	ITALIAN AMERICANS: Into the Twilight of Ethnicity
FITZPATRICK	PUERTO RICAN AMERICANS: The Meaning of Migration to the Mainland, *Second Edition*
KITANO	JAPANESE AMERICANS: The Evolution of a Subculture, *Second Edition*
MOORE	MEXICAN AMERICANS, *Second Edition*
PINKNEY	BLACK AMERICANS, *Third Edition*
WAX	INDIAN AMERICANS: Unity and Diversity

The American Negro is a unique creation;
he has no counterpart anywhere and no
predecessors.

JAMES BALDWIN

CONTENTS

PREFACE   vii

CHAPTER ONE
HISTORICAL BACKGROUND   1

    Slavery, *1*   The Civil War, *15*   The Reconstruction, *19*
    Institutionalized White Supremacy, *23*   Selected Bibliography, *31*
    Notes, *33*

CHAPTER TWO
CHARACTERISTICS OF THE POPULATION   36

    Size and Growth, *36*   Fertility, *37*   Health and Mortality, *39*
    Age and Sex Composition, *41*   Distribution, *43*
    Selected Bibliography, *49*   Notes, *49*

CHAPTER THREE
THE BLACK COMMUNITY   51

    Growth and Development, *51*   Rural Black Communities, *53*
    The Urban Black Community, *56*   Social Stratification, *59*
    Selected Bibliography, *66*   Notes, *67*

CHAPTER FOUR
SOCIOECONOMIC STATUS   69

    Education, *69*   Occupational Status, *77*   Income, *86*
    Selected Bibliography, *91*   Notes, *92*

CHAPTER FIVE
SOCIAL INSTITUTIONS   95

    The Family, *95*   Politics, *106*   Religion, *115*
    Selected Bibliography, *125*   Notes, *126*

Contents

CHAPTER SIX
SOCIAL DEVIANCE   130

Crime and Delinquency, *131*   Mental Illness, *138*
Drug Addiction (Substance Abuse), *143*   Selected Bibliography, *148*
Notes, *149*

CHAPTER SEVEN
ASSIMILATION INTO AMERICAN SOCIETY   153

Cultural Assimilation, *154*   Structural Assimilation, *156*
Marital Assimilation, *158*   Identificational Assimilation, *159*
Attitude-Receptional Assimilation, *161*
Behavior-Receptional Assimilation, *163*   Civic Assimilation, *168*
Selected Bibliography, *171*   Notes, *172*

CHAPTER EIGHT
THE BLACK REVOLT AND ITS CONSEQUENCES   175

Beginnings of the Revolt: Black Persistence and White Resistance, *175*
The Civil Rights Movement, *179*   Despair in the Slums, *183*
Black Power, *186*   The Consequences, *192*   Selected Bibliography, *201*
Notes, *202*

CHAPTER NINE
FROM BLACK NATIONALISM TO AFFIRMATIVE ACTION   205

The Black Nationalist Tradition, *206*
Expressions of Black Nationalism, *209*
Affirmative Action and Its Opponents, *212*
Selected Bibliography, *219*   Notes, *221*

INDEX   223

PREFACE

When this book was first published in 1969 black Americans faced a serious crisis arising from the assassination of Martin Luther King, Jr. Angered by this act, blacks took to the streets in cities around the country, demonstrating their outrage by massive acts of property destruction. In general, white Americans and educational institutions responded to the tragedy of the assassination by attempting to make some amends for past injustices. Colleges and universities recruited black students in larger numbers than ever before, and programs for Afro-American and African studies were organized on a wide scale. It appeared that equality for blacks had finally become an issue of critical importance.

However, by the time the second edition appeared in 1975 little change in the status of black people relative to that of white people had come about, but many changes in the mind and mood of Afro-American people had occurred, mainly in the ascendancy of nationalist sentiment in the black community. Black nationalist organizations thrived until the Federal Bureau of Investigation and other government agencies commenced a systematic campaign to destroy this movement. Because of this campaign and the inevitable internal dissension within these organizations, the movement virtually collapsed. Nevertheless, with the advent of affirmative action some progress was made in the status of blacks in the United States.

With this, the third edition, it appears that the mood of the country has changed, and that conservatism has become the dominant ethos of American politics and of the country as a whole. The right-wing administration of Ronald Reagan and the egocentricity of the American people have combined to mount a serious attack on affirmative action for minorities and women. These forces have even attempted to eradicate some of the citizenship gains that blacks and other minorities have accomplished through intensive struggle. The third edition incorporates these events as well as some alterations in the author's perspective on some aspects of the black experience in the United States. Since the last edition, it should be added, many of the statistics on blacks in the United States are no longer available.

While this book is a sociological study of Afro-Americans, it addresses the general reader as well as the professional student of society. Therefore, lay language has been used throughout. It is hoped that sociological perspective and analysis have not been sacrificed.

While many persons, especially my Prentice-Hall editor, Bill Webber, have contributed to whatever virtues the book may have, its shortcomings are mine alone.

Alphonso Pinkney

CHAPTER ONE
HISTORICAL
BACKGROUND

Historians insist that a knowledge of the past is essential for understanding the present. This axiom is especially relevant insofar as black Americans are concerned, for theirs is a unique history. Virtually all aspects of their history are without parallel when compared to those of other minority groups in the United States. The very circumstances which led to their departure from their homeland, to the Middle Passage between Africa and the New World, and to the institution of slavery which developed on their arrival in what is now the United States are unique to black Americans out of all U.S. minority groups. The institution of slavery, with all its peculiarities, has left a legacy which continues to play a dominant role in the life of Americans. After nearly three and a half centuries white Americans continue to react to Afro-Americans with a mass irrationality which precludes the complete entrance of blacks into the larger society. Yet it would be difficult to imagine members of a group putting forth more diligent and persistent efforts for acceptance than those put forth by black Americans. A variety of approaches has been attempted throughout the years, and some gains have been made; but a series of historical circumstances has preserved the low status of Afro-Americans in the society.

The history of black people in the United States is complex, and no attempt to record this detailed sequence of events in one chapter can succeed. However, certain occurrences have greater bearing on the present status of black people in American society than others.

SLAVERY

Black people were among the earliest participants in the Spanish explorations of what is now the United States, but the first Africans to settle on its shores arrived in 1619. In that year a Dutch vessel landed in Jamestown, and the captain sold twenty blacks to the Virginia settlers. This was twelve years after the establishment in Virginia of the first permanent British colony in America and one year before the *Mayflower* landed the Pilgrims at Plymouth Rock (Massachusetts). Inasmuch as there was no precedent for slavery in English law, these blacks and those who followed for some time had the same legal status as white indentured servants. Their term of service was prescribed by local laws. Throughout much of the seventeenth century the status of blacks was not at all clearly defined, and the institution of chattel slavery gradually evolved into one in which black people, in part because of their physical differences, were to hold a caste position in society. Like white indentured servants, it was possible for them to gain their freedom after working for a specified number of years or after converting to Christianity. The ambiguity of this status as indentured servant rather than slave, combined with the uncertainties attached to the Indian and white indentured servant supply, led to the ultimate relegation of black people to a status of perpetual servitude.[1]

Slavery as practiced in North America was a complex institution. In some respects the practices varied by state, region (Deep South vs. Border South), size of plantation, number of slaves involved, season of the year, and, of course, the convictions of the individual slaveholder. However, many practices were common throughout the slaveholding states. Furthermore, many of the restrictions imposed on the slaves were also applicable to "free" blacks in the United States, both in the South and elsewhere in the country. In addition to the general characteristics of slavery in the South, of special relevance to the present discussion are the slaves' loss of their native culture, the attitude of white people toward slaves, the reaction of slaves to their status, and the status of black people who technically were not slaves.

General Characteristics of Slavery

The first statutory recognition of slavery in North America occurred in Virginia in 1661. This lead was soon followed by the other colonies, and by the time the colonies gained independence, chattel slavery and a body of law defining the status of slaves had become institutionalized. These laws covered every aspect of a slave's life. In general, slavery in North America developed into the harshest form of social relations ever to exist. Slaves received none of the protections of organized society because they were not considered to be persons; rather, they were considered to be property, and only to the extent that a citizen's property must be protected could the slave expect society's consideration. Slaveholders maintained absolute power over their property. They were endowed by law with rights over the slave, and in return were expected to assume certain obligations toward the slave. "The law required that masters be humane to their slaves, furnish them with adequate food and clothing, and provide care for them during sickness and old age."[2] Therefore slaves were at one and the same time human beings and property, and "throughout the antebellum South the cold language of statutes and judicial decisions made it evident that, legally, the slave was less a person than a thing."[3] In such a status the slaves were denied virtually all rights, both civil and political. Perhaps the most important element in defining the status of slaves was the perpetual nature of slavery; slaves were destined to occupy this status throughout their lives and to transmit it to their children, who in turn transmitted their inherited status to their children. Slavery and Afro-American became synonymous, and since slaves were defined as innately inferior, blacks were defined as inferior beings.

Because slaves were forbidden by law to enter into contractual arrangements, their marriages were not legally binding relationships. Husbands, wives, and children could be separated at the discretion of the slaveholder, as was frequently the case. Thus it was impossible to maintain a stable family system. The slave family had little importance as regards the traditional functions which marriage was expected to perform for those who entered into the relationship. Parents had little to say or do about rearing children or controlling other forces leading to cohesion in family life. The nature of the institution of slavery was such that no family in the usual sense can be said to have existed. Children derived their condition from the status of the mother. The father ". . . was not the head of the family, the holder of the property, the provider, the protector."[4] His wife could be undressed and either whipped or violated by the slaveholder or overseer in his presence and in the presence of the children.

Slaves were property which could be sold, traded, or given as gifts, and slave families were frequently dissolved for economic reasons. As Stampp has written, "They were awarded as prizes in lotteries and raffles; they were wagered at gambling tables and horse races. They were, in short, property in fact as well as in law."[5] Female slaves were encouraged to engage in promiscuous relations with other slaves. Although these relations occasionally developed into stable ones, they were more often associations entered into for the express purpose of reproduction. In the words of Frazier: "To the slave trader, who had only an economic interest in the slave, the Negro was a mere utility."[6] Clearly no stable family system could develop under such circumstances. The permanency of marriage depended on those rare opportunities slaves had to live and work together within a situation of common experiences and trust.

According to the laws of the antebellum South, slaves had no civil or property rights. "A slave might not make a will, and he could not, by will, inherit anything. Slaves were not to hire themselves out, locate their employment, establish their own residence, or make contracts for any purpose. . . ."[7] They could not be a party to suits involving free persons. Strict interpretations of laws regulated every aspect of their lives, and the enforcement machinery was such that violation rarely went unpunished. These strict laws were geared toward the behavior of the slaves, but they also clearly regulated the behavior of whites who might interfere with slave discipline. To slaves who were found guilty of violating the slave codes a variety of punishment was meted out, the most frequent being whipping for minor crimes and harsher forms of punishment, including burnings and mutilation, for more serious crimes. The death penalty was common and resulted from such offenses as striking whites.

Stampp views the rigidity of the codes and the harshness of the punishments as serving to instill fear in the slaves. This atmosphere of fear, he maintains, was accomplished through a series of steps designed by the slaveholders to preserve absolute control over their "human property": "accustom him to rigid discipline, demand from him unconditional submission, impress upon him his innate inferiority, train him to adopt the master's code of good behavior, and instill in him a sense of complete dependence."[8]

The work performed by the slaves depended on whether they were on a large plantation or a small farm; whether they were rural or urban; whether the slaveholder specialized in cotton, tobacco, rice, sugar cane, hemp, or other agricultural products; whether they were male or female; whether they were assigned to the slaveholder's house or to the fields; and, of course, what the season of the year was. Regardless of the foregoing conditions, however, slaves were generally required to work from sunrise until dusk. They usually worked under the supervision of a white overseer whose job it was to maintain strict discipline. All slaves were required to work, and the slaveholder decided at what age children should go into the fields. In general, by the age of five or six children were expected to follow their parents into the fields. When a slave woman was too old to work in the fields, she was expected to perform domestic tasks for the other slaves, such as caring for small children and preparing food. Old men tended gardens and cared for the animals.

On larger plantations an elaborate division of labor developed. There were skilled craftsmen, such as carpenters, mechanics, and blacksmiths; a variety of domestic servants, such as coachmen, housemaids, butlers, cooks, and laundresses; and, of course, there were field hands who cultivated and harvested the crops. In the cities slaves worked in construction and maintenance work, in domestic work, at various crafts such as carpentry and cabinetmaking, in laundries, and in cotton presses.[9]

There were few occupational tasks in the antebellum South that slaves did not perform, and, although some slaves managed to evade the fourteen-to-sixteen-hour day by malingering, the system was such that most of them were forced into a rigorous routine of hard labor.

Because of the division of labor among slaves, status distinctions developed among them. Status was frequently derived from the wealth and extent of holdings of the slaveholder, but the most important distinctions were those between domestic slaves and those relegated to field work. The "house slaves" enjoyed higher status that the "field slaves," and they jealously guarded their superior positions. Slaveholders tended to attach greater significance to the appearance of these slaves. Being around the slaveholder's family afforded "house slaves" the opportunity to assimilate the external forms of behavior which they observed.[10] Slaveholders and their families, who usually preferred mulatto house servants, encouraged the division between "house slaves" and "field slaves" as a means of maintaining control.[11]

The living conditions of the slaves were generally in keeping with their almost total lack of status. Most of them lived in small crude huts without the most elementary provisions for sanitation and safety, such as floors, windows, and interior walls. Whole families were frequently crammed into one-room cabins. According to Stampp, "The common run of slaves cabins were cramped, crudely built, scantily furnished, un-painted, and dirty."[12] Cabins were generally without stoves, beds, or other essentials. Writing about his childhood as a plantation slave, Booker T. Washington recalled: "I cannot remember having slept in a bed until after our family was declared free by the Emancipation Proclamation. Three children—John, my older brother, Amanda, my sister, and myself—had a pallet on the dirty floor, or, to be more correct, we slept in and on a bundle of filthy rags laid upon the dirt floor."[13] He reports that his mother, the plantation cook, prepared food for all the slaves and whites on the plantation on an open fire in their small cabin. The crowded conditions under which slaves were forced to live were a constant threat to health and sanity. "One Mississippi planter had 24 huts, each measuring 16 feet by 14 feet, for his 150 slaves."[14]

On some of the larger plantations, slaveholders maintained communal kitchens for all slaves, but in general the food provided was the least expensive possible and no consideration was given to its nutritional value. "A peck of cornmeal and three or four pounds of salt pork or bacon comprised the basic weekly allowance of the great majority of adult slaves."[15]

Because they lived under such adverse conditions, the morbidity and mortality rates among slaves were high. Malaria, yellow fever, cholera, pneumonia, tuberculosis, and tetanus were widespread. Infant and maternal mortality were commonplace. Some of the larger plantations maintained medical doctors for the care of the slaves, but folk medical practices were usually resorted to. Even when doctors were available, the practice of medicine among the slaves was something short of scientific. The doctors frequently complained that they were unable to administer treatment because the slaves were not amenable to the same medical treatment as white patients. Frances Kemble summarized the conditions in a slave infirmary on one plantation: "In all, filth, disorder, and misery abounded; the floor was the only bed, and scanty begrimed rags of blankets the only covering."[16]

Loss of Native Culture

The Africans who arrived in North America represented many cultures. Contrary to popular belief, they were representative of a variety of highly advanced civilizations.[17] These slaves carried with them to North America a knowledge of the complex cultures they left behind. How much of these original cultures was able to survive the brutality of antebellum slavery has been disputed by scholars. There is general agreement, however, that systematic attempts were made to strip these people of their culture. In the first place, slaves were widely scattered on plantations, small farms, and cities throughout the colonies and later throughout the United States. Second, slaves arriving in North America were from a diversity of cultural backgrounds. These cultures might have contained many common elements, but they contained even more distinctive characteristics. Furthermore, since young male slaves predominated in the earliest importations, it was virtually impossible for the slaves to recreate the cultures they knew. Frazier summarizes the impact of slavery on the slaves as follows:

> The African family system was destroyed, and the slave was separated from his kinsmen and friends. Moreover, in the United States there was little chance that he could reknit the ties of friendship and old associations. If by chance he encountered fellow slaves with whom he could communicate in his native tongue, he was separated from them. From the very beginning he was forced to learn English in order to obey the commands of his white masters. Whatever memories he might have retained of his native land and native customs became meaningless in the New World.[18]

It is not suprising, therefore, that much of the Old World culture failed to survive. However, the circumstances under which slaves lived did not preclude their retaining some cultural characteristics. For example, Franklin sees African survivals in language, folk tales, music, social organization, and aesthetic endeavors.[19] Other scholars maintain that many other survivals of African culture were so pervasive that they have remained to the present day.[20]

Clearly, some aspects of African cultures survived in the antebellum South, but the adjustments these new arrivals were required to make were of such a magnitude that an essentially new way of life developed. Whatever a slave's occupation had been in Africa, he or she was usually forced to enter farming or domestic service in North America. Slaves were forbidden to practice their traditional religions and were required to practice the religion of their oppressors. Although they were denied formal instruction, they had to learn English. The foods they had eaten in Africa were unavailable on Southern plantations. Family patterns they had practiced were not permitted. Given these circumstances, and denied participation in the culture of the South, the slaves somehow had to survive in a world that was both hostile and strange. This struggle for survival forced them to create their own patterns of culture, which represented a mixture of elements brought from Africa and those created by their life experiences in the New World.

Attitudes of White People toward Slaves

Although the first Africans to arrive in North America were not treated differently from white indentured servants, as the institution of slavery developed, it became exclusively Afro-American. The process was gradual, and some historians attribute it to economic forces,[21] although others see race as the primary motivating factor.[22] Regardless of whether the precipitating factor was economic or racist, the attitudes which ultimately developed toward the slaves, and the behavioral component of these attitudes, led to a system of human bondage without parallel in human history.[23] As Tannenbaum has noted, slavery in North America differed from other systems of human slavery, especially that practiced in Latin America, in that the North American slaves were denied, in law and in practice, moral personalities. He writes: "While the impact of the law did not and could not completely wipe out the fact that the Negro slave was human, it raised a sufficient barrier to make the humanity of the Negro difficult to recognize and legally almost impossible to provide for. This legal definition carried its own moral consequences and made the ultimate redefinition of the Negro as a moral person most difficult."[24] Hence, rather than being reacted to as human beings possessing moral personalities, slaves in North America were considered simply "beasts of the field."

Not all attitudes toward slaves were strongly negative; however, throughout most of the period of slavery the blacks were considered uniquely suited for human slavery as a result of certain racial traits which, it was thought, made it impossible for them to adjust to the "civilized" world of the Anglo-Saxons.[25] Hence they were "destined by God" to serve Caucasians. This attitude became dominant and governed the behavior directed toward them. Racial inferiority thus became *the* justification for the institution of slavery in North America. Furthermore, the "free" blacks were, like the slaves, responded to in similar fashion. Throughout the slave era black people were accorded different treatment from whites, regardless of degree of achievement. Black status was based on ascribed, i.e., racial, characteristics.

During the antebellum period slaves came into contact with a variety of white people: slaveholders and their families; overseers, who were poor and landless whites; and religious leaders. Although slaveholders differed in their treatment of slaves, they were in general convinced of the innate inferiority of the slaves and treated them accordingly. If the slaves disobeyed orders, they were to be whipped. According to Franklin, "Some planters went so far as to specify the size and type of lash to be used and the number of lashes to be given for specific offenses. Almost none disclaimed whipping as an effective form of punishment, and the excessive use of the lash was one of the most flagrant abuses of the institution."[26]

Slaveholders maintained absolute control over their slaves. As a means of social control, punishment was felt to be most effective. Violation of the norms set by the slaveholder was met with a variety of forms of punishment. Stampp describes some of the more ingenious methods: "A Maryland tobacco grower forced a hand to eat the worms he failed to pick off the tobacco leaves. A Mississippian gave a runaway a wretched time by requiring him to sit at the table and eat his evening meal with the white family. A Louisiana planter humiliated disobedient male field hands by giving them 'women's work' such as washing clothes, by dressing them in women's clothing, and by exhibiting them on a scaffold wearing a red flannel cap."[27]

Frederick Douglass, as ex-slave who became an Abolitionist, a writer, and a minister to Haiti, recalled that the first slaveholder on whose plantation he lived frequently engaged in acts of cruelty toward his slaves. For example,

> I have often been awakened at the dawn of day by the most heart-rending shrieks of an own aunt of mine, whom he used to tie up to a joist, and whip upon her naked back till she was literally covered with blood. No words, no tears, no prayers, from his gory victim, seemed to move his iron heart from its bloody purpose. The louder she screamed, the harder he whipped and where the blood ran the fastest, there he whipped the longest. He would whip her to make her scream, and whip her to make her hush; and not until overcome by fatigue, would he cease to swing the blood-clotted cowskin.[28]

Stampp cites many examples of psychopathic slaveholders who thoroughly enjoyed the practice of inflicting extreme brutality on their slaves.[29]

Because slaves represented an important capital investment in the plantation economy, slaveholders naturally protected their investments, and some reports of the relations between the slaves and the slaveholders indicate ambivalent feelings on the part of the latter. Many of them developed affectionate relations toward their slaves—an affection always tempered by antipathy.

On small plantations slaves had direct contact with the slaveholders. On larger plantations overseers, generally recruited from among the poorer whites, maintained discipline among the slaves. Their treatment of slaves was indicative of the low esteem in which they held these people. On plantations where overseers were employed, cruelty and brutality were institutionalized. Reports of the treatment of slaves by overseers are filled with instances of torture. The overseers were in a peculiar position because they felt exploited by the system, and they tended to displace their frustration onto the slaves. It is reported that fights between slaves and overseers were common, and slaves frequently forced overseers to leave plantations.[30] The brutality of the overseers was indeed widespread, and relations between them and the slaves were rarely amicable.

Although many religious leaders ultimately adopted antislavery positions, most of them perceived of slavery as being divinely sanctioned and thereby a natural condition. Most slaveholders approved of religious training for their slaves, but a series of codes developed whereby religious services were rigidly regulated. One of the most universal of these practices was that blacks were prohibited from becoming ministers. Services were conducted by white ministers, who interpreted their function as one of teaching the slaves to adjust to their condition of servitude. Frequently, slaves were required to attend the church of the slaveholder. Through the medium of the church, slaveholders sought to maintain slavery intact. As Franklin has written, compelling the slaves to attend church with the slaveholder was "the method the whites employed to keep a closer eye on the slaves."[31] Slaveholders employed ministers who instructed slaves to be obedient and subservient. Bishops and other religious leaders themselves frequently owned slaves; for example, an Episcopal bishop in Louisiana owned four hundred slaves.[32] Although slaveholders were generally responsible for the religious life of their slaves and the selection of clergymen to preach to them, they had little difficulty finding allies among the clergy. The Scriptures were employed to justify slavery, and many books were written in its defense.[33] In general, the clergymen with whom the slaves came into contact were men who used their religion as a means of maintaining the status quo.

Reactions of Slaves

Owners of slaves, supporters of slavery, and believers in the innate inferiority of the Afro-American justified slavery on a variety of grounds. One such ground was that the slaves, being docile and childlike, approved of their status. Slavery advocates cited the infrequency and failure of serious insurrections to support their contention that the slaves were indeed happy with their lot in life. Evidence which failed to support their contention was generally ignored. That their beliefs were not rooted in reality is evidenced by the extreme measures they were forced to resort to in order to maintain slavery. Slave revolts occurred in the earliest record of the period and continued throughout the era. Indeed, evidence indicates that the slave traders in Africa experienced both constant resistance to capture from the slaves and numerous revolts during the Middle Passage between Africa and the New World.[34] In addition, many thousands of slaves managed, often against extraordinary odds, to escape from chattel slavery. That slaves reacted to their status with constant attempts to alter it meant that throughout the period they managed to be "a troublesome property" for slaveholders. Attempts to gain freedom took many forms, two of which were insurrections and flights from captivity.

Altogether some 250 slave insurrections and conspiracies are reported to have occurred in the history of Afro-American slavery, and although some of these were more serious than others, the history of slavery in North America is not without widespread popular revolts on the part of slaves.[35] The first such revolt occurred as early as 1663, and such uprisings continued throughout the slavery era. Some revolts were well planned and organized, and others were haphazardly planned.[36] The 250 revolts reported involved numbers estimated as ranging from ten to fifty thousand slaves.

Three of the many slave revolts stand out because of the seriousness of the attempts, the number of slaves involved, and the reaction they generated throughout slaveholding North America. In 1800 a slave named Gabriel, a worker on a plantation near Richmond, Virginia, who perceived of himself as having a divine mission, organized the first major slave insurrection in North America. Gabriel is said to have possessed unusual intelligence.[37] For weeks he met on Sundays with fellow slaves at parties and dances. On these occasions he selected special slaves to serve as assistants to work on plans with him. Gabriel picked what he felt to be the most advantageous date for the insurrection. The plan called for the use of few weapons. They were to murder the slaveholders and their families on the nearby plantations. Initially, all whites were to be killed, but as the revolt spread, landless whites were to be recruited to fight against wealthy landowners. Strategy was mapped for the spread of the revolt and the enlistment of additional slaves into Gabriel's army. Gabriel had been inspired to insurrection by reading the Bible and by the French Revolution. It is reported that ". . . he was said to have planned to buy a piece of silk cloth to have the egalitarian slogan 'Liberty or Death' printed on it."[38] The revolt never materialized because two fellow slaves on the plantation informed on the slave rebels, and the organizers and other participants were killed.

The second major plan for a slave insurrection occurred in Charleston, South Carolina, in 1822. Denmark Vesey, an ex-slave who had purchased his freedom with money won in a lottery, planned this insurrection. He was a gifted carpenter and, like Gabriel, was said to have been endowed with exceptional intelligence.[39] In his early years in Charleston he used his shop as a meeting place for black people, and he spent much of his time attempting to strengthen his feelings of self-confidence. He was irritated by complacency among both slaves and "free blacks." He became a member of the African Methodist Episcopal Church and later a preacher, for the purpose of recruiting prospects for the rebellion he was planning. Altogether he spent four years planning his revolt, and slowly he selected those in whom to confide. This insurrection, like that of Gabriel's, failed because a "faithful" house servant informed on his fellow slaves. The planners were rounded up; thirty-five of them were killed, and thirty-four were deported.

The third and probably the best-known slave revolt occurred in Southampton County, Virginia, in 1831. The leader of this outbreak was Nat Turner, also an intelligent and talented man.[40] Turner had escaped from slavery but had voluntarily returned because of religious convictions. He became a mystic and frequently buried himself in prayer. Through visions he felt that he had been divinely ordained to lead his people out of bondage. Because of his mysticism, little time and effort went into planning the revolt. Therefore it involved fewer participants than previous revolts, but it became the biggest slave uprising in North America. Armed with an ax and clubs, six men first murdered the plantation owner and his family and then proceeded to nearby houses, killing all through the night. Altogether they murdered fifty-five whites. By the time the rebellion had been quelled, Turner's troops numbered more than sixty. The Army of the United States was finally called to put down the rebellion, and the soldiers were joined by other whites, who attacked the slaves indiscriminately.

The attack on Harpers Ferry by John Brown, a white man, was an important uprising and no doubt played a major role in the abolition of slavery. However, few slaves joined Brown in his attempt to liberate the slaves. Brown devoted his entire life to the elimination of slavery; once he became convinced that moral appeals were of no avail to slaveholders, he concentrated on armed revolt. As with Nat Turner's revolt, John Brown's raid on Harpers Ferry was subdued by the armed militia.

Although there were many revolts by the slaves in North America, few of them gained significant momentum, and all failed. In no case did they succeed in improving the status of the slaves; rather, they generally brought forth repressive measures. Some reasons for the failure of the slave revolts may be advanced. The very nature of slavery and its effects on the slave were such that successful insurrection was impossible. As

Elkins has written, "American slavery operated as a 'closed' system—one in which, for the generality of slaves in their nature as men and women, *sub specie aeternitatis,* contacts with free society could occur only on the most narrowly circumscribed of terms."[41] Such a system had a demoralizing effect on the slaves' personalities, thereby rendering widespread participation in revolts unlikely and, in many cases, unthinkable. As has been mentioned, slaveholders encouraged status differences among slaves as a means of dividing and conquering them. Revolts were most often betrayed by that category of slaves most closely allied to the owner—the house slaves. Because the plantation was a closed system, communication among slaves on the various plantations was impossible. Whenever slaves met, for whatever reason, they were under the constant surveillance of whites. Finally, of crucial importance was the ratio of slaves to whites in North America. Slaves were usually outnumbered, and where they happened to be in a majority, any slaveholder had the full force of the military at his or her disposal for the purpose of maintaining order. This was the situation after the colonies gained independence, and it was during this period that organized slave revolts were common. Therefore the lack of success of slave revolts cannot be taken as an indication of blacks' acceptance of their status. As Stampp has written, "In truth, no slave uprising ever had a chance of ultimate success, even though it might have cost the master class heavy casualties. The great majority of the disarmed and outnumbered slaves, knowing the futility of rebellion, refused to join in any of the numerous plots. Most slaves had to express their desire for freedom in less dramatic ways."[42]

Recognizing the futility of organized rebellion, most slaves expressed their antipathy for slavery in individual acts. Most frequently these acts took the form of escape. From the very inception of the institution until its end, runaway slaves posed problems for the slaveholders. The newspapers of the period were full of advertisements in search of escaped slaves. The exact number of slaves to escape is not known, but it is estimated that thousands fled each year. Estimates of the total number of escapees in the four decades between 1810 and 1850 run as high as one hundred thousand, with a value of more than $30 million.[43] So great was the number of runaway slaves that in 1793 Congress enacted the Fugitive Slave Law, which empowered a slaveholder to seize runaway slaves who had crossed state lines and ultimately return them to the state from which they had fled. The persistence of slaves in risking their lives to escape serves as dramatic evidence of their reaction to their status.

A significant proportion of the slaves to escape was aided by "free" blacks and white Abolitionists. The Underground Railroad, an organized effort to assist slaves attempting to escape, is said to have been incorporated in 1804.[44] It was operated in defiance of federal fugitive slave laws, and thousands of slaves were able to escape to the North and to Canada through its utilization. So well organized was it that funds for its operation were solicited from philanthropists. Employing several thousand workers, the Underground Railroad operated hundreds of stations in the East and West. The number of slaves to escape through the Underground Railroad is not known but estimates run into the hundreds of thousands, with an estimated forty thousand passing through Ohio alone.[45] There are recorded instances in which individual "conductors" on the Underground Railroad assisted thousands of black people in their escape from slavery.

Although some slaves successfully accommodated to their status, the persistence of runaway slaves posed continuous problems for slaveholders. So widespread was this phenomenon that a southern doctor was convinced that blacks suffered from a "disease of the mind," which he called "drapethomania," which caused them to run away.[46] In reality, however, aside from the general harshness and degradation inherent in the institution of slavery, several of its special features served to motivate slaves to flee.[47] Arbitrary separation of slaves from their families induced many of them to escape. Other slaves resented being moved against their will. Still others reacted to such factors as attempts to work them too severely, fear of punishment, and fear of being sold into the Deep South. The major motivation, however, was a desire to escape from the inhumanity which the institution of slavery imposed. The constant fleeing of slaves is hardly compatible with the view of them held by a leading historian of slavery during the first three decades of the twentieth century. Ulrich B. Phillips saw the slaves as possessing "a readiness for loyalty of a feudal sort," and he viewed them as a people who were eager to please the slaveholders by working "sturdily for a hard boss."[48] He saw them as a people "who for the most part were by racial quality submissive rather than defiant."[49] The views expressed by Phillips were widely shared among slaveholders and writers of the period.

The "Free" Blacks

Not all black people in the United States were enslaved prior to the Civil War. Indeed, the population of the free blacks increased steadily from the middle of the seventeenth century until emancipation. Although they were generally referred to as "free," their status was only slightly higher than that of the slaves and was significantly lower than that of their white fellow countrymen. And although their status resembled that of the slaves, they were indeed neither slave nor free. As one historian of the period has written, "Since the Constitution made no mention of race or color, the states and the federal government separately defined the legal status of free Negroes. Both generally agreed, however, that the Negro constituted an inferior race and that he should occupy a legal position commensurate with his degraded social and economic condition."[50] The population of free blacks in the United States numbered 59,557 at the time of the first census in 1790, and by the census of 1860 (the last before the Civil War) it had increased to 448,070.[51] They were, roughly, evenly divided between the South and non-South regions of the country.[52]

Several factors account for the steady increase in the population of free blacks[53]: (1) manumission of slaves, which had been practiced since the beginning of slavery, became a major factor in the increase in the free black population; (2) children born to free blacks inherited the status of their parents; (3) mulatto children born of free black mothers were free; (4) children of free black and Indian parentage were born free; (5) mulatto children born to white mothers were free; and (6) slaves continued to escape to freedom. Although the population of free blacks came from several sources, their African heritage still relegated them to a precarious position in society.

Perhaps the most difficult task for the free blacks was that of maintaining their freedom. Franklin describes this condition as follows:

> A white person could claim, however fraudulently, that a Negro was a slave, and there was little the Negro could do about it. There was, moreover, the danger of his being kidnapped, as often happened. The chances of being reduced to servitude or slavery by the courts were also great. A large majority of free Negroes lived in daily fear of losing what freedom they had. One slip or ignorance of the law would send them back into the ranks of slaves.[54]

Free blacks were denied many of the rights that white Americans enjoyed. The degree of freedom they enjoyed depended on whether they lived in the South or North, and within these regions it varied from state to state. Their movements were generally resricted, especially in the South, where they were required to carry passes. Most states enacted laws forbidding them to convene meetings unless whites were in attendance. It was especially difficult for them to earn a living. Several states restricted the occupations they could engage in. In spite of these restrictions, the blacks engaged in a number of skilled and professional pursuits; they became druggists, dentists, lawyers, teachers, tailors, carpenters, barbers, shopkeepers, salesmen, and cabinetmakers.

Southern states generally excluded free blacks from the franchise, and most Nothern states made it difficult for them to vote. Only one state (Georgia) forbade free blacks to own property, and many of them amassed great wealth.[55] Indeed, many of the free blacks owned slaves. In general, however, black ownership of slaves differed from white ownership in that the free blacks usually also purchased their slaves' spouses, relatives, or friends. While many of the free blacks attended religious services with whites, in segregated sections of the churches, several all-black congregations and denominations were established during this period. In the South, religious worship, except in the segregated white churches, was difficult for free blacks because it was feared that all-black services were used to organize insurrections among slaves.

It was difficult for the free blacks to secure education. All Southern states made it virtually impossible, and in the North segregated education was the norm. In spite of the difficulties involved, many blacks managed to achieve the highest realm of scholarship. Black people were graduated from college as early as 1827.[56] Before the Civil War two colleges, Lincoln University in Pennsylvania and Wilberforce University in Ohio, were established for the education of free blacks.

In general, laws reinforced the low status of the free blacks, but where this was not the case, violence was resorted to. Between 1830 and 1850 race riots were widespread throughout the United States. Roaming bands of whites frequently invaded the black sections of cities, burning homes and churches and beating and killing the residents. Violence was resorted to where whites felt that free blacks were competing for jobs, and whites commonly drove free blacks from cities. Rarely were blacks protected from these acts of violence by law-enforcement officials.[57]

Although life for the free blacks was somewhat less circumscribed than for the slaves, they were forced to live within a set of rigid rules which made it virtually impossible for them to fulfill the obligations of citizenship. Yet the highest degree of civic responsibility was demanded of them, always at the risk of jail or slavery. In spite of the restrictions on their lives and the uncertainties of their status, many notable achievements were registered. Several free blacks distinguished themselves as Abolitionists; many emerged as educators, poets, playwrights, historians, and newspaper editors.

THE CIVIL WAR

By the middle of the nineteenth century slavery had become a serious problem for the United States at home and in its relations wtih other countries. Antislavery sentiment within the country reached significant proportions, and, since the British government had already emancipated the slaves in its colonial possessions, relations between the two countries gradually deteriorated. Various proposals for dealing with slaves were discussed by federal officials, and intersectional strife had reached the point where a bloody confrontation seemed inevitable. The Abolitionists gained ground in their cause of freedom for the slaves, and the slaveholding states maintained their determination to perpetuate the institution. Antislavery societies mushroomed throughout the nonslaveholding states, and the supporters of slavery responded to the challenge by widespread acts of violence. Furthermore, at about this time slavery had ceased to be profitable as a system.[58] By the time the president-elect, Abraham Lincoln, arrived in Washington in 1861, he had become well acquainted with the institution of slavery through travels in the South. He had expressed opposition to slavery and vowed, on occasion, to put an end to it. At other times Lincoln expressed segregationist views. It appears that he was both opposed to the institution of slavery and opposed to racial integration. When he assumed the presidency, the country had already become divided on the issue, and since seven of the slaveholding states had already seceded from the Union, a civil war was imminent. The Civil War was an all-important development for the slaves, and of special significance were the participation of blacks in the war, the emancipation it brought about, and the destruction wrought by this armed conflict.

Participation by Blacks

At the beginning of the Civil War blacks rushed to enlist in the Union army, but they were rejected. In several instances, after being rebuffed, they organized themselves and trained for service in the expectation that they would ultimately be permitted to participate in a war which they were convinced would end with the freeing of the slaves. In the early stages of the war they were rejected because it was felt that to permit them to fight would endow them with a status comparable to that of white soldiers. Furthermore, blacks were considered incapable of fighting wars. As Du Bois has pointed out, "Negroes on the whole were considered cowards and inferior beings whose very presence in America was unfortunate."[59] As the war developed, however, army commanders were permitted to use their own discretion about utilizing blacks. Some commanders insisted on returning runaway slaves to their owners, and others permitted them to fight. As the Union army moved South, where the war was being fought, blacks rushed to the Union lines.[60] When they were finally permitted to enlist in Union armies, blacks did so enthusiastically. By the end of the Civil War, approximately 186,000 black troops had been enrolled. These troops took part in 198 battles and suffered 68,000 casualties.[61] It is estimated that 300,000 blacks were involved in the war effort, including servants, laborers, and spies. The troops were organized into various regiments, including artillery, cavalry, infantry, and engineers. They fought in segregated units and were known as the United States Colored Troops. Most of the black troops served under white officers, but Woodson estimated that "Negroes held altogether about 75 commissions in the army during the Civil War."[62] In addition to being segregated, they were paid differentially for their services. "The Enlistment Act of 1862 provided that whites in the rank of private should receive $13 a month and $3.50 for clothing, but Negroes of the same rank were to receive only $7 and $3, respectively."[63] Such discrimination was protested by black troops and by their white commanding officers. During the Civil War blacks were engaged in combat in every major battle area and suffered significantly higher casualty rates than did white troops. It is generally conceded that they made significant contributions to the victory of the Union armies.

The Confederate armies, like those of the Union, at first denied blacks the right to fight in the Civil War, but unlike the Union armies, the Confederacy was afraid that if blacks were armed, they would rebel. Furthermore, few, if any, blacks expressed willingness to fight for the cause of the Confederacy. One of the major problems faced by this region was the widespread desertion of the slaves to join the ranks of the Union armies. Confederate army units utilized blacks for cooking and other menial tasks, and several Confederate soldiers took their black servants to war with them.[64] Toward the end of the Civil War, in 1865, the Confederate senate enacted a bill calling for the enlistment of 200,000 black troops who were to be freed if they remained loyal throughout the war. In addition, a bill calling for the conscription of 300,000 additional troops, including blacks, proved unsuccessful. Few blacks volunteered, and many fled to avoid conscription. Furthermore, by this time the Union armies were virtually assured of victory.

The role of the black soldiers in the Civil War has been deprecated. However, one historian of the period summarized their participation as follows: "Without their help, the North could not have won the war as soon as it did, and perhaps it could not have won at all. The Negro was crucial to the whole Union war effort."[65]

The Emancipation

In the midst of the Civil War, on January 1, 1863, President Lincoln proclaimed that "all persons held as slaves within any State, or designated part of the State, the people whereof shall be in rebellion against the United States, shall be then, thenceforward, and forever free." The President made it clear that this action was taken in order to preserve the Union and not to destroy slavery. The newly freed blacks were asked to refrain from violence and to seek employment at reasonable wages. The Emancipation Proclamation gave impetus to increasing black participation in the ongoing Civil War.

News of the Emancipation Proclamation was received by the slaves with bewilderment. There were nearly four million slaves in the South at that time, and life for them had been such that few of them had ever expected to be set free. They did not know what to do. The state of illiteracy which had been perpetuated for most slaves served to complicate their new lives. In many instances they were powerless to protect themselves against the violence directed toward them by white persons. It is reported: "Many of the slaves immediately left the plantations when they learned that they were free. This was seen as natural since one of the tests of freedom was the ability to move around freely. On the other hand, the attitude of subordination was still strong in some slaves and they were afraid to assert their newly acquired rights."[66] It is perhaps fair to say that emancipation initially came as a shock to the slaves because they were unprepared for it. However, evidence indicates that by and large they welcomed their new status.

The slaveholders and other southern whites, on the other hand, were not pleased with the disruption of the way of life they had grown to cherish and upon which they were dependent. It was reported that "some planters held back their former slaves on the plantations by brute force. Armed bands of white men patrolled the country roads to drive back the Negroes wandering about. Dead bodies of murdered Negroes were found on or near highways and byways. . . . A veritable reign of terror prevailed in many parts of the South."[67] Some slaveholders accepted the change in status of the slaves without such vindictiveness but with reluctance, and others appeared to be relieved that they could now reject a system which had long ago become unpleasant for them.

Destruction Caused by the Civil War

Whatever the causes of the Civil War, the destruction wrought by the conflict was vast. When the Confederate army surrendered in 1865, it signaled the end to the costliest war in which the United States had ever engaged and, indeed, the bloodiest civil war in human history.[68] Its end marked a victory for the Abolitionists and for the blacks, for it ended a system of human slavery which had persisted for almost 250 years. However, since the war had been fought in the South, that area had suffered widespread destruction. With the end of the war came widespread social disorganization among the whites as well as among the slaves. This social disorganization was matched by massive physical destruction. "Fields were laid waste, cities burned, bridges and roads destroyed. Even most of the woefully inadequate factories were leveled. . . . And if the Union forces did not loot quite as many smokehouses and pantries as they were blamed for, what they did do emphasized the helplessness of the once proud Confederates."[69]

One reporter, traveling in the South immediately after the Civil War, recorded the physical destruction of that region. Arriving in Richmond, Virginia, he reported:

> All up and down, as far as the eye could reach, the business portion of the city bordering on the river lay in ruins. Beds of cinders, cellars half filled with bricks and rubbish, broken and blackened walls, impassable streets deluged with debris, here a granite-front still standing and there the iron fragments of crushed machinery—such was the scene which extended over 30 entire squares and parts of other squares.[70]

Of Atlanta, Georgia, he wrote:

> "Every business block in Atlanta was burned, except one. The railroad machine shops, the foundries, the immense rolling mill, the tent, pistol, gun carriage, shot-and-shell factories and storehouses of the Confederacy had disappeared in flames and explosions. Half a mile of the principal street was destroyed.[71]

Such descriptions as these could be matched for each of the principal cities of the Confederacy, and loss of lives was staggering. The South had suffered a humiliating defeat by a superior power. Added to this military defeat was the destruction of a way of life, the most serious aspect of which was the liberation of the slaves, a situation which posed social, economic, and political problems of enormous magnitude. Although General Robert E. Lee accepted the terms of the surrender imposed by General Ulysses S. Grant, Southerners were determined that defeat in battle would not significantly alter their relations with the newly freed ex-slaves. They considered the blacks to be free but were convinced of their inferiority, and they were also convinced that, given time, southerners would decide their status to their own satisfaction.

THE RECONSTRUCTION

The efforts to rehabilitate the South and the role of black people in these efforts loom as two of the most controversial aspects of American history. Since economic, political, and social life were disrupted by the Civil War, problems posed by Reconstruction were not limited to the South, nor was their outcome determined solely by the role played by the nearly four million ex-slaves. It is primarily to the role of the Afro-American in Reconstruction and to the effects of this period on the present status of black people in the United States that attention is now directed.

Presidential Reconstruction

The year following the Civil War was an especially difficult one for the newly freed blacks. President Lincoln had envisioned Reconstruction as a function of the office of the president, but his assassination in April 1865 put an end to the plans he had formulated. The South was in a state of almost total disorganization, and Lincoln's successor, President Andrew Johnson, appeared to be less concerned about Afro-American rights than about other aspects of reconstruction.[72] Meanwhile, the condition of the black people gradually deteriorated. Southern whites grew more violent, and as one historian has written, "It seems as though in 1866 every Southerner began to murder or beat Negroes."[73] The president was indifferent to the treatment of black people because his conception of democracy did not include the blacks. The southerners, who had waged a war to keep blacks enslaved, proceeded to pass a series of laws which became known as Black Codes. These laws were specifically designed to restrict the rights of blacks. As Du Bois has written, they represented an attempt ". . . on the part of the Southern states to make Negroes slaves in everything but name."[74] The Black Codes varied from state to state, but in general they dealt with virtually every aspect of the lives of ex-slaves, and were designed to take advantage of the precarious position of the ex-slaves. These codes covered such diverse features as whether blacks could enter certain states, the conditions under which they were allowed to work, their rights to own and dispose of property, conditions under which they could hold public assemblies, the ownership of firearms, vagrancy, and a variety of other matters. In some states any white person could arrest an Afro-American. In Opelousas, Louisiana, one ordinance provided that "no Negro or freedman shall be allowed to come within the limits of the town of Opelousas without special permission from his employer, specifying the object of his visit and the time necessary for the accomplishment of the same." It continued, "Every Negro freedman who shall be found on the streets of Opelousas after ten o'clock at night without a written pass or permit from his employer, shall be imprisoned and compelled to work five days on the public streets or pay a fine of five dollars."[75]

The southern ex-slaveholders enacted such laws for a variety of reasons, one of them being their irritation at the presence of black troops with bayonets stationed in the South. This practice was only slightly more offensive to them than the establishment by Congress in 1865, over the veto of the president, of the Bureau of Refugees, Freedmen, and Abandoned Lands, commonly known as the Freedmen's Bureau. This agency had as its responsibility aiding refugees and freedmen by "furnishing supplies and medical services, establishing schools, supervising contracts between freedmen and their employers, and managing confiscated or abandoned lands."[76] The Freedmen's Bureau suspended the Black Codes before they became effective. Nevertheless, it became clear to northern observers, Abolitionists, and Congressmen that the president maintained little interest in protecting the rights of the freedmen. Violence directed against them became widespread. During the summer of 1866, for example, bloody race riots erupted throughout the South during which time hundreds of black people were killed. Congress therefore voted itself responsibility for Reconstruction.

Radical Reconstruction

Congress established a procedure whereby the South was divided into military districts, and the freedmen became wards of the government. Military commanders of each of the five districts were empowered to suspend the functions of civil government when deemed necessary and to call constitutional conventions consisting of delegates selected without regard to race or previous condition of servitude. The South was finally moving toward democratic reconstruction. In 1865 the Thirteenth Amendment to the Constitution, which abolished slavery, had been enacted and ratified, and in 1866 Congress passed, again over the president's veto, the Civil Rights Act of 1866, which made blacks citizens and gave them the same rights enjoyed by white Americans. This law ultimately became the Fourteenth Amendment to the Constitution, which prohibited states from depriving any person "of life, liberty, or property, without due process of the law," and forbade states from denying blacks "the equal protection of the laws."

Perhaps the most revolutionary aspect of Reconstruction was the participation by blacks in the political arena. In the former Confederate states the black people registered to vote in greater numbers than whites did. The series of Reconstruction Acts enacted by Congress between 1866 and 1868 and the Fifteenth Amendment, which became part of the Constitution in 1870, guaranteed them the right to vote. During the first registrations, when delegates were elected to state conventions in 1868, 703,000 black voters registered as compared with only 627,000 white voters.[77] Blacks were in a majority in the South Carolina state convention and made up half of the delegates in Louisiana. In the other states they constituted minorities ranging from 10 percent of the delegates to 19 percent.[78]

During the period of Radical Reconstruction black people participated in politics to a greater extent than in any other period in American history. The masses of blacks, however, were illiterate and depended on southern landowners for support. The landowning class capitalized on the traditional anti-black prejudices of the poor whites, with whom the blacks were in competition, and thereby sought to maintain their position of dominance. Ultimately the landowning class was successful in these efforts, but the blacks managed to play a significant role in the political life of the South. Although they made up numerical majorities in the population of several states, they never effectively controlled the affairs of any states. They often held important offices, but there was never a black governor. There were two lieutenant governors, and several blacks represented their states in the U.S. Congress.

Many of the black leaders in the South were well educated. For example, a black state treasurer in South Carolina had been educated in Glasgow and London; one of that state's black representatives in Congress had been educated at Eton College in England; and a black man who was a state supreme court justice held a law degree from the University of Pennsylvania. Florida's black secretary of state had graduated from Dartmouth College. According to one historian, "One of the really remarkable features of the Negro leadership was the small amount of vindictiveness in their words and their actions. There was no bully, no swagger, as they took their places in the state and federal governments traditionally occupied by white planters of the South. The spirit of conciliation pervaded most of the public utterances the Negroes made."[79] In the realm of social relations, black people gave no indication of serious interest in interpersonal relations with white people. Their chief concern was with being accorded a position of equality with southern whites.

In spite of the constant attempts at counterreconstruction, especially by such avowed white supremacy organizations as the Ku Klux Klan, the Red Shirts, and the Knights of the White Camelia, the newly freed slaves in the South enjoyed a kind and degree of freedom they had not known before and have not known since. Of paramount concern to them was the question of education. In five states black men were elected to the state superintendency of education, and throughout the South both the young and the old flocked to schools. They freely attended places of public accommodation, they voted in large numbers, and they elected intelligent and capable blacks to public office. In effect, they enjoyed a significant measure of political, economic, and social freedom.

The Compromise of 1877: Turn toward Slavery

Throughout the period of Radical Reconstruction attempts were made by ex-Confederates to impede the progress being made toward racial democracy in the South. Conservatives frequently seized power in state governments, and by 1876 they had succeeded in coming to power and effectively destroying Reconstruction programs in eight states.[80] Federal troops had been withdrawn from all but three states. Violence directed against blacks was widespread. It was clear that the South was determined to maintain white supremacy at all cost. They were effectively assisted in this endeavor by the outcome of the disputed presidential election of 1876, in which Rutherford B. Hayes was the Republican candidate and Samuel Tilden the Democratic candidate. This disputed election was settled in Congress by the Compromise of 1877, in which Hayes was finally declared the winner. In effect, the Compromise of 1877 saw the Republican party (the so-called Party of Emancipation) abandon the blacks to former slaveholders.[81] It was felt by the party leaders to be necessary to avert another civil war. Nevertheless, for all practical purposes this compromise signaled a return toward slavery which was to characterize the relations between blacks and whites in the South for decades to follow. The remaining troops were withdrawn from the South, and the South was accorded complete home rule and other political favors. The most important favor to the southerners was the promise which the compromise brought in the realm of race relations: "It did assure the dominant whites political autonomy and nonintervention in matters of race and policy. . . ."[82]

The leaders of the South promised that the rights of blacks would be protected, and especially that the newly ratified amendments to the Constitution would be adhered to. Political leaders in Washington, who were aware of the course the South had been taking since emancipation appeared to be more interested in political stability than in human rights. Thus virtually all the accomplishments of Radical Reconstruction were gradually overturned. Black people had been most effective in political life, and the southern whites were determined to disfranchise them. It was not long before they succeeded. For the blacks the South proceeded on a backward course. As summarized by Franklin, "Reconstruction was over. The South was back in the Union, with a leadership strikingly like that of the South which had seceded in 1860."[83]

INSTITUTIONALIZED WHITE SUPREMACY

From 1877 to 1954 virtually all the events pertaining to black people in the United States adversely affected their status. While this period of more than seven decades saw profound changes in the society as a whole, the Afro-American's status remained relatively fixed. Americans persisted in their prejudiced attitudes toward blacks, and these attitudes were translated into acts of segregation and discrimination in virtually every aspect of life. Where segregation and discrimination were not required by law, they became deeply ingrained in the mores. Such behavior became part of the "American way of life," and few white Americans challenged these sacred practices. Black people, on the other hand, constantly challenged them, especially those which were enacted into law; but they were consistently rebuffed. They had been relegated to a caste position in society, and no black, no matter what his or her level of achievement, could expect to be accorded treatment equal to that of a white person.

The Emergence of "Jim Crow"

With the end of Reconstruction in the South the restoration of white supremacy was underway. Race became the crucial factor in political, economic, and social life. Although the South was in the vanguard of this movement, it had many allies throughout the country. In 1883, for example, the Supreme Court declared the Civil Rights Act of 1875 unconstitutional. This act made it a crime for a person to deny any citizen equal access to accommodations in inns, public conveyances, theaters, and other places of amusement. Several other judicial rulings of the nation's highest court served to institutionalize white supremacy in the United States.

Principal among these was the decision of the Court in the *Plessy v. Ferguson* case in 1896. In this case the Court ruled that separate (i.e., segregated) facilities for blacks and whites were not a violation of the constitutional guarantees of the Thirteenth and Fourteenth Amendments. "If one race be inferior to the other socially, the Constitution of the United States cannot put them upon the same plane," declared the majority opinion.[84] This ruling set the pattern for attitudes toward blacks and treatment of them in the United States that have persisted to the present. It became known as the "separate but equal" ruling of the Supreme Court, and southerners were more concerned with the separation of blacks than with equality. This decision had been foreshadowed by that in a previous case, *Hall v. de Ceur,* in 1877, which stated that "a state could not *prohibit* segregation on a common carrier," and in the case of *Louisville, New Orleans, and Texas Railroad v. Mississippi,* in 1880, when the Court ruled that "a state could constitutionally *require* segregation on carriers."[85]

Jim Crow laws had existed in the South since the fall of the Confederacy, but they were quickly repealed by Reconstruction legislatures. However, with the Compromise of 1877 they reappeared, gradually at first, and by 1890 they were mushrooming throughout the South. In the two decades between 1890 and 1910 these laws served to relegate black people to subordinate status in virtually all apects of life.[86]

Added impetus to the institutionalization of white supremacy was given by the black educator Booker T. Washington, who advocated accommodation on the part of black people at a time when accommodation meant continued relegation to a subordinate position in society. He encouraged other blacks to accept, as he himself had done, the subordinate position of the Afro-American. "Cast down your bucket where you are," he admonished black people. Washington's position was clearly set forth in a speech he delivered at the Cotton States Exposition in Atlanta, Georgia, in 1895. Among other things, he told his predominantly white audience: "As we have proved our loyalty to you in the past, in nursing your children, watching by the sickbed of your mothers and fathers, and often following them with tear-dimmed eyes to their graves, so in the future, in our humble way, we shall stand by you. . . ." He continued, "In all things that are purely social we can be as separate as the fingers, yet one as the hand in all things essential to mutual progress."[87] Upon completion of his address it is reported that the white audience "came to its feet, yelling" approvingly, while the blacks in the audience wept.[88] The "Atlanta Compromise" speech, as it became known, assured Americans that the recently mushrooming Jim Crow laws defined the proper form of relations between blacks and whites. Washington was acknowledged as the "leader" of the black population of the United States. The outcome of Washington's program of accommodation to white supremacy was accurately predicted by his most formidable critic, William E. B. Du Bois.[89]

As a leader, Booker T. Washington enjoyed wide popularity among both black and white Americans. He was highly respected by white philanthropists and government officials. As adviser to two presidents (Theodore Roosevelt and William H. Taft), he is reported to have recommended virtually all appointments of blacks to high office during their administrations. Washington achieved prominence at a time when relations between black and white Americans were deteriorating, and although many aspects of his self-help program might have seemed to improve the status of the freedmen, his lack of concern with equal rights for blacks did not represent an insightful long-range plan.[90]

A wave of terror, stemming from violence directed against blacks, spread throughout the South. As Frazier has noted, during the Reconstruction blacks responded to violence by organized action, which often led to race riots, but because of the precariousness of their position at this time, organized action was rare. Hence whites resorted to lynching and terror as means of containing the blacks. Lynchings in the South increased between 1882 and 1890, and the last decade of the nineteenth century witnessed a sharp increase. This increase coincided with the many legislative acts in that region which institutionalized the subordinate status of the blacks.[91]

White Americans in the North had apparently lost interest in the welfare of black people. Indeed, many who had championed the cause of the blacks defended the southern view of race relations. Many periodicals, such as *The Nation, Harper's Weekly,* the *North American Review,* and the *Atlantic Monthly,* carried articles by "Northern liberals and former Abolitionists mouthing the shibboleths of white supremacy regarding the Negro's innate inferiority, shiftlessness, and hopeless unfitness for full participation in the white man's civilization."[92] Meanwhile, disfranchisement of black people proceeded rapidly, and the number of blacks holding elective offices declined. By the turn of the century the last black congressman had left office, and virtually all black people in the South were disfranchised.

The Black Response

Because of their economic plight and the widespread violence directed against them, many black people sought to improve their status through migration. In 1900 nearly nine-tenths of the blacks in the United States were in the South, the vast majority of them living in the rural areas. The migration took several forms: rural blacks sought safety in the relative anonymity of cities, southern blacks moved North, and many blacks moved to countries in Africa. Because of their economic plight, the absence of skills, and discrimination elsewhere in the United States, most blacks remained in the rural South.

The campaign to prove that black people were innately inferior was under way. Southerners led the campaign, but they were by no means alone in this endeavor. Northern newspapers and magazines supported their efforts by running a steady stream of editorials in which blacks were caricatured as subhuman beings. Meanwhile, a talented group of black intellectuals, led by William E. B. Du Bois, challenged the leadership of Booker T. Washington and organized to protest the subordinate position to which black people had been relegated. Du Bois's response to Washington's teachings was stated as follows:

> . . . so far as Mr. Washington apologizes for injustice, North or South, does not rightly value the privilege of voting, belittles the emasculating effects of caste distinctions, and opposes the higher training of our brighter minds,— so far as he, the South, or the Nation does this,— we must increasingly and firmly oppose them. By every civilized and peaceful method we must strive for the rights which the world accords men.[93]

Despite the widespread campaign to prove the innate inferiority of black people, and despite the efforts of Booker T. Washington in counseling them to accommodate to the status quo, many blacks reached the highest realms of scholarship and organized to protest the many Jim Crow laws being enacted throughout the country. By that time disfranchisement in the South was virtually complete, and a system of rigid segregation had been enacted into law. In 1905 these intellectuals met and organized the Niagara Movement, an organization that demanded for blacks the same rights enjoyed by white Americans. This movement convinced numerous white Americans that many black people had rejected the leadership of Booker T. Washington. Furthermore, Washington's program of accommodation appeared to be ineffective in dealing with the widespread antiblack mob violence and other acts of white supremacy spreading throughout the United States. Consequently, a group of whites and blacks met in 1909 and organized the National Association for the Advancement of Colored People (NAACP). They adopted a platform calling for the abolition of segregation, equal educational opportunities, the right to vote, and the enforcement of the Fourteenth and Fifteenth Amendments.[94]

World War I and Its Aftermath

The participation by the United States in World War I did little to improve the status of black people. It did, however, influence their geographic distribution. From 1914 to 1920 an estimated 400,000 to 1,000,000 black people left the South to work in industries of the North.[95] The steady stream of immigrants from Europe had virtually ceased, and blacks in the South were recruited by northern industries. In addition to economic opportunities, continued lynching and intimidation in the South stimulated the northward migration of blacks. As these migrants settled in northern cities, they were forced into segregated neighborhoods. Although continued southern violence had in part motivated this migration, violence also greeted them in their new locations. For example, a mob of whites in East St. Louis, Illinois, massacred and burned 125 blacks in 1917. While black troops fought abroad, their civilian counterparts were forced to defend themselves in the streets back home. Lynching continued in the South. A crowd of three thousand white spectators in Tennessee responded to a newspaper invitation to watch a black man being burned alive.[96] Violence directed against black people during this period was not limited to civilians; black soldiers in uniform were the subjects of continued violence, including lynching, especially in the South.

Meanwhile, nearly 400,000 blacks registered for military service in World War I. In characteristic American fashion, they were enrolled in segregated units and trained at segregated camps. They served mainly in the army, being barred from the marines and utilized in the most menial capacities in the navy. In the army they served in nearly all branches except the Aviation Corps. Service in the army was difficult for blacks because they were constantly insulted by white officers. Throughout the war severe clashes between black and white soldiers erupted. Despite these difficulties, they remained loyal, and some 100,000 of them served on overseas duty. Those who served overseas, like those who remained in the United States, were subject to indignities from white soldiers. Nevertheless, many of them performed heroically in battle and received praise for their services from the French.[97]

The year following the end of World War I was also difficult for blacks. More than seventy black persons, including ten servicemen in uniform, were lynched. The summer of 1919 was called the Red Summer because of the racial violence which took place. From June to September some twenty-five race riots erupted in American cities, and fourteen blacks were publicly burned alive. The most serious outbreak occurred in Chicago, where thirty-eight persons were killed, twenty-three of them blacks. The postwar antiblack violence convinced many blacks that it was necessary to defend themselves from these attacks; therefore armed self-defense was widespread, especially in cities.[98]

After the war many blacks remained in Europe, especially in France, where they experienced racial democracy for the first time. Those who returned expected to find changed attitudes in the United States but found instead that white supremacy was still the norm. There had been a deliberate effort to belittle their roles in the war effort, and their scores on the army intelligence tests were widely interpreted as proving their innate inferiority.

The widespread economic prosperity of the 1920s had little effect on the low status to which black people were relegated. By then much of the country was completely segregated along racial lines, and antiblack violence, including lynching, continued unchecked. In response to those conditions, scores of black people in the North and South rallied to the support of Marcus Garvey and the Universal Negro Improvement Association.[99] Garvey was able to build the largest mass movement among blacks in American history. The number of black people who actually became members of the organization is not known; however, estimates range up to six million.[100] Garvey's popularity was based on his nationalistic appeal to poorer blacks. He advocated pride in blackness and the eventual establishment of a black nation in Africa. Middle-class blacks, especially the leadership of the NAACP, were his strongest critics, for they envisioned the complete integration of black people in American society. After a persistent stream of rebuffs, however, many black people maintained doubts about this eventuality. One historian has written in appraisal of Garvey's program: "Its significance lies in the fact that it was the first and only real mass movement among Negroes in the United States and that it indicates the extent to which Negroes entertained doubts concerning the hope for first-class citizenship in the only fatherland of which they knew."[101] The Universal Negro Improvement Association finally declined in 1923, when Garvey was convicted on a charge of using the mails to defraud in raising money for the shipping line which he founded. He was subsequently deported to the West Indies and eventually died in London in 1940.

The post-World War I decade witnessed, in addition to the phenomenal growth of the Universal Negro Improvement Association, what has been called a Negro renaissance. During the 1920s a number of blacks, especially those in Harlem, were active in publishing books, magazines, and newspapers. The theme of the writings and music of this period was an attack on the injustices imposed on blacks by the larger society. Although black authors had published books prior to this time, it was this period of extraordinary literary activity which convinced the owners of publishing companies that black people were capable of high-caliber literary achievement. Although most of their efforts may be termed social protest, the artistic merit of their work marked them as among the outstanding contributors to American literature and music.

The Depression, The New Deal, and World War II

The Great Depression of the 1930s virtually ended the massive migration of blacks from the South. Although most Americans suffered from the depression, it was especially difficult for those in low-status occupations, and the overwhelming majority of blacks fell within this category. By the mid-1930s great masses of blacks were receiving public assistance; in some sections of the country the figure was as high as 80 percent. When the unemployed and hungry blacks applied for public assistance, they again met with discrimination. In many sections of the country there was a significant differential between the allocations they received and those received by white Americans.[102]

The government agencies created to deal with problems brought about by the depression were effective in aiding those poor people who were in greatest need, including a significant proportion of blacks. Whatever assistance was provided by the New Deal generally occurred within a framework of segregation. President Franklin D. Roosevelt appointed what became known as his Black Cabinet to advise him on matters pertaining to the welfare of black people. Many blacks held high (although primarily symbolic) positions in such agencies as the National Youth Administration and the Department of the Interior. Because of the interest of Roosevelt and of Eleanor Roosevelt in the general welfare of the poor, and of blacks in particular, black people began to shift in large numbers from the Republican party to the Democratic party. The northward migration and the residential segregation of blacks in large cities stimulated political rejuvenation for the first time since Reconstruction. The New Deal policies of the Roosevelt administration ushered in a new conception of the role of government toward citizens. Many of the social welfare measures enacted during the period helped bring the country out of the depression and have since become firmly established social policy.

In many ways the New Deal signaled a turning point in attitudes toward blacks.[103] Many of the prominent politicians of this period expressed an interest in the plight of the black population as part of a broader humanitarian interest in the problem of poverty. For example, one individual who expressed great interest in the welfare of black people was Harold L. Ickes, secretary of the interior and a former president of a local chapter of the NAACP. In addition, black voting strength in northern cities reached a point where their welfare could not be easily ignored. Furthermore, blacks organized to protect their interests. In 1933 the Joint Committee on National Recovery, a coalition of black-rights organizations, was founded to fight discriminatory policies in federal works projects. One of its main accomplishments was exposing differential wages paid to black and white workers.

In general the New Deal benefited black people by creating a favorable climate of opinion for increased civil rights, by increasing the material benefits paid to the unemployed, and by reducing discrimination in employment. However, discrimination continued in federal works projects and in the policies of the Agricultural Adjustment Administration; moreover, segregation was maintained in public accommodations in the South and in housing financed by the Federal Housing Administration.[104]

The rise of industrial unionism, especially the formation of the Congress of Industrial Organizations (CIO), had its impact on race relations during the 1930s. Although separate locals were maintained in the South, the CIO made interracial trade unionism respectable. It gave black and white workers a sense of common interest, and for the first time black and white workers worked together, receiving equal pay for comparable jobs.[105]

As the United States became increasingly involved in the war in Europe, a period of widespread prosperity was enjoyed by most Americans, including blacks. Again the southern blacks migrated north by the millions. As they sought employment in the war industries, they were faced with characteristic acts of discrimination. It took the threat of a massive march on Washington by blacks to force President Roosevelt to issue an executive order barring discrimination against blacks in industries with government contracts. Since many black people had received technical training during the New Deal administration, they were well prepared to work in industries supporting the war effort.

More than a million black men and women served in the military service during World War II. Approximately 500,000 of them served overseas. As usual, the military services were rigidly segregated, although toward the end of the war a practice of integrating black platoons into white units overseas was established. Widespread violence and discrimination continued, causing black servicemen to question their participation in a war being fought for "four freedoms" by a country which denied them the very principles for which they were fighting on behalf of others. Servicemen in uniform were beaten and murdered by southern policemen and citizens. Attempts on their part to resist segregation and discrimination resulted in frequent clashes on military installations, both at home and abroad, that sometimes led to race riots. One of the more humiliating practices for black servicemen was that of restaurant owners' serving German prisoners of war in places of public accommodation in the United States while denying similar service to black servicemen.[106]

The continued adherence to white supremacy in the face of widespread participation by blacks in World War II, as well as the support of the war effort by black civilians, raised doubts in the minds of many black people about the seriousness of cultural pronouncements of such concepts as "freedom," "justice," and "equality." Meanwhile, as the war was being waged in Europe and Asia, European colonial powers were beginning to lose their black colonies in Africa. At the close of the war the United Nations was established, and the United States became increasingly concerned about its "image" abroad.

During the years immediately following World War II, because of the combination of increased black militancy and changing world conditions, several events occurred which gave black people some hope that their depressed status might somehow be altered. New York State enacted the first state Fair Employment Practices Law in 1945. President Harry S.

Truman created the first national committee on civil rights in 1946, and in 1948 he issued an executive order banning segregation and discrimination in the armed forces. Meanwhile, the Supreme Court, beginning in 1946, issued a series of decisions outlawing segregation in various aspects of American life, culminating in the decision in 1954 which prohibited racial segregation in public education.

• • •

This brief sketch of significant historical events in the lives of Afro-Americans since the first permanent black settlement in North America has focused on those circumstances which are responsible for the present state of race relations in the United States. Blacks were enslaved and subjected to a system of bondage with few parallels in human history. Formal slavery ended in a costly war, and a caste system developed which continued to relegate the former slaves and their descendants to a subordinate position in society. By the middle of the twentieth century the oppressed status of black people had finally been recognized as a social problem of some magnitude, and there were attempts by both black and white Americans to deal with the problem. These approaches will be discussed in a later chapter. The next several chapters deal with the immediate results of the peculiar history of black people in the United States.

SELECTED BIBLIOGRAPHY

APTHEKER, HERBERT. *A Documentary of the Negro People in the United States.* New York: Citadel Press, 1951.

———. *American Negro Slave Revolts.* New York: International Publishers Co., 1963.

ARMSTRONG, GEORGE D. *The Christian Doctrine of Slavery.* New York: Charles Scribner's Sons, 1857.

BENNET, LERONE, JR. *Before the Mayflower.* Baltimore: Penguin Books, 1966.

BROWN, INA C. *The Story of the American Negro.* New York: Friendship Press, 1957.

BUCKMASTER, HENRIETTA. *Let My People Go: The Story of the Underground Railroad and the Growth of the Abolition Movement.* New York: Harper & Brothers, 1941.

CRONON, EDMUND DAVID. *Black Moses: The Story of Marcus Garvey and the Univeral Negro Improvement Association.* Madison: University of Wisconsin Press, 1955.

DAVIS, DAVID B. *The Problem of Slavery in Western Culture.* Ithaca, N.Y.: Cornell University Press, 1966.

DEGLER, CARL N. *Out of Our Past.* New York: Harper & Row, Publishers, 1959.

DOUGLASS, FREDERICK. *Narrative of the Life of Frederick Douglass, An American Slave.* Edited by Benjamin Quarles. Cambridge, Mass: Harvard University Press, 1960.

DOUNAN, ELIZABETH. *Documents Illustrative of the History of the Slave Trade to America.* Washington, D.C.: Carnegie Institution in Washington, 1935.

DU BOIS, W. E. B. *Black Folk, Then and Now.* New York: Henry Holt & Co., 1939.

———. *Black Reconstruction.* New York: Harcourt, Brace & Co., 1935.

———. *The Souls of Black Folk.* Chicago: A.C. McClurg & Co., 1903.

ELKINS, STANLEY. *Slavery: A Problem in American Institutional and Intellectual Life.* Chicago: University of Chicago Press, 1959.

EMBREE, EDWIN R. *Brown Americans.* New York: Viking Press, Inc., 1946.

FEHRENBACHER, DON. *Slavery, Law, and Politics: The Dred Scott Case in Historical Perspective.* New York: Oxford University Press, 1981.

FITZHUGH, GEORGE. *Cannibals All! Or Slaves Without Masters.* Richmond, Va.: A. Morris, 1857.

FRANKLIN, JOHN HOPE. *From Slavery to Freedom.* New York: Alfred A. Knopf, 1948.

————. *Reconstruction after the Civil War.* Chicago: University of Chicago Press, 1961.

FRAZIER, E. FRANKLIN. *Black Bourgeoisie.* Glencoe, Ill.: Free Press, 1957.

————. *The Negro Family in the United States.* Chicago: University of Chicago Press, 1966.

————. *The Negro in the United States.* New York: Macmillan Co., 1957.

FREYRE, GILBERTO. *The Masters and the Slaves: A Study in the Development of Brazilian Civilization.* New York: Alfred A. Knopf, 1964.

GENOVESE, EUGENE D. *The Political Economy of Slavery: Studies in the Economy and Society of the Slave South.* New York: Pantheon Books, 1965.

GRANT, JOANNE. *Black Protest.* New York: Fawcett World Library, 1968.

HALASZ, NICHOLAS. *The Rattling Chains: Slave Unrest and Revolt in the American South.* New York: David McKay Co., 1966.

HARLAN, LOUIS R. *Booker T. Washington: The Making of a Black Leader, 1865–1901.* New York: Oxford University Press, 1973.

HARRIS, MARVIN. *Patterns of Race in the Americas.* New York: Walker & Co., 1964.

HERSKOVITS, MELVILLE. *The Myth of the Negro Past.* New York: Harper & Brothers, 1941.

HIGGINBOTHAM, A. LEON. *In the Matter of Color: Race and the American Legal Process: The Colonial Period.* New York: Oxford University Press, 1978.

HUGHES, LANGSTON. *Fight for Freedom: The Story of the NAACP.* New York: Berkley Publishing Corp., 1962.

KEMBLE, FRANCES A. *Journal of a Residence on a Georgia Plantation in 1838–1839.* Edited by John A. Scott. New York: Alfred A. Knopf, 1961.

LITWACK, LEON F. *North of Slavery.* Chicago: University of Chicago Press, 1961.

LOGAN, RAYFORD W. *The Negro in the United States.* Princeton, N.J.: D. Van Nostrand Co., 1957.

McPHERSON, JAMES M. *The Negro's Civil War.* New York: Random House, 1965.

MEIER, AUGUST, and RUDWICK, ELLIOT. *From Plantation to Ghetto.* New York: Hill and Wang, 1966.

MYRDAL, GUNNAR. *An American Dilemma: The Negro Problem and Modern Democracy.* New York: Harper & Brothers, 1944.

NOEL, DONALD L., ed. *The Origins of Slavery and American Racism.* Columbus, Ohio: Charles E. Merrill Co., 1972.

OLMSTEAD, FREDERICK L. *The Cotton Kingdom.* Edited by Arthur M. Schlesinger. New York: Alfred A. Knopf, 1953.

PHILLIPS, ULRICH B. *American Negro Slavery.* New York: D. Appleton & Co., 1918.

ROSS, FRED A. *Slavery Ordained by God.* Philadelphia: J.B. Lippincott Co., 1857.

SIEBERT, WILBUR H. *The Underground Railroad from Slavery to Freedom.* New York: Macmillan Co,. 1898.

SIMKINS, FRANCIS B. *A History of the South.* New York: Alfred A. Knopf, 1959.

STAMPP, KENNETH M. *The Peculiar Institution: Slavery in the Ante-Bellum South.* New York: Alfred A. Knopf, 1965.

TANNENBAUM, FRANK. *Slave and Citizen: The Negro in the Americas.* New York: Alfred A. Knopf, 1946.

TROWBRIDGE, JOHN T. *The Desolate South.* New York: Meredith Press, 1956.

U.S. BUREAU OF THE CENSUS. *Negro Population 1790–1915.* Washington, D.C.: Government Printing Office, 1918.

WADE, RICHARD C. *Slavery in the Cities.* New York: Oxford University Press, 1964.

WASHINGTON, BOOKER T. *Up From Slavery.* New York: Doubleday & Company, 1900.

WOODSON, CARTER G. *The African Background Outlined.* Washington, D.C.: Association Press, 1936.

————. *The Negro in Our History.* Washington, D.C.: Associated Publishers, 1922.

WOODWARD, C. VANN. *Reunion and Reaction.* Boston: Little, Brown & Co., 1951.

————. *The Strange Career of Jim Crow.* New York: Oxford University Press, 1957.

NOTES

[1]Joseph Boskin, "Race Relations in Seventeenth Century America: The Problem of the Origins of Negro Slavery," *Sociology and Social Research* 49 (July 1965), 446–55; John Hope Franklin, *From Slavery to Freedom* (New York: Knopf, 1948), pp. 70–71; Wilbert E. Moore, "Slave Law and the Social Structure," *Journal of Negro History* 26 (1941), 171–202.

[2]Kenneth M. Stampp, *The Peculiar Institution* (New York: Knopf, 1956), p. 192.

[3]Ibid., p. 193.

[4]Ibid., p. 343.

[5]Ibid., p. 201.

[6]E. Franklin Frazier, *The Negro Family in the United States* (Chicago: University of Chicago Press, 1966), p. 360.

[7]Arnold A. Sio, "Interpretations of Slavery," *Comparative Studies in Society and History,* 7 (1965), p. 294.

[8]Stampp, *Peculiar Institution,* p. 148.

[9]Richard C. Wade, *Slavery in the Cities* (New York: Oxford University Press, 1964), pp. 28–54.

[10]E. Franklin Frazier, *The Negros in the United States* (New York: Macmillan, 1957), p. 55.

[11]See Frederick L. Olmstead, *The Cotton Kingdom,* ed. Arthur M. Schlesinger (New York: Knopf, 1953), p. 184; Stampp, *Peculiar Institution,* pp. 151–53.

[12]Stampp, *Peculiar Institution,* p. 294.

[13]Booker T. Washington, *Up from Slavery* (New York: Doubleday, 1900), pp. 3–4.

[14]Franklin, *From Slavery to Freedom,* p. 194.

[15]Stampp, *Peculiar Institution,* p. 282.

[16]Frances A. Kemble, *Journal of a Residence on a Georgia Plantation in 1838–1839,* ed. John A. Scott (New York: Knopf, 1961), p. 71.

[17]See Lerone Bennett, Jr., *Before the Mayflower* (Baltimore: Penguin, 1966); Edwin R. Embree, *Brown Americans* (New York: Viking, 1946); Franklin, *From Slavery to Freedom;* Melville Herskovits, *The Myth of the Negro Past* (New York: Harper, 1941); August Meier and Elliott Rudwick, *From Plantation to Ghetto* (New York: Hill and Wang, 1966), pp. 4–22; Charles Silberman, *Crisis in Black and White* (New York: Random House, 1964), especially chap. 6.

[18]E. Franklin Frazier, *Black Bourgeoisie* (Glencoe, Ill.: Free Press, 1957), p. 12.

[19]Franklin, *From Slavery to Freedom,* p. 40.

[20]Herskovits, *Myth of the Negro Past;* Carter G. Woodson, *The African Background Outlined* (Washington, D.C.: Association Press, 1936).

[21]See, e.g., Stanley Elkins, *Slavery* (Chicago: University of Chicago Press, 1959); Eugene Genovese, *The Political Economy of Slavery: Studies in the Economy and Society of the Slave South* (New York: Pantheon, 1965); Rayford W. Logan, *The Negro in the United States* (Princeton, N.J.: Van Nostrand, 1957); Stampp, *Peculiar Institution.* A recent anthology presents convincing evidence that American racism was more a product than a cause of slavery. See Donald L. Noel, ed., *The Origins of American Slavery and Racism* (Columbus, Ohio: Chas. E. Merrill, 1972).

[22]Two of the chief proponents of this view are Frank Tannenbaum and Stanley Elkins. See Tannenbaum's *Slave and Citizen* (New York: Knopf, 1946); and Elkins, *Slavery,* p. 52–89. In a recent work the author puts forth the thesis that slavery in Brazil was not radically different from slavery in North America. See Marvin Harris, *Patterns of Race in the Americas* (New York: Walker, 1964). See also David B. Davis, *The Problem of Slavery in Western Culture* (Ithaca, N.Y.: Cornell University Press, 1966), pp. 223–61; Carl N. Degler, *Out of Our Past* (New York: Harper & Row, 1959).

[23]See Nathan Glazer's introduction to Elkins, *Slavery;* David B. Davis, *Slavery in Western Culture,* p. 60.

[24]Tannenbaum, *Slave and Citizen,* p. 103.

[25]Ulrich B. Phillips, *American Negro Slavery* (New York: Appleton, 1918), pp. 342–43.

[26]Franklin, *From Slavery to Freedom,* p. 192.

[27]Cited in Stampp, *Peculiar Institution,* p. 172.

[28]Frederick Douglass, *Narrative of the Life of Frederick Douglass, an American Slave,* ed. Benjamin Quarles (Cambridge, Mass.: Belknap Press of Harvard University Press, 1960), p. 29.

[29]Stampp, *Peculiar Institution,* pp. 181–82.

[30]Franklin, *From Slavery to Freedom,* pp. 192–93.

[31]Ibid., p. 199.

[32]Ibid., p. 200.

[33]George D. Armstrong, *The Christian Doctrine of Slavery* (New York: Scribner, 1857); George Fitzhugh, *Cannibals All! Or Slaves Without Masters* (Richmond, Va.: A. Morris, 1857); Fred A. Ross, *Slavery Ordained by God* (Philadelphia: Lippincott, 1857). Both Armstrong and Ross were ministers.

[34]See Frazier, *Negro in the United States,* chap. 5; and Elizabeth Dounan, *Documents Illustrative of the History of the Slave Trade to America,* 4 vols. (Washington, D.C.: Carnegie Institution, 1935).

[35]Herbert Aptheker, *American Negro Slave Revolts* (New York: International Publishers, 1963), p. 162.

[36]For a typology of slave revolts see Marion D. deB. Kilson, "Towards Freedom: An Analysis of Slave Revolts in the United States," *Phylon* 25 (Summer 1964), 175–87.

[37]Nicholas Halasz, *The Rattling Chains* (New York: McKay, 1966), pp. 87–97.

[38]Ibid., p. 91.

[39]Ibid., pp. 116–38.

[40]Ibid., chap. 8.

[41]Elkins, *Slavery,* pp. 81–82.

[42]Stampp, *Peculiar Institution,* p. 140.

[43]Franklin, *From Slavery to Freedom,* pp. 255–56. See also Wilbur H. Siebert, *The Underground Railroad from Slavery to Freedom* (New York: Macmillan, 1898).

[44]Henrietta Buckmaster, *Let My People Go* (New York: Harper, 1941).

[45]Franklin, *From Slavery to Freedom,* p. 256.

[46]Stampp, *Peculiar Instituiton,* p. 109.

[47]Ibid., pp. 109–24.

[48]Phillips, *American Negro Slavery,* pp. 291–92.

[49]Ibid., pp. 341–42.

[50]Leon F. Litwack, *North of Slavery* (Chicago: University of Chicago Press, 1961), p. 30.

[51]U.S. Bureau of the Census, *Negro Population, 1790–1915* (Washington, D.C.: Government Printing Office, 1918).

[52]Meier and Rudwick, *From Plantation to Ghetto,* p. 66.

[53]Frazier, *Negro in the United States,* pp. 59ff.

[54]Franklin, *From Slavery to Freedom,* pp. 215–16.

[55]Ibid., pp. 221–23; Phillips, *American Negro Slavery,* pp. 432–36.

[56]Logan, *Negro in the United States,* p. 14.

[57]Franklin, *From Slavery to Freedom,* pp. 231–34.

[58]See Carter G. Woodson, *The Negro in Our History* (Washington, D.C.: Associated Publishers, 1922), especially chap. 19.

[59]W. E. B. Du Bois, *Black Reconstruction* (New York: Harcourt, Brace, 1935), p. 56.

[60]Franklin, *From Slavery to Freedom,* p. 269.

[61]See Logan, *Negro in the United States,* p. 22; James M. McPherson, *The Negro's Civil War* (New York: Random House, 1965), p. ix.

[62]Woodson, *Negro in Our History,* p. 374.

[63]Franklin, *From Slavery to Freedom,* p. 287.

[64]Ibid., p. 284.

[65]McPherson, *The Negro's Civil War,* pp. ix–x. Copyright 1965, Random House, Inc.

[66]Frazier, *Negro in the United States,* p. 111.

[67]Quoted in Du Bois, *Black Reconstruction,* p. 671.

[68]See Francis B. Simkins, *A History of the South* (New York: Knopf, 1959), p. 243.

[69]John Hope Franklin, *Reconstruction after the Civil War* (Chicago: University of Chicago Press, 1961), p. 2.

[70]John T. Trowbridge, *The Desolate South: 1865–1866* (New York: Meredith Press; and Boston: Little, Brown, 1956), pp.84–85.

[71]Ibid., p. 238.

[72]Simkins, *History of the South,* especially chap. 17.

[73]Ibid., p.265.

[74]Du Bois, *Black Reconstruction,* p. 167.

[75]Ibid., p. 177.

[76]Franklin, *Reconstruction after the Civil War,* pp. 36–37.

[77]Simkins, *History of the South,* p. 271.

[78]Frazier, *Negro in the United States,* p. 132.

[79]Franklin, *Reconstruction after the Civil War,* pp. 89–90.

[80]Ibid., p. 209.

[81]C. Vann Woodward, *Reunion and Reaction* (Boston: Little, Brown, 1951), Chap. 11.

[82]From p. 246 of *Reunion and Reaction* by C. Vann Woodward, copyright 1951, © 1966 by C. Vann Wooward, reprinted by permission of Little, Brown and Company, Publishers.

[83]Franklin, *Reconstruction after the Civil War,* p. 226.

[84]Logan, *Negro in the United States,* document no. 9A.

[85]C. Vann Wooward, *The Strange Career of Jim Crow* (New York: Oxford University Press, 1957), p. 54.

[86]Ibid., pp. 49–95.

[87]Logan, *Negro in the United States,* document no. 8.

[88]Bennett, *Before the Mayflower,* pp. 228–29.

[89]W. E. B. Du Bois, *The Souls of Black Folk* (Chicago: A. C. McClurg, 1903), especially Chap. 3: "Of Mr. Booker T. Washington and Others."

[90]A strong defense of Booker T. Washington's leadership is put forth in Howard Brotz, *The Black Jews of Harlem* (New York: Free Press, 1964), pp. 72–83. For a different appraisal see Louis R. Harlan, *Booker T. Washington: The Making of a Black Leader, 1865–1901* (New York: Oxford University Press, 1973); Meier and Rudwick, *From Plantation to Ghetto,* pp. 181–86.

[91]Frazier, *Negro in the United States,* p. 159.

[92]Woodward, *Strange Career of Jim Crow,* pp. 52–53.

[93]Du Bois, *The Souls of Black Folk,* p. 59.

[94]Langston Hughes, *Fight for Freedom* (New York: Berkley Publishing Corp., 1962).

[95]Franklin, *From Slavery to Freedom,* p. 465; Logan, *Negro in the United States,* p. 70.

[96]Franklin, *From Slavery to Freedom,* p. 467.

[97]Woodson, *Negro in Our History,* pp. 526–27.

[98]Franklin, *From Slavery to Freedom,* pp. 471–76.

[99]See Edmund David Cronon, *Black Moses* (Madison: University of Wisconsin Press, 1955). x0

[100]Ibid., pp. 205–7.

[101]Franklin, *From Slavery to Freedom,* p. 483.

[102]Ina C. Brown, *The Story of the American Negro* (New York: Friendship Press, 1957), p. 120; Franklin, *From Slavery to Freedom,* p. 488.

[103]Meier and Rudwick, *From Plantation to Ghetto,* pp. 210–17; Gunnar Myrdal, *American Dilemma* (New York: Harper, 1944), pp. 1000–1001.

[104]Meier and Rudwick, *From Plantation to Ghetto,* pp. 212–13; Myrdal, *American Dilemma,* pp. 464–66.

[105]Meier and Rudwick, *From Plantation to Ghetto,* p. 213.

[106]Franklin, *From Slavery to Freedom,* pp. 570–73.

CHAPTER TWO
CHARACTERISTICS OF THE POPULATION

The peculiar history of black Americans is, in part, responsible for their present status. In many ways black Americans, as a group, differ from white Americans.[1] These differences invariably stem from the low status to which they have been relegated in society. In no instance are these differences more pronounced than in population characteristics. In the United States there are several fundamental differences between black and white population characteristics. When black and white Americans share similar socioeconomic status positions in society, they are remarkably similar in fertility and mortality rates, for example, but the overrepresentation of black people in the lowest status category serves to make for significant group differences between them and their white fellow citizens on population characteristics.

SIZE AND GROWTH

In 1980 black people made up 11.7 percent of the American population. Their total population of 26.5 million is exceeded on the world scene by only 28 of the more than 154 independent nation-states and self-governing territories. Only 5 of the more than 40 independent African states have total populations which exceed the number of blacks in the United States. Within the United States, blacks are the largest visible minority group. They constitute approximately 90 percent of the "nonwhite" population of the country. The size of the black population is frequently cited as a factor influencing their integration into American society. Since they have been retained in a subordinate position, and since they are responded to as a group, the very magnitude of their numbers may be considered both a handicap and an asset to their advancement in the United States.[2]

At the time of the first population census, in 1790, nearly 1 out of every 5 (19.3 percent) Americans was black. Slightly more than 750,000 blacks were enumerated by that census. With each following census the number increased to the point where, in less than two hundred years, nearly 27 million blacks now reside in the United States. The pattern of growth has been consistent, with the percentage of increase being greatest in the earlier years. During the decade from 1800 to 1810, for example, the black population increased by 37.5 percent. The decade with the lowest percentage of increase (6.5 percent) was from 1910 to 1920. The greatest single historical contributor to the increase in the black population has been the excess of births over deaths (natural increase). Since the first census, immigration has been an insignificant element in black population growth.

The proportion of black people in the total population of the United States remained relatively stable up through the census of 1810, when there was a gradual decline which persisted up through the census of 1930. This decline in the proportion of black people in the population resulted mainly from two factors: the decline and ultimate cessation in the importation of slaves and the increase in the number of white immigrants to the United States. In the decade from 1930 to 1940 there was a gradual increase in the proportion of black people in the population. In 1930 they comprised 9.7 percent of the population, and by 1980 the proportion was approximately 12 percent. (See table 2-1.)

The growth pattern of the black population may be attributed to two major factors: (1) a consistent increase in numbers from the first census until the present time and (2) fluctuation as regards proportion of the total population. The proportion was reasonably steady between 1790 and 1830, decreased moderately from 1830 to 1930, and increased gradually since 1930.

FERTILITY

The black population of the United States is increasing at a more rapid rate than the white population. The major element in the black population growth rate is the increase in births over deaths. Throughout the present century the birth rate among blacks has remained consistently higher than the white birth rate. In 1980 the birth rate among non-whites was 22.5 per 1000 population while among whites the rate was 14.9. Since 1920 the nonwhite birth rate has been at least six points greater than the white birth rate. (See table 2-2.)

TABLE 2-1   The Black Population of the United States, 1790–1980

Year	Total U.S. Population	Total Black Population	Percent Black
1980	226,545,805	26,945,025	11.7
1970	203,211,926	22,580,000	11.0
1960	179,323,175	18,871,831	10.5
1950	150,697,361	15,042,286	10.0
1940	131,669,275	12,865,518	9.8
1930	122,775,046	11,891,143	9.7
1920	105,710,620	10,463,131	9.9
1910	91,972,266	9,797,763	10.7
1900	75,944,575	8,833,994	11.6
1890	62,974,714	7,488,676	11.9
1880	50,155,783	6,580,973	13.1
1870	39,818,449	5,392,172	13.5
1860	31,443,321	4,411,830	14.1
1850	23,191,876	3,638,808	15.7
1840	17,069,453	2,873,648	16.8
1830	12,866,020	2,328,642	18.1
1820	9,638,453	1,771,656	18.4
1810	7,239,881	1,377,808	19.0
1800	5,308,483	1,002,037	18.9
1790	3,929,214	757,208	19.3

Source: Computed from the following U.S. Bureau of the Census publications: *Historical Statistics of the United States, Colonial Times to 1957*, series A 17-21, p. 8; *1980 Census of Population, Characteristics of Population, U.S. Summary*, table 46; *Statistical Abstract of the United States, 1982–83*, tables 17, 24.

Another measure of the difference between black and white fertility is the number of children born per 1000 women between the ages of 35 and 44. For black women in 1983 the number was 2879 while for white women it was 2327.[3]

The black fertility rate, like that of whites, is affected by social factors. Blacks and whites who share the same economic status positions and the same residence patterns, show similar fertility patterns. Historically, blacks have been concentrated in the rural South and have occupied low-status economic positions. Therefore their fertility rate has been higher than that of whites. When they migrate to cities, and when they improve their economic status, the birth rate declines. The economic status has apparently been a more salient variable than whether they lived in rural or urban areas, because within urban areas blacks have a higher birth rate than do whites.

After World War II the birth rate among blacks increased sharply. This trend continued up to 1960, when it dropped, and the decline persisted up to 1964. As black people are becoming urbanized at an even greater rate than whites, their fertility might be expected to continue to

TABLE 2-2   Birth Rate Per 1000 Population in The United States, By Color, 1920–1980

Year	Total	White	Nonwhite	Difference
1980	15.9	14.9	22.5	7.6
1970	18.2	15.5	25.2	9.7
1965	19.4	18.3	27.6	9.3
1960	23.7	22.7	32.1	9.4
1955	25.0	23.8	34.8	11.0
1950	24.1	23.0	33.6	10.6
1945	20.4	19.7	26.5	6.8
1940	19.4	18.6	27.6	9.0
1935	18.7	17.9	25.8	7.9
1930	21.3	20.6	27.5	6.9
1920	27.7	26.9	35.0	8.1

Source: U.S. Bureau of the Census, *Statistical Abstract of the United States, 1972*, tables 63, 67; *Statistical Abstract, 1985*, table 82.

decline. However, because the economic gap between blacks and whites is broadening rather than narrowing and because the fetal death rate is declining more rapidly among blacks than among white persons, the differential fertility rate might be expected to persist.

HEALTH AND MORTALITY

Reliable statistics on the death rate of black people were not available until about 1900. Although blacks have a higher death rate than white Americans, the death-rate differential is not so great as for births. In 1900 the death rate among blacks was 25.0 per 1000 population, while among whites it was 17.0 per 1000 population. Since that time the gap between whites and blacks has gradually narrowed to the point where, in 1982, the rate for blacks was 7.8 as compared with 5.3 for whites.[4]

Blacks still die in greater proportion than whites from diseases which are controllable through the use of modern medical techniques. In 1980 the general mortality rate for blacks was significantly higher than for whites in virtually every category.[5] Tuberculosis is no longer a major cause of death in the United States, but black people die from tuberculosis at a rate nearly three times that for whites. Similarly, the death rate from syphilis is nearly three times as great among black people as among whites. Blacks are also much more likely to die from diabetes, gastritis, infections of the kidney, measles, influenza, and pneumonia.

In recent years the death rate among blacks from hypertension has increased rapidly. By 1980 blacks were four times as likely as whites to die from hypertension and other cardiovascular diseases. The same pattern holds for malignant neoplasms (cancer). In addition, blacks were more likely to die from accidents, including motor vehicle deaths. The homicide rate for blacks is more than eight times that for whites.

Black mothers die during delivery and from complications of pregnancy at a rate six times greater than do white mothers. While the differential in general mortality rates for blacks and whites is no longer great, black infants have considerably higher mortality rates than do white infants. Since reasonably accurate statistics have been available, the infant mortality rate for black people has been consistently higher than whites. In 1915, for example, for every 1000 live births among blacks, 181 babies died during infancy; the corresponding figure for white babies was 97. This difference has persisted through the years, although between 1920 and 1955 the differences were not so great. Beginning in 1960, however, black babies were again twice as likely to die during infancy as white babies. In 1980 the infant mortality rates for white and black babies per 1000 live births were 10.5 and 17.8, respectively. (See table 2-3.) There has been a steady reduction in infant mortality rates for both blacks and whites, but the differential between the two has persisted.

A reasonably accurate measure of the health and living standards of a people is their life expectancy. In this regard black Americans have always fared less well than white Americans. In 1900 the life expectancy at birth for blacks was 33 years, while for whites it was 47.6 years. By 1980 it was 69.5 for blacks and 74.4 for whites.[6] In both cases the life expectancy at birth has substantially increased, largely because of declining infant mortality, and there has been a reduction in the difference between blacks and whites from nearly 15 years to approximately 5 years. That white Americans can expect to live longer than black Americans remains a significant indicator of the differences in living standards between these two groups.

The Department of Health and Human Services (formerly Health, Education, and Welfare) on October 15, 1985, released a report prepared by a special task force on the health of blacks and other minorities. The major findings relating to the black population included the following:[7] Homicide (defined as a public health problem) is the leading cause of death for black males ages 15 to 44. Blacks account for 43 percent of homicide victims, even though they represent only about 12 percent of the population. Cardiovascular disease is the number one killer for all Americans, with a greater total heart disease death rate for blacks than whites. A serious disparity exists between blacks and whites for cancer deaths. The increase was attributed to greater smoking among blacks than among whites. Infant mortality rates are at an all-time low for Americans but are twice as high for blacks as for whites.

According to the report, much of the health gap suffered by minority Americans is related to knowledge and lifestyle. Smoking, alcohol, diet, and obesity are clearly linked to the higher cancer, cirrhosis, cardiovascu-

TABLE 2-3   Infant Mortality Rates per 1000 Live Births, United States, By Color, 1915–80

Year	Total	White	Nonwhite	Difference
1980	12.6	10.5	17.8	7.3
1970	19.8	17.4	31.4	14.0
1965	24.7	21.5	40.3	18.8
1960	26.0	22.9	43.2	20.3
1955	26.4	23.6	42.8	19.2
1950	29.2	28.6	44.5	15.9
1945	38.3	35.6	57.0	21.4
1940	47.0	43.2	73.8	30.6
1935	55.7	51.9	83.2	31.3
1930	64.6	60.1	99.9	39.8
1925	71.7	68.3	110.8	42.5
1920	85.8	82.1	131.7	49.6
1915	99.9	98.6	181.2	82.6

Source: From 1915 to 1955, U.S. Bureau of the Census, *Historical Statistics of the United States, Colonial Times to 1957*, series 101–112, p. 25; from 1960 to 1970, U.S. Bureau of the Census, *Statistical Abstract of the United States, 1972*, p. 57; *Statistical Abstract, 1985*, p. 73.

lar, infant mortality, and other disease rates afflicting minorities. The report describes the disparity in terms of "excess deaths"—deaths which would not have occurred had mortality rates for minorities been as low as for whites. The task force has found that there are more than sixty thousand "excess deaths" each year among America's minority citizens.

In regard to cancer, lung cancer is 45 percent higher among minorities; cancer of the esophagus is three times higher; stomach cancer is one and a half times higher; prostate cancer is twice as high; and cervical cancer is two and a half times higher. Finally, the report disclosed that low birth weight is one explanation for the disparity in infant mortality.

In both health standards and mortality rates, black Americans share unequally in the social rewards of American society. The discrepancy between black Americans and their white fellow citizens in this regard is another manifestation of the racist nature of American society. While the difference in crude death rates is not great, this is a function of the younger age structure of the black population than of the white population.

AGE AND SEX COMPOSITION

The median age of the black population, like that of the white population, steadily increased in the United States until 1950. In 1850 the median age of blacks in the United States was 17.3, and by 1950 it had increased to 26.1. In 1960 the median age had decreased to 23.5, and by 1980 the decline had continued to 24.9.[8] The increase in median age of blacks resulted from an increase in the average length of life and a gradual decrease in the proportion of children. The decrease since 1950 resulted from an increase in the birth rate.

The recent decline in the median age of black people is paralleled by a similar trend among white Americans. The black population, however, is somewhat younger than the white population. There are relatively more young people and fewer old people among blacks. In 1980, for example, 39.3 percent of the black population was under 18 years of age, compared with 30 percent of the white population. On the other hand, among people 65 years of age and over in 1980, 12.1 percent of the total white population fell into this age category, compared with only 7.9 percent of the black population.[9] When the black populations under 18 and over 65 are combined, nearly one-half of the total black population falls within this dependent category; that is, almost half the black population of the United States is either too young or too old for the labor force. With the high unemployment rate for blacks eligible for the labor force, such a condition poses serious problems of economic support for the black population as a whole.

The age distribution of the black population is not uniform throughout the country. Blacks in the South are somewhat younger than those living elsewhere. The South contains a greater proportion of blacks in the dependent-children (under 18 years of age) and the dependent-aged (65 years of age and over) categories. Forty-three percent of the blacks in the South were under 18 years of age in 1980, and 8 percent were 65 and over. Comparable figures for non-southern states were considerably lower. Consequently, in that region of the country, where social welfare services are the least well developed, the need is greatest.

Blacks and whites differ in age distribution on farms and in nonfarm areas. The median age for blacks living on farms is 24 years, while for whites it is 31 years. Furthermore, blacks living on farms are younger than nonfarm blacks. The median age for urban blacks in 1980 was 25 years. This pattern is reversed for white Americans, with the median age being younger in nonfarm regions than on farms. Among black people who live on farms, 54.2 percent are under 18 years of age, and 5.6 percent are 65 years of age and over. Among nonfarm blacks, on the other hand, 43.9 percent were under 18 and 6.2 percent were 65 and over.[10] Again, where social welfare services are the least well developed (i.e., in rural areas), the need is greatest. A higher proportion of blacks than whites who fall within the dependent-children category are farm residents, while in the dependent-aged category a higher proportion of whites than blacks are nonfarm residents.

Black females outnumber black males. In 1980 there were more than 1.5 million more black females than males in the United States. Furthermore, black females are somewhat older than black males. In 1980, for example, the median age for black males was 23.6 while the median age for black females was 26.2. Among blacks, 37 percent of the females were under 18 years of age, compared with 42 percent of the males. Also, 9 percent of black females were 65 years of age and over, while 6.7 percent of the males were in this age category.[11] Throughout the United States, in all geographical regions, black females tend to be older than black males.

Because of the age differences between black males and black females and the later age of marriage for males there is a higher proportion of single males than females (34.3 percent and 30.5 percent, respectively). There is also a greater percentage of black males than black females who are married (54.6 percent vs. 48.7 percent). But, among the widowed, a significantly greater proportion of black females fall into this category than black males (14.3 percent vs. 3.2 percent).[12] These figures reflect the greater life expectancy among females than among males.

A higher proportion of black farm residents under the age of 18 are likely to be female. On the other hand, among black nonfarm residents, a higher proportion of males than females are under 18 years of age. Adult males (those 18 years of age and over) are more likely than their female counterparts to live on farms, while adult females are more likely than adult males to live in nonfarm regions.[13]

The black population is younger than the white population, and, although there are substantially more females than males in the black population, the males are younger. With the continuing difficulties that blacks face in securing and maintaining employment, such a population composition is likely to contribute to increased disillusionment and disorder in American cities.

DISTRIBUTION

Black Americans differ from white Americans in their regional and rural-urban distribution in the United States. Furthermore, redistribution in both these two categories is occurring at a more rapid rate for black Americans than for white Americans.

South—Non-South

Throughout most of American history black people have been heavily concentrated in the agricultural South. At the end of the Civil War more than 92 percent of all blacks lived in the South. There has been a gradual reduction in the black population in the South since the beginning of the twentieth century. At the turn of the century (1900), nine out of ten blacks in the United States were still in the South. Throughout the present century, however, blacks have migrated from the South to other regions, principally to the Northeast and to the North Central states. So widespread has been this migration that by 1980 only slightly more than half (53 percent) of the blacks remained in the South.[14]

Except for the South, where they constitute 19 percent of the population, blacks represent small proportions in other regions of the country. In the Northeast 10 percent of the population in 1980 was black; in the North Central states it was 9 percent; and in the West the blacks constituted only 5 percent of the total population.[15] While the South has experienced a decline in the proportion of blacks living in that region, each of the other regions has experienced increases. (See table 2-4.) The first significant exodus of black people from the South occurred during World War I. This trend has continued, declining somewhat during the depression of the 1930s and greatly accelerating during World War II. In the two decades following World War II, the proportion of blacks living in the South declined from more than three-fourths to slightly less than one-half. Altogether 3.3 million blacks left the South between 1940 and 1963.[16] The region with the greatest percentage of increase has been the West. For example, in 1940 slightly more than 1 percent of the blacks in the United States lived in this region, but by 1980 more than 9 percent lived in these states. The proportion of blacks in the North Central states nearly doubled during the same period, from 11 percent to 20 percent. The proportion of blacks in the northeastern states increased in this period from 10.6 percent to 18 percent.

Migration of blacks from the South has recently decreased. Those remaining in that region are heavily concentrated in the Deep South states. In 1980 in seven states—Alabama, Georgia, Louisiana, Maryland, Mississippi, North Carolina, and South Carolina—the population was at least one-fourth black.[17] In the country as a whole twelve states—California, Georgia, Florida, Illinois, Louisiana, Ohio, Pennsylvania, Michigan, New York, North Carolina, Texas, and Virginia—each had more than a million blacks. Seven other states had black populations in excess of five hundred thousand but less than one million.[18]

The regional redistribution of blacks generally results from the search for greater economic opportunities. Although they may not earn salaries comparable to white Americans, they can expect to earn significantly more outside the South than in that region. Furthermore, the "North" (i.e., non-South) has generally been more attractive to blacks because of the relatively lesser degree of institutionalized violence directed against them.

TABLE 2-4 Number (in thousands) and Percentage of Distribution of the Black Population in the United States, by Region, 1860–1980

Region	1980 Number	1980 Percent	1970 Number	1970 Percent	1960 Number	1960 Percent	1940 Number	1940 Percent	1900 Number	1900 Percent	1860 Number	1860 Percent
United States	26,495	100.0	22,580	100.0	18,860	100.0	12,866	100.0	8,834	100.0	4,442	100.0
Northeast	4,848	18.0	4,344	19.0	3,028	16.1	1,370	10.6	385	4.4	156	3.5
North Central	5,337	20.0	4,571	20.0	3,446	18.3	1,420	11.0	496	5.6	184	4.1
South	14,048	53.0	11,970	53.0	11,311	60.0	9,905	77.0	7,923	89.7	4,097	92.2
West	2,262	9.0	1,695	8.0	1,074	5.7	171	1.3	30	0.3	4	0.1

Source: U.S. Bureau of the Census, *Census of Population, 1960, General Population Characteristics, United States Summary*, PC (1)-1B, pp. 1–64; *Census of Population, 1980, General Population Characteristics, United States Summary*, tables 45, 50.

Rural-Urban

The internal redistribution of black people from rural areas to urban centers has been even more dramatic than their exodus from the South. Indeed, those blacks who leave the South usually settle in urban areas in other regions. Furthermore, within the South the blacks have tended to leave rural areas and settle in cities. Before the Civil War blacks were heavily concentrated in the rural sections of the South, but after 1860 they began to migrate to cities. In 1900 slightly more than one in five (22.7 percent) blacks lived in urban areas. This figure was in contrast to two out of five for the American population as a whole.[19] By 1980, however, four out of every five (80 percent) blacks lived in urban areas, compared to 73 percent of the total population. Blacks have been becoming urbanized at a faster rate than the population as a whole. In the eighty years between 1900 and 1980 the black population has been transformed from a predominately rural people to a predominately urban people.

When black people move from the rural South, they settle in the centers of the largest cities. As of 1980, twenty-eight of the largest cities in the United States had black populations of between 100,000 and 1,000,000. (See table 2-5.) These cities varied in the proportion of black people in their population anywhere from 71 percent in Gary, Indiana, to 17 percent in Los Angeles, California. Of the twenty-two American cities with populations of at least 500,000, only Phoenix, Arizona, San Antonio, Texas, and the California cities of San Diego, San Francisco, and San Jose, had fewer than 100,000 black people.

Today nearly one-half of the blacks live outside the South, and while two-fifths of those who remain in the South live in rural areas, in the North, 96 percent of blacks live in cities. If the urbanization rate among black people continues, and if whites continue to flee to the suburbs, in a matter of decades the centers of most large American cities will represent black communities. The pace of this urbanization is rapid. The black population of Los Angeles County, for example, increased by 600 percent between 1940 and 1960, and the black population of Newark, New Jersey, increased from one-third to one-half between 1960 and 1965.[20] by 1980 Newark's population was up to 58 percent black.

The widespread redistribution of blacks, combined with the enactment of civil rights legislation, has tended to broaden the focus of race relations from the South to the entire country. Because of the practices of segregation and discrimination throughout the United States, virtually every major city faces serious problems in the areas of *de facto* segregated education, inadequate and segregated housing, and unemployment in black communities. Problems in race relations are being transformed into urban problems, and the problems which were at one time referred to as

TABLE 2-5   Cities in the United States with 100,000 or more Blacks, 1980

City	Total Population	Black Population	Percentage Black Population
New York, N.Y.	7,071,639	1,784,337	25.2
Chicago, Ill.	3,005,072	1,197,000	39.8
Detroit, Mich.	1,203,339	758,939	63.1
Philadelphia, Pa.	1,688,210	638,878	37.8
Los Angeles, Calif.	2,966,850	505,210	17.0
Washington, D.C.	638,333	448,906	70.3
Houston, Texas	1,595,138	440,346	27.6
Baltimore, Md.	786,775	431,151	54.8
New Orleans, La.	557,515	308,149	55.3
Memphis, Tenn.	646,356	307,702	47.6
Atlanta, Ga.	425,022	282,911	66.6
Dallas, Texas	904,078	265,594	29.4
Cleveland, Ohio	573,822	251,347	43.8
St. Louis, Mo.	453,085	206,386	45.6
Newark, N.J.	329,248	191,745	58.2
Oakland, Calif.	339,337	159,281	46.9
Birmingham, Ala.	284,413	158,224	55.6
Indianapolis, Ind.	700,807	152,626	21.8
Milwaukee, Wis.	636,212	146,940	23.1
Jacksonville, Fla.	540,920	137,324	25.4
Cincinnati, Ohio	385,457	130,467	33.8
Boston, Mass.	562,994	126,229	22.4
Columbus, Ohio	564,871	124,880	22.1
Kansas City, Mo.	448,159	122,699	27.4
Richmond, Va.	219,214	112,357	51.3
Gary, Ind.	151,953	107,644	70.8
Nashville-Davidson, Tenn.	455,651	105,942	23.3
Pittsburgh, Pa.	423,938	101,813	24.0

Source: U.S. Bureau of the Census, *America's Black Population: 1970 to 1982: A Statistical View* (Washington, D.C.: Governemnt Printing Office), 1983, p. 2.

problems of race relations are increasingly being discussed as the problems of cities.

Through redistribution the black population is becoming more aware of its status relative to that of white Americans. In the black communities throughout the United States the residents are organizing themselves and are protesting in a manner which was not possible when they were scattered throughout the rural South. As organized urban residents, their protests are likely to be more effective. Furthermore, they are in a better position to demand that elected officials address themselves to the problems they face. Recently, these citizens have demonstrated that they are capable of posing problems in large cities with which municipal officials, acting alone, are incapable of dealing. In each of the major uprisings in black communities since 1965 it has been necessary for municipal officials to seek assistance from state governments and from the federal government. (See chapter 8.)

Finally, the migration of black people alters their status insofar as employment and medical care are concerned. In cities their employment is likely to be upgraded when compared to farm employment in the rural South, and medical care is significantly improved.

•   •   •

Black people constitute 12 percent of the American population. Within the United States, however, they are not just 26.5 million citizens out of a total population 226.5 million. Rather, they form a minority group which when compared with the larger population, occupies the lowest status in the society. They have been relegated to a harsh environment not unlike that of the peoples in the so-called developing nations of the world. In many ways they are a nation apart from white Americans. The similarities between blacks in the United States and peoples in the developing nations, on demographic characteristics, are striking. For example, both have a high birth rate and a declining death rate. Infant mortality is especially high (compared to white Americans), and life expectancy is low. Black people continue to die at a disproportionately high rate from diseases that can easily be controlled by modern medical techniques. A high proportion of the black population falls within the dependent-aged and dependent-children categories. They are migrating from rural to urban areas at a rapid rate and are being crowded into special sections of the largest cities in the country. In many regards, then, black Americans resemble the peoples of Africa, Asia, and Latin America. This resemblance has implications for protest movements and other expressions of discontent found among nonwhite peoples throughout the world.

Finally, the Census Bureau, after an analysis of the 1970 census, reported in 1973 that it had overlooked approximately 5,300,000 Americans, or 2.5 percent of the total.[21] Two-thirds of those missed were white; but because of the smaller size of the total black population, 7.7 percent of all blacks were missed in 1970, compared with 1.9 percent of the white population. The Census Bureau arrived at its undercount by checking such sources as birth records, immigration and death statistics, and Medicare and Social Security applications. Altogether some 1.88 million blacks, largely in urban areas, were not counted. The undercount of blacks was greatest among children under 10 years of age, and the major explanation offered for the sizable number of blacks not counted was the reluctance of some census enumerators to enter the black community.

SELECTED BIBLIOGRAPHY

Bogue, Donald J. *The Population of the United States.* New York: Free Press, 1959.

Frazier, E. Franklin. *The Negro in the United States.* New York: Macmillan Co., 1957.

Hauser, Philip M. "Demographic Factors in the Integration of the Negro." In *The Negro American,* edited by Talcott Parsons and Kenneth B. Clark. Boston: Houghton Mifflin Co., 1966.

Kaiser, Clyde V., ed. *Demographic Aspects of the Black Community.* New York: Milbank Memorial Fund, 1970.

Klineberg, Otto. *Negro Intelligence and Selective Migration.* New York: Columbia University Press, 1935.

Lieberson, Stanley. *Ethnic Patterns in American Cities.* New York: Free Press, 1963.

Pettigrew, Thomas F. *A Profile of the Negro American.* Princeton, N.J.: D. Van Nostrand Co., 1964.

Taeuber, Conrad, and Irene Taeuber. *The Changing Population of the United States.* New York: John Wiley & Sons, 1958.

Taeuber, Conrad, and Alma Taeuber. *Negroes in Cities.* Chicago: Aldine Publishing Co., 1965.

U.S. Bureau of the Census, *America's Black Population, 1970 to 1982: A Statistical View.* Washington, D.C.: Government Printing Office, 1983.

———. *General Social and Economic Characteristics, 1980 Census of Population, United States Summary.* Washington, D.C.: Government Printing Office, 1981.

———. *1980 Census of Population: General Population Characteristics, United States Summary 1980.* Washington, D.C.: Government Printing Office, 1981.

———. *The Social and Economic Status of the Black Population in the United States, 1972.* Washington, D.C.: Government Printing Office, 1973.

———. *Historical Statistics of the United States, Colonial Times to 1957.* Washington, D.C.: Government Printing Office, 1960.

———. *Statistical Abstract of the United States, 1985.* Washington, D.C.: Government Printing Office, 1984.

NOTES

[1] Data on the black population in the United States are sometimes entered as "Negro" and sometimes combined with other "nonwhite" minorities. Since blacks have made up at least 94 percent of the nonwhite population since the first census, "nonwhite" and "Negro" are frequently used interchangeably.

[2] See Philip M. Hauser, "Demographic Factors in the Integration of the Negro," in *The Negro Americans,* ed. Talcott Parsons and Kenneth B. Clark (Boston: Houghton Mifflin, 1966).

[3] U.S. Bureau of the Census, "Fertility of American Women: June 1983," *Current Population Reports,* series P-20, no. 395, (Washington, D.C.: Government Printing Office, 1983).

[4] U.S. Bureau of the Census, *Historical Statistics of the United States, Colonial Times to 1957* (Washington, D.C.: Government Printing Office, 1960), p. 27; U.S. Bureau of the Census, *Statistical Abstract of the United States, 1972* (Washington, D.C.: Government Printing Office, 1972), p. 57; *Statistical Abstract, 1985,* p. 71.

[5] U.S. Department of Health, Education, and Welfare, *Vital Statistics of the United States, 1968* (Washington, D.C.: Government Printing Office, 1969), pp. 7-114–7-127; *Statistical Abstract, 1985,* p. 71.

[6] U.S. Bureau of the Census, *Historical Statistics, Colonial Times to 1957,* p. 25; *Statistical Abstract, 1985,* p. 73.

[7] U.S. Department of Health and Human Services, *HHS News* (Washington, D.C.: Department of Health and Human Services, 1985).

[8] *Statistical Abstract, 1972,* p. 24; *Statistical Abstract, 1985,* p. 28.

[9]Ibid., p. 28.

[10]U.S. Bureau of the Census, *General Social and Economic Characteristics, 1980 Census of Population, United States Summary* (Washington, D.C.: Government Printing Office, 1981), table 74.

[11]*Statistical Abstract, 1985,* p. 28.

[12]Ibid., p. 28.

[13]U.S. Bureau of the Census, *General Population Characteristics, United States Summary, 1980* (Washington, D.C.: Government Printing Office, 1981), table 44.

[14]As defined by the U.S. Bureau of the Census, the South consists of Alabama, Arkansas, Delaware, the District of Columbia, Florida, Georgia, Kentucky, Louisiana, Maryland, Mississippi, North Carolina, Oklahoma, South Carolina, Tennessee, Texas, Virginia, and West Virginia.

[15]U.S. Bureau of the Census, *Statistical Abstract, 1985,* p. 29.

[16]U.S. Department of Labor, Bureau of Labor Statistics, *The Negroes in the United States: Their Economic and Social Situation* (Washington: D.C.: Government Printing Office, 1966), p. 2.

[17]*Statistical Abstract, 1985,* table 34, p. 31.

[18]Ibid., table 26, pp. 23–25.

[19]See Conrad Taeuber and Irene Taeuber, *The Changing Population of the United States* (New York: Wiley, 1958), p. 124.

[20]Charles Silberman, *Crisis in Black and White* (New York: Random House, 1964), p. 31.

[21]*New York Times,* April 26, 1973, p. 1.

CHAPTER THREE
THE BLACK COMMUNITY

The black community as a distinctive social entity can be understood only within the larger context of the status of black people in American society. Paramount among the factors contributing to its development, continuance, and growth has been the role of racism in American life. Having been systematically excluded from full participation in the larger society, black Americans found it necessary to develop separate (although frequently parallel) community institutions. The task of developing these institutions was simplified by residential segregation imposed upon blacks. As with some other minorities, blacks were never given a choice between developing separate institutions or participating in those of the larger society. They either developed their own segregated institutions or existed without them. Since their very survival depended, to some extent, on mutual dependence and aid, they developed within their own communities institutions geared toward their own self-interest and well-being.[1]

This chapter focuses on the physical character of the black community and on social stratification. The social institutions which have developed within the black community will be discussed in greater detail in later chapters.

GROWTH AND DEVELOPMENT

Until the second half of the twentieth century, blacks were predominantly rural people, concentrated in the South. Although interregional and intraregional redistribution of blacks has persisted since the turn of the century, so heavy was the concentration of blacks in the rural South that only in recent years have they become heavily urbanized and reasonably evenly distributed between the South and non-South regions of the country. At the present time the proportion of blacks living in urban areas exceeds that of the population as a whole living in urban areas. If the present rate of urbanization continues, virtually all blacks will be urban dwellers by the year 2000.

Whether urban or rural, black people in the United States have always been forced to live with other blacks. Freedom of chioce in residence has always been and continues to be an issue about which white Americans maintain strong negative views.[2] White Americans live in communities based on education, income, occupation, and other criteria of status, but blacks, whatever their status, have always been forced to live with other blacks. Voluntary associations among black people tend to be limited to those of similar status, but the general residential pattern has been one in which black people of all status levels must live side by side, in the section of the city to which they have been relegated. Residential segregation is as characteristically American as any other aspect of the culture. No matter what the city, the rule is that the "black section of town" is a distinctive one. Kenneth Clark, in discussing the concept "ghetto" as originating among Jews in Europe, has written: "America has contributed to the concept of ghetto the restriction of persons to a special area and the limiting of their freedom of choice on the basis of skin color."[3] The residential segregation of black people is virtually complete, but there is some evidence that it is gradually diminishing.

A major trend among the black population in the twentieth century has been its increasing urbanization. This process has occurred with the migration of blacks from rural areas of the South to urban areas of the North and West and from the rural areas of the South to urban centers within that region. The northward migration gained impetus during the second decade of the twentieth century and accelerated with the entry of the United States into World War I. At a time of restrictive immigration laws against Europeans and Asians in the 1920s, the blacks' northward movement continued, subsiding during the depression of the 1930s but accelerating again when the United States entered World War II. This regional redistribution and urbanization continued, with more than three million black people moving from the South to the North in the period from 1940 to 1960.

All-black neighborhoods develop mainly as a result of racial discrimination. One outgrowth of discrimination is "racial succession," that is, Afro-Americans taking over homes formerly occupied by whites. This phenomenon is especially prevalent outside the South. In Southern cities new housing is generally built for either blacks or for whites on a segregated basis. Housing developments are characteristically built in black neighborhoods for blacks and in white neighborhoods for white Americans. In either process, blacks and whites ultimately live in separate neigh-borhoods, but the difference in regions is that "in most Southern cities, Negroes have continuously been housed in areas set aside for them, whereas in the North, most areas now inhabited by Negroes were for-merly occupied by whites."[4]

In addition to residential discrimination, violence and intimidation keep black people within a restricted neighborhood. New York City pro-vides a case in point. In 1900 many blacks lived in the same neighborhood with working-class white people. This section, known as the Tenderloin, was located in midtown Manhattan. During the summer violence erupted in the neighborhood when a black man was charged with the murder of a white plainclothes policeman. In the ensuing violence, black residents were indiscriminately beaten by mobs of angry white Americans. The police, instead of protecting the blacks, joined the mobs. Hence the blacks realized the difficulties involved in living peacefully with their white neighbors; they moved north to Harlem at the first opportunity.[5] Anti-black violence, resulting from resistance to desegregation in housing, is so widespread throughout the United States that Afro-Americans can, in most cases, expect to live peacefully only when they remain in black neighborhoods. Although there has been some change in recent years, the general pattern still holds.

RURAL BLACK COMMUNITIES

Throughout much of the period following emancipation, a vast majority of black Americans lived in rural areas of the South. However, several rural developments were also found in the Northeast and North-Central regions.[6] These communities were generally made up of families of mu-latto ex-slaves and of blacks indigenous to the North. They were located in New Jersey, New York, Ohio, and Michigan. At one point these were thriving communities, held together by family and kinship ties, but with increasing urbanization they have virtually disappeared.

In the rural South black communities have persisted. Although there is some diversity within communities, and from community to com-munity, depending on the region, these residents represent the closest American approximation to a peasant class. They generally work in agri-culture, domestic service, and the lowest-paid jobs in industry. Houses are generally of poor construction, unpainted, in need of repairs, and without indoor sanitary facilities and electricity. They are usually over-crowded, with several children sharing the same bed, often in the same room with other beds for adults or children. One of the civil rights volunteers who spent the summer of 1964 in Mississippi described the community of Itta Bena: "The Negro neighborhood hasn't got a single paved street in it. It's all dirt and gravel roads. The houses vary from beat-up shacks to fairly good-looking cottages. The beat-up places predominate. There are lots of smelly outhouses, and many of the houses have no inside water."[7] Another volunteer described the living arrangements in the home of a relatively prosperous independent black farmer with whom he lived during the summer: "In the two-bedroom house in which I live we have 5 small girls, a baby, 3 teen-age girls, the mother and father, one 11-year-old boy, and a grandmother, plus two of us volunteers. The five children slept pinwheel fashion in one bed."[8]

The economic conditions of rural blacks are best illustrated by the fact that more than one-fourth of all nonwhite farm residents had family incomes of less than $5,000 in 1980, and the median income for such families was $8,600.[9] The average family size of blacks in the South, rural and urban is 3.7, and 8 percent of the families contain more than seven persons.[10] The rural southern black man is generally poor and landless and dependent on the white landowner for both employment and housing.

Rural black communities are physically distinguishable from white communities. On entering virtually any small town, it is possible to distinguish the black section from the white section because the former usually contains unpaved streets, slum housing, and outdoor sanitary facilities. A civil rights volunteer in Mississippi in 1964 describes her impressions on entering the black community in which she was to work: ". . .then the pavement bellied out and sidewalks disappeared or fell away in broken pieces: Niggertown. Rows of shanties perched on stones and bricks and joined together in precarious asymmetry were interrupted, though not often, by a spacious lawn adorned with [an] air-conditioned ranch house and a fence. The better-off Negroes had no choice of neighbors. The only other structures with anything of the right angle housed grocery stores with Chinese names and churches."[11]

In rural black communities in the South there is little organizational life except the church and the school. Of these two institutions, the church has played the dominant role. Johnson writes on the influence of the church in the rural South:

> The church has been, and continues to be, the outstanding social institution in the Negro community. It has far wider function than to bring spiritual inspiration to its communicants. Among rural Negroes the church is still the only institution which provides an effective organization of the group, an approved and tolerated place for social activities, a forum for expression on many issues, an outlet for emotional repressions, and a plan for social living. It is a complex institution meeting a wide variety of needs.[12]

One of the primary functions of the church is that of making the individual's difficulties somehow tolerable. The frustrations inherent in the precarious existence of rural blacks are many, and the constant intimidations and threats of intimidation from rural white Americans add up to lives of hardship. Through the church their lives are made worthwhile, and relief is promised in the afterlife. One of its major functions, then, is providing emotional relief for a difficult life.

Most black people in rural communities are affiliated with either Baptist or Methodist churches, with Baptists outnumbering Methodists. In recent years the church in the rural black community has been in the forefront of the drive for greater civil rights. Individual rural clergymen, under the inspiration and leadership of the late Rev. Martin Luther King, Jr., have played important roles in such movements as voter-registration drives and selective-buying campaigns. The civil rights movement was orginally organized around religious principles of nonviolence and the disarming of one's adversary through love.

Education has played an insignificant role in the life of the rural black community. Schools, where available, have generally been housed in old buildings that frequently were originally built for other purposes. The schools have traditionally been rigidly segregated racially. No attempt was made to equalize facilities until the states were threatened by a series of antisegregation decisions by the Supreme Court in the 1950s. Johnson describes what he calls a typical rural black school:

> It is in a dilapidated building, once whitewashed, standing in a rocky field unfit for cultivation. Dust-covered weeds spread a carpet all around, except for an uneven, bare area on one side which looks like a ball field. Behind the school is a small building with a broken, sagging door. As we approach, a nervous middle-aged woman comes to the door of the school. She greets us in a discouraged voice marred by a speech impediment. Escorted inside, we observe that the broken benches are crowded to three times their normal capacity. Only a few battered books are in sight, and we look in vain for maps or charts. We learn that four grades are assembled here.[13]

Teachers are often poorly trained, and until about fifteen years ago compulsory school attendance for black pupils was not enforced. Young children accompanied their parents to work in agriculture during the harvesting season. For all practical purposes, the schools did little in the way of providing education for black pupils. Those who managed to receive quality education did so in the face of extraordinary difficulties. Despite the difficulties, studies indicate considerable eagerness on the part of rural black youth for formal education.[14]

Relations between the rural black community and the larger community tend to be economic rather than social or political. Traditionally matters of politics or education were accomplished for the black community by a few black "leaders," whose main function has been to contain the black community. Social relations between the black and white communities on a basis of equality have never existed. Law and custom have decreed that a rigid caste line separate the two communities socially and that no association between blacks and whites, as equals, take place. In matters of economics the black community, with few exceptions, had been totally dependent on the white community for survival. Throughout much of the agricultural region of the South, blacks have traditionally served as sharecroppers or tenant farmers for white landowners. In this relationship they are totally dependent on the white farmer. In small towns they are usually employed in low-status positions in industry, business, and domestic and public service. A vast majority of the black women have traditionally performed domestic services. A recent survey indicated that as late as 1985 segregation in the rural South remained the norm.[15]

Through a variety of techniques rural blacks are kept in a subordinate caste position to white landowners in the rural South. Relatively few landowners control large numbers of black tenant farmers. When land is "sold" to black tenants, the white landlord profits by taking the land back by illegal means. Virtually all land is thereby held by white farmers. Farm labor is considered to be the work of blacks, who generally work from sunup to sundown. Even females and children are expected to work long hours to assist in supporting large families. Tenants receive loans in the form of food or cash which must be spent for food. Salary advances and the withholding of loans serve as a means of maintaining the subordinate caste position of the black tenants. Intimidation is also an element of economic control. Physical violence in the form of whipping has not been uncommon.[16]

THE URBAN BLACK COMMUNITY

By 1980 the black population of the United States was predominantly (80 percent) urban. Northern and western blacks were more highly urbanized (95 percent) than their southern counterparts, but even in the South three out of every five blacks lived in urban areas. Even more than their rural counterparts, urban blacks are likely to live in a rigidly segregated section of the city in deteriorated or deteriorating housing. Within the urban areas blacks are heavily concentrated in central cities with high population densities. Already, twenty-eight of the largest cities in the United States have black population in excess of 100,000. These cities vary in the proportion of blacks in the total population anywhere from 17 percent in Los Angeles to 71 percent in Gary, Indiana. In each of the cities the pattern holds: blacks are moving into the center while whites are moving to the suburbs.

Urban black communities in the North and West differ somewhat from those in the South, especially because blacks are relative newcomers to these regions, but in one crucial respect they are strikingly similar:

blacks are forced to live in areas with other blacks. In a 1965 study Taeuber and Taeuber developed a "segregation index," which was applied to census data for 207 cities in the United States.[17] This index included every city with a population of at least 50,000 and several smaller cities. The segregation index is based on the extent of racial residential segregation in city blocks. If blacks and whites are equally distributed (proportionately) in a block, the segregation index assumes a value of zero, indicating no racial residential segregation. If, on the other extreme, city blocks contain only blacks or only whites, the segregation index assumes a value of 100, indicating complete segregation. For the cities studied the index values ranged from 60.4 (San Jose, California) to 98.1 (Fort Lauderdale, Florida). "Only a few cities had values in the lower range of observed scores—8 cities with values below 70 and 31 cities with values below 79. Half the cities have values above 87.8 and a fourth above 91.7."[18]

Regionally, the South attained the highest degree of racial residential segregation (mean of 90.0), followed by the North Central states (mean of 87.7), the West (mean 79.3), and the Northeast (mean 79.2). Thus it can be demonstrated that racial segregation in housing is characteristically American, and regional differences are minor. The likelihood is that the rural black who migrates from the South will settle in an urban black slu   elsewhere. Likewise, when the children become adults, they too are   le in the black community, for ". . . Negroes are by far the   regated urban minority group in recent Ameri   dent in the virtually complete exclusion of Negr   ew suburban developments of the past 50 year   block expansion of Negro residential areas in the   ny large cities."[19] Unlike the situation among wh   re segregated residentially for racial reasons al   and rich blacks alike are usually confined to the s   nd unlike some of the earlier immigrant groups,   city, whatever his or her status, cannot expect to   to other sections of the city or to the suburbs.   ary characteristics of urban black areas is the high   umber of persons per square mile). In four of the   ies or subsections of cities with black populations   00 to 813,000 in 1960, in which blacks constituted   o 54 percent of the population, the density of the   d the general urban black pattern.[20] In Chicago, with a   of 813,000, blacks constituted 23 percent of the popula-   rcent of these blacks, or 15 percent of Chicago's popula-   ck census tracts, which comprised only eight square miles   of the city's land area. In Los Angeles blacks constituted 14   population. Some 22 percent of the blacks, or 3 percent of the Los Angeles's total population, lived in an area of one square mile and occupied less than 0.5 percent of the city's land area. In the borough of Manhattan in New York City, where blacks made up 23 percent of the population, 59 percent of them, or 14 percent of the total population, lived in an area of two square miles and occupied 9 percent of the borough's land area. In Washington, D.C., where blacks represented 54 percent of the population, 50 percent of them or more than 25 percent of the population, lived in an area of three square miles and occupied only 5 percent of the city's land area. The population density for each of these black census tracts was among the highest in the world: Chicago, 68,000; Los Angeles, 73,000; Manhattan, 118,000; and Washington, D.C., 68,000. These black communities were at least five times as dense as the cities as a whole.

One of the more dramatic statistics on black population density came from the United States Civil Rights Commission in 1959: "If the population density of some of Harlem's worst blocks obtained for the rest of New York City, the entire population of the United States could fit into three of New York's boroughs."[21] Not much, if anything, has changed in the intervening three decades.

Statistics on housing in the urban black community are as revealing as those on population density. In 1980 the median value of black-occupied housing units was slightly more than one-half that of white Americans. Of households lacking complete plumbing facilities, 5.5 percent were ocupied by blacks while 1.7 percent were occupied by whites. Sixteen percent of black households were without telephones, more than one-half (57.3 percent) lacked air-conditioning, and about one-third (32.6 percent) had no vehicles. Only 44.4 percent were owner occupied, while the ownership for white families was more than two-thirds (68 percent).[22]

Chief among the characteristics of the urban black community are its powerlessness and its dependence on the frequently hostile white community which surrounds it. These enclaves are kept powerless by powerful individuals and institution in the white community.[23] The dwellings of the urban black community are usually owned by absentee white landlords and institutions, and no attempt is made to maintain the buildings or to provide the customary services to their inhabitants. Residential buildings, for which the occupants are charged high rents, frequently do not provide safe and adequate shelter. Often they are owned by wealthy and politically prominent suburban residents. Community services, such as garbage collection and street cleaning, are provided less frequently than in the white community.

The residents continue to provide a cheap labor supply. Most often they must find employment outside the black community. Within the community, business establishments, like residential buildings, are owned by whites who live outside the community. The school system is operated and maintained by individuals who live outside the area and who are often unresponsive to the needs of the local residents. Law and order are maintained by a police force who is often hostile and prejudiced.

Such conditions, coupled with the day-to-day frustrations inherent in living in a racist society, contribute to the social problems of the black community. (See chapter 6.) These communities experience high rates of crime and delinquency, alcoholism, drug addiction, and family disruption.

In recent years the educational attainment of pupils in the black community has become a center of controversy, stemming from the underachievement of black pupils as compared with white pupils.[24] Teachers tend to place the blame on the home life of the pupils, whereas parents see the school as the source of the problem. Whatever the source, which is probably a combination of social factors, parents in the black community are pressing their demands for equal educational oportunities for their children.

Existing conditions in the urban black community thus bear many parallels to those in the so-called developing nations. Collectively, the many urban black communities in the United States resemble a colonial territory which is seeking to achieve independence from forces beyond its control. Such claims to territoriality may be seen in the urban rebellions of the 1960s in which blacks attempted to remove the agents of colonialism from the black community; that is, they may be seen as moves toward decolonialization.[25]

SOCIAL STRATIFICATION

The black community, like the white community which surrounds it, has always maintained a degree of social stratification. During slavery the primary distinctions among the slaves were based on those who worked as house servants and those forced to work as field hands. The house servants were most often mulattoes, a favored class in the eyes of the slaveholders. The field hands were the black illiterates who were considered less than human beings. This distinction between slaves frequently fostered by slaveholders, served as a divisive force between the slaves.

Among the "free" blacks during slavery, several types of distinctions were discernible. As among the slaves, distinctions were made between mulattoes and blacks, with the former enjoying higher status. There were also distinctions between skilled workers and artisans and domestic workers and unskilled laborers. Finally, many of the free blacks were direct descendants of wealthy white planters. They frequently maintained extensive property holdings and slaves.[26] Although white ancestry was not enough to confer high social status among free blacks, it was frequently associated with greater education and mechanical skills.

After emancipation, class distinctions among blacks frequently followed the patterns established during slavery: those based on wealth, occupation, "respectability," and skin color. However, another factor assumed prominence. Blacks who had been free before the Civil War distinguished themselves from those who were freed with the emancipation.[27] The restoration of white supremacy, as well as the migrations of the blacks from rural to urban areas and from South to North, had the effect of minimizing class distinctions among blacks. Yet the black community, like its white counterpart, has continued, through a variety of criteria, to distinguish among its members.

Several studies have focused attention on status distinctions in the black community.[28] In judging one another, black people use many of the conventional social-class criteria utilized by white Americans, such as income, occupation, education, wealth, family background, style of life, refinement, property ownership, organizational affiliations, respectability, and morality. Some criteria, however, such as white ancestry, skin color, and cultural similarity to whites, are peculiar to the black community. In recent years black nationalism has made inroads into the black community especially in urban areas. This development has led to a deemphasis, if not a cessation, of these characteristics as criteria for status.

The Rural Blacks

Studies of rural black communitites reveal the presence of the three social-class levels found in the society at large. In a study of rural Afro-Americans in eight counties in five southern states, Charles S. Johnson delineated three classes and estimated the percentage of blacks in each class as follows: upper class, 6 percent; middle class, 12 percent; lower class, 82 percent.[29] The upper-class blacks were those possessing a family social heritage that was known and respected in the community and a high educational and occupational status. These persons were usually medical doctors, schoolteachers, and successful landowners. The middle class consisted of proprietors of small businesses, white-collar workers, schoolteachers, and some skilled artisans. The lower class was composed of unskilled and semiskilled workers and domestic workers. Also within this group were the sharecroppers and tenant farmers.

Dollard also posited the existence of three social classes among Afro-Americans in the small town which he studied in the 1930s, but he concentrated on the middle- and lower-class blacks.[30] In this community the lower-class blacks were those individuals with the lowest skill levels, forming the "broad base on which society in this area rests." The middle-class people were mainly teachers and ministers, who attempted to isolate themselves from the lower class and what they considered lower-class values.

Davis, Gardner, and Gardner report that in rural Mississippi social classes were present among blacks but that the differentiation among classes was slight.[31] In rural southern communities fewer criteria exist for distinguishing among blacks than are found in urban areas. However, such criteria as education and property ownership still constitute a basis for social stratification.

The Urban Blacks

Since the vast majority of black people are urban dwellers, and since the complexity of urban life is conducive to stratification, it might be expected that somewhat more elaborate stratification may be discerned among blacks in urban areas than among rural blacks. Although there are regional differences in stratification among urban blacks, in general the class distinctions hold in the South and elsewhere. Frazier makes the point that skin color diminishes as a status variable as one progresses from the Deep South to the Border South to the North.[32] In addition, economic opportunities for blacks have generally been greater in the North than in the South; therefore, greater occupational differentiation has made for some differences in stratification. Finally, compared to the South, the black in the northern city is a relative newcomer. Southern blacks in some ways have a more established system of stratification. It is possible, however, to make some general statements about class distinctions which hold for urban blacks throughout the United States.

Most of the studies of social stratification among urban blacks delineate a small upper class, a proportionately small but growing middle class, and a larger lower class that encompasses the vast majority of blacks. The black upper class includes professionals, especially medical doctors, dentists, and lawyers; public administrators; civic leaders; businesspeople; educators; and politicians. (These people would be considered middle class in terms of their standing in the general society if race were irrelevant.) In describing the upper-class blacks in Chicago, Drake and Cayton say:

> If one wished to ascertain just what people constitute Bronzeville's upper class, it might seem practicable to group together those persons who have the most money, those with the greatest amount of education, those with the "best" family backgrounds, and those who wield the greatest political power—and attach to this group the label UPPER CLASS.[33]

This group, they write, included some five thousand people in the 1940s, most of whom were medical doctors, lawyers, newspaper editors, civic leaders, and politicians. Their prestige was based on education, professional status, and style of life, rather than on income, although some of them earned as much as $50,000 yearly.

Frazier describes the black upper class in Washington, D.C., which he feels to be typical of other border cities, as composed of "a relatively large professional class and a clerical group of the same relative size as Chicago and New York. Consequently, those of upper-class status include almost entirely people of professional status, businessmen, and those in clerical occupations."[34]

Upper-class blacks tend to associate with other upper-class blacks. Entertaining is done in the home, except for the public events they sponsor. They are Protestants, usually Congregationalists, Episcopalians, and Presbyterians. They are active in social clubs, especially fraternities and sororities, and support civil rights activities through the National Association for the Advancement of Colored People (NAACP) or the Urban League.

Middle-class status among blacks in Chicago, according to Drake and Cayton, is not necessarily limited to those persons of appropriate income and occupation. "Rather, the middle class is marked off from the lower class by a pattern of behavior expressed in stable family and associational relationships, in great concern with 'front' and 'respectability,' and in a drive for 'getting ahead.' All this finds an objective measure in standard of living—the way people spend their money, and in *public behavior*."[35] The middle class in Chicago consisted of a wide variety of occupational categories, including professionals, independent businesspeople, clerical workers, service workers, and laborers. Frazier agrees that style of life is the most crucial element in identifying the black middle class. He writes, "Because of their fairly secure and adequate incomes, Negroes of middle-class status are able to maintain what they regard as a desirable mode of life. This desirable mode of living includes . . . certain standards of home and family life."[36]

With increasing urbanization there has emerged a rather well defined middle class among blacks. In large cities there is a large group of clerical, skilled, and public-service workers, in addition to professional workers in virtually every field. Because these occupations provide adequate incomes and economic security, the black middle class has developed stable family lives. There is among the black middle class an overriding concern with "respectability" and a serious desire that their children receive the educational advantages which they were frequently denied.

Middle-class blacks value home ownership and are concerned about maintaining the proper associational relationships necessary for advancing themselves. They are likely to be members of church congregations, including Congregationalist, Episcopalian and Presbyterian, but unlike the upper-class blacks, most middle-class blacks are Methodists and Baptists. Within these two denominations they frequently attend churches which cater to the middle class. Like the upper-class blacks, the middle class expend considerable time and energy on social clubs and other social organizations, especially fraternities and sororities.

Because of the precariousness of the status of the middle-class blacks, their overriding concern is with maintaining repectability. This concern has frequently led to a self-hate characterized by contempt for lower-class blacks. One writer takes a rather harsh view of the rising black middle class and the fantasy world which, he insists, they share with upper-class blacks. He writes:

> The emphasis upon "social" life or "society" is one of the main props of the world of make believe into which the black bourgeoisie has sought to escape from its inferiority and frustrations in American society. This world of make believe, to be sure, is a reflection of the values of American society, but it lacks the economic basis that would give it roots in the world of reality. In escaping into a world of make believe, middle-class Negroes have rejected both identification with the Negro and his traditional culture. Through delusions of wealth and power they have sought identification with white America, which continues to reject them. But these delusions leave them frustrated because they are unable to escape from the emptiness and futility of their existence.[37]

The lower-class black, comprising nearly two-thirds of the urban black population, is at the bottom of the class structure in the black community. It is of the lower-class black that so many stereotypes have developed. These are the blacks who are chronically unemployed, who work at the lowest-paid jobs in industry and domestic service—i.e., who do the back-breaking jobs and are still defined as "lazy"—and who make up a disproportionately high proportion of the welfare rolls in urban areas. The lower-class black is most often the recent migrant from the rural South seeking to improve his or her status in the city. Among lower-class blacks, what has been characterized as disorganized family life is prevalent.[38] It is also to the lower-class blacks that widespread social problems are attributed.[39] Finally, it is the lower-class black who in many ways was the major target of the "war on poverty." For, historically, these are the individuals who have received fewer social rewards than any other group. They are crowded into the slums of the largest cities and are noticed only when acts of violence (real or imagined) are attributed to them.

Drake and Cayton describe the complexity of the lower class in the black community in Chicago. In addition to those with middle-class aspirations and to the stable "church folk," one finds "the denizens of the underworld—the pimps and prostitutes, the thieves and pickpockets, the dope addicts and the reefer smokers, the professional gamblers, cutthroats, and murderers."[40]

Writing about the residents in America's urban black slums, especially New York's Harlem, Kenneth Clark describes the lower class as being "subject peoples, victims of greed, cruelty, insensitivity, guilt, and fear of the masters."[41] Perhaps the most salient characteristics of the lower-class blacks are their powerlessness, hopelessness, and despair.

They lack the organization and organizational participation of middle- and upper-class blacks. Even religious institutions have failed to assist them in coping with their many problems, especially in urban areas. They tend to affiliate themselves with "store front" Fundamentalist churches, which are generally powerless in the larger community. Furthermore, they tend to be rejected by middle- and upper-class blacks, who feel that identification with the lower class would lower their status.[42] Again, the ascendancy of black nationalist ideology throughout the black community has had its impact on middle- and upper-class blacks. Even in such elite summer resorts catering to Afro-Americans as Oak Bluffs on Martha's Vineyard, Sag Harbor on Long Island, and Arundel on the Maryland shore, the black residents have become as involved in the problems of urban blacks as they once were with their yachts and dinner parties. Similarly, with the spread of nationalist sentiment, black fraternities and sororities have become socially conscious.

Differences in Social Stratification: Blacks versus Whites, and Some Myths

Social stratification in the black community differs in some regards from that found in the white community. Because of the overrepresentation of blacks in the lower class, stratification tends to be based to a greater degree on behavioral patterns and social factors rather than on income and occupation, which usually are considered crucial determinants in the white community. Social stratification in the black community is more likely to be determined by style of life and family background. Although a few blacks who have amassed great wealth or achieved fame in the larger society might be considered upper class by objective standards, most blacks who are considered upper class within their own community would not be so considered if they were white. Schoolteachers are a notable example. Within the black community they are frequently considered to be upper class; white schoolteachers are rarely so considered. Similarly, many individuals working as skilled workers, service workers, and even laborers are considered to be middle class because of their behavior patterns.

However, behavior patterns, while still salient, are losing force. Support for this contention is found in a review of published literature dealing with prestige criteria among blacks. This study reveals that in sixteen of the better-known community studies, blacks traditionally used different criteria for evaluating one another than did whites.[43] However, the trend is clearly toward increasing acceptance of the same three main criteria used in the general community. Thus education is emphasized more frequently than any other status element, followed by occupation and income, respectively. Other criteria reported (in order of importance) are respectability or morality, refinement or "culture," skin color or white ancestry, family background, and property ownership.[44] Among white Americans occupation and income have received importance equal to that of education, and frequently more so.

With increasing urbanization, regional redistribution, educational achievement, and occupational differentiation, there is a trend toward the development of socioeconomic status groupings among urban blacks that will parallel those among white Americans. However, some recent accounts in books, magazines, and newspapers of black social stratification, have exaggerated the progress Afro-Americans have made since the advent of affirmative-action programs in the decade of the 1970s. Perhaps the most unwarranted account is provided by Wattenberg and Scammon, who maintain that a majority of blacks are now in the middle class.[45] An equally unreasonable position is taken by another writer who maintains that the black middle class has increased rapidly and the today "the life chances of blacks have less to do with race than with economic class affiliation."[46]

These writers include in their definition of the black middle class such occupational positions as plasterers, bus drivers, lathe operators, secretaries, bank tellers, and automobile-assembly-line workers. Education is considered largely irrelevant, and some utilize incomes as low as $7,500 in 1975.[47]

The data show that in 1977 slightly more than 17 percent of black persons in the United States had completed at least one year of college, that 23 percent of all black men held white-collar occupations, and that 21 percent of all black families had incomes between $15,000 and $25,000.[48] Given the correlation between education, income, and occupation in determining socioeconomic status, it is fair to say that at that time some one-fourth of all blacks in the United States were middle class.[49]

While the 1970s may have witnessed a slight increase of blacks into the middle class, there are ample data to indicate that the poor blacks are becoming poorer, and there appears to be a growing permanent underclass among blacks.[50] This is largely a function of lack of education, racism, and the changing structure of the economy. In any event, figures differ on the extent of this social problem, but the unemployment rate among black teenagers and young adults has been estimated to be as high as 60 percent. This situation was commented upon in a *New York Times* editorial: "No society can call itself civilized when so many of its young are being maimed and destroyed so early in life."[51]

• • •

As with American communities in general, the black community varies depending on whether it is in the South or outside that region and on whether it is urban or rural. However, certain recurrent patterns exist in the black community throughout the United States. In a study of the black community in eleven cities of varying sizes and different regions, Williams reports clearly discernible patterns appearing in each of them.[52] Several of these characteristics are of relevance to the present chapter. The black community tends to be socially isolated from the larger community. Separate social institutions have developed among blacks to meet needs not served by the larger community. The church continues to play a dominant role in the institutional life of the rural black community but a declining role in the urban community. The black community adheres to a system of social stratification not unlike the larger community. Its members distinguish among themselves on the basis of certain achieved and ascribed criteria.

In addition, the black community in America is like a colonial possession: it tends to be economically and politically dependent upon the larger community. Its residents provide a source of cheap labor, and depending on the needs of the larger community, unemployment is usually widespread. The residents of the black community are crowded into a geographical area distinguishable from the general community by poor housing conditions and the lack of services provided. Education is controlled from the outside, and the police often assume the posture of occupying forces. In short, all important decisions—political, economic, and educational—affecting the black community are made for its residents by white Americans who have become known as the "white power structure." In periods of disorder (usually in summer) specially trained and equipped police and military forces are rushed in to quell the disturbances with armed force, but public officials give little thought to the conditions that produce these disorders.

SELECTED BIBLIOGRAPHY

BELFRAGE, SALLY. *Freedom Summer.* New York: Viking Press, 1965.
BLACKWELL, JAMES. *The Black Community: Diversity and Unity.* New York: Dodd, Mead & Co., 1975.
BLAUNER, ROBERT. *Racial Oppression in America.* New York: Harper & Row, Publishers, 1972.
CLARK, KENNETH. *Dark Ghetto.* New York: Harper & Row, Publishers, 1965.
DAVIS, ALLISON, BURLEIGH GARDNER, AND MARY GARDNER. *Deep South.* Chicago: University of Chicago Press, 1941.
DOLLARD, JOHN. *Caste and Class in a Southern Town.* New Haven, Conn: Yale University Press, 1937.
DRAKE, ST. CLAIR, AND HORACE CAYTON. *Black Metropolis.* New York: Harcourt, Brace & Co., 1945.
DU BOIS, W. E. B. *The Philadelphia Negro.* Philadelphia: University of Pennsylvania Press, 1899.
FRAZIER, E. FRANKLIN. *Black Bourgeoisie.* Glencoe, Ill.: Free Press, 1957.
———. *The Negro in the United States.* New York: Macmillan Co., 1957.
———. *Negro Youth at the Crossways.* Washington, D.C.: American Council on Educaiton, 1940.

HESSLINK, GEORGE K. *Black Neighbors: Negros in a Northern Rural Community.* Indianapolis and New York: Bobbs-Merrill Co., 1968.

HILL, ROBERT. *The Illusion of Black Progress.* Washington, D.C.: National Urban League, 1978.

JOHSON, CHARLES. *Growing Up in the Black Belt.* Washington, D.C.: American Council on Education, 1941.

LEWIS, HYLAN. *Blackways of Kent.* Chapel Hill: University of North Carolina Press, 1955.

OSOFSKY, GILBERT. *Harlem: The Making of a Ghetto.* New York: Harper & Row, Publishers, 1965.

PINKNEY, ALPHONSO. *The Myth of Black Progress.* New York and London: Cambridge University Press, 1984.

POWDERMAKER, HORTENSE. *After Freedom.* New York: Viking Press, 1939.

ROHRER, JOHN, AND MUNRO EDMONDSON. eds. *The Eighth Generation Grows Up.* New York: Harper & Row, Publishers, 1960.

SUTHERLAND, ELIZABETH, ed. *Letters From Mississippi.* New York: McGraw-Hill Book Co., 1965.

TAEUBER, KARL E., AND ALMA TAEUBER. *Negroes in Cities.* Chicago: Aldine Publishing Co., 1965.

U.S. BUREAU OF THE CENSUS. *The Social and Economic Status of the Black Population in the United States, 1972.* Washington, D.C.: Government Printing Office, 1973.

U.S. DEPARTMENT OF LABOR, OFFICE OF POLICY PLANNING AND REASERCH. *The Negro Family: The Case for National Action.* Washington, D.C.: Government Printing Office, 1965.

WARNER, ROBERT. *New Haven Negroes.* New Haven, Conn.: Yale University Press, 1940.

WILLIAMS, ROBIN M., JR. *Strangers Next Door: Ethnic Relations in American Communities.* Englewood Cliffs, N.J.: Prentice-Hall, 1964.

Youth in the Ghetto. New York: Harlem Youth Opportunities Unlimited, 1964.

NOTES

[1]See Hylan Lewis, *Blackways of Kent* (Chapel Hill: University of North Carolina Press, 1955).

[2]"A Study of Attitudes toward Racial and Religious Minorities and toward Women," Harris Poll, 1978, p. 15.

[3]Kenneth Clark, *Dark Ghetto* (New York: Harper & Row, 1965), p. 11.

[4]Karl E. Taeuber and Alma F. Taeuber, *Negroes in Cities* (Chicago: Aldine, 1965), p. 5.

[5]See Gilbert Osofsky, *Harlem: The Making of a Ghetto* (New York: Harper & Row, 1965), pp. 46–50.

[6]E. Franklin Frazier, *The Negro in the United States* (New York: Macmillan, 1957), pp. 197–98.

[7]Elizabeth Sutherland, ed., *Letters from Mississippi* (New York: McGraw-Hill, 1965), p. 39.

[8]Ibid., p. 41.

[9]Bureau of the Census, *General Social and Economic Characteristics, 1980 Census of Population, United States Summary* (Washington, D.C.: Government Printing Office, 1981), table 93.

[10]Bureau of the Census, *Statistical Abstract of the United States, 1985* (Washington, D.C.: Government Printing Office, 1984), p. 42.

[11]Sally Belfrage, *Freedom Summer* (New York: Viking, 1965), p. 39.

[12]Charles S. Johnson, *Growing Up in the Black Belt* (Washington, D.C.: American Council on Education, 1941), p. 135; Sutherland, *Letters from Mississipi,* pp. 50–52.

[13]Johnson, *Growing Up in the Black Belt,* p. 104.

[14]Ibid., pp. 114–19; Sutherland, *Letters from Mississippi,* pp. 90–117.

[15]Reported in the *New York Times,* April 27, 1985, p. 1.

[16]Allison Davis, Burleigh Gardner, and Mary Gardner, *Deep South* (Chicago: University of Chicago Press, 1941).

[17]Taeuber and Taeuber, *Negroes in Cities,* pp. 28–31.

[18]Ibid., p. 34.

[19]Ibid., p. 2.

[20]U.S. Department of Labor, Bureau of Labor Statistics, *The Negroes in the United*

States: Their Economic and Social Situation (Washington, D.C.: Government Printing Office, 1966), p. 20.

[21]Quoted in Michael Harrington, *The Other America: Poverty in the United States* (New York: Macmillan, 1963), p. 62.

[22]*Statiscal Abstract, 1985*, p. 734.

[23]Clark, *Dark Ghetto*, pp. 11–20; *Youth in the Ghetto* (New York: Harlem Youth Opportunities Unlimited, 1964).

[24]U.S. Office of Education, *Equality of Educational Opportunity* (Washington, D.C.: Government Printing Office, 1966).

[25]See Robert Blauner, *Racial Oppression in America* (New York: Harper & Row, 1972), especially chap. 3.

[26]Frazier, *Negro in the United States*, pp. 275–76.

[27]Ibid., pp. 276–78.

[28]See, for example, James Blackwell, *The Black Community: Diversity and Unity* (New York: Dodd, Mead, 1975); Davis, Gardner, and Gardner, *Deep South;* John Dollard, *Caste and Class in a Southern Town* (New Haven, Conn,: Yale University Press, 1937); St. Clair Drake and Horace Cayton, *Black Metropolis* (New York: Harcourt, Brace, 1945); W. E. B. Du Bois, *The Philadelphia Negro* (Philadelphia: University of Pennsylvania Press, 1899); E. Franklin Frazier, *Negro Youth at Crossways* (Washington, D.C.: American Council on Education, 1940); Robert Hill, *The Illusion of Black Progress* (Washington, D.C.: National Urban League, 1978); Lewis, *Blackways of Kent;* Alphonso Pinkney, *The Myth of Black Progress* (New York and London: Cambridge University Press, 1984); Hortense Powerdermaker, *After Freedom* (New York: Viking Press, 1939); Robert Warner, *New Haven Negroes* (New Haven, Conn.: Yale University Press, 1940).

[29]Johnson, *Growing Up in the Black Belt*, p. 77.

[30]Dollard, *Caste and Class*, p. 83.

[31]Davis, Gardner, and Gardner, *Deep South*, p. 238.

[32]Frazier, *Negro in the United States*, p. 291.

[33]Drake and Cayton, *Black Metropolis*, p. 526.

[34]Frazier, *Negro in the United States*, p. 286.

[35]Drake and Cayton, *Black Metropolis*, pp. 661–662 (italics in the original).

[36]Frazier, *Negro in the United States*, p. 301.

[37]E. Franklin Frazier, *Black Bourgeoisie* (Glencoe, Ill.: Free Press, 1957), p. 237.

[38]See especially U.S. Department of Labor, Office of Policy Planning and Research, *The Negro Family: The Case for National Action* (Washington, D.C.: Government Printing Office, 1965).

[39]Clark, *Dark Ghetto*, chap. 5; Frazier, *Negro in the United States*, pp. 286–87, 303–4.

[40]Drake and Cayton, *Black Metropolis*, p. 600.

[41]Clark, *Dark Ghetto*, p. 11.

[42]Middle- and upper-class blacks repeatedly express contempt for lower-class blacks. Such feelings are frequently expressed in the case histories reported in Abram Kardiner and Lionel Ovesey, *The Mark of Oppression* (New York: World Publishing, 1962), especially chap. 6; see also Frazier, *Black Bourgeoisie*, pp. 224–29.

[43]Norval Glenn, "Negro Prestige: A Case Study in the Bases of Prestige," *American Journal of Sociology*, 68 (May 1963), 645–57.

[44]Ibid., p. 647.

[45]Ben Wattenberg and Richard Scammon, "Black Progress and Liberal Rhetoric," *Commentary*, April 1973, p. 35.

[46]William Wilson, *The Declining Significance of Race* (Chicago: University of Chicago Press, 1978), p. 9.

[47]For a critique of these studies, see Pinkney, *Myth of Black Progress*, chap. 6.

[48]U.S. Bureau of the Census, *The Social and Economic Status of the Black Population in the United States: An Historical View, 1790–1978* (Washington, D.C.: Government Printing Office, 1979), pp. 189, 218.

[49]Pinkney, *Myth of Black Progress*, chap. 6.

[50]Ibid., chap 7; and chap. 4 of this book.

[51]*The New York Times*, March 15, 1979, p. A22.

[52]Robin M. Williams, Jr., *Strangers Next Door* (Englewood Cliffs, N.J.: Prentice-Hall, 1964), pp. 252–54.

CHAPTER FOUR
SOCIOECONOMIC STATUS

Compared with most of the other countries in the world at the present time, the United States is essentially a middle-class society. In 1983 the median number of years of school completed for adult Americans (25 years of age and over) was 12.6; in the same year more than four-fifths of all workers were employed in white-collar and blue-collar occupational categories; and the median family income was $24,580. Furthermore, the middle class sets standards of behavior which persons of lesser status emulate. Within this middle-class society, however, black Americans as a group are generally relegated to a lower-class position.[1] They differ significantly from white Americans on all status indicators. Some black citizens have attained high status in the United States, but they are the exceptions. The majority of black Americans occupy the lowest status positions in society. Through the practice of racism, American society has succeeded in relegating a significant segment of its population to a subordinate position.

Education, occupation, and income are three of the most reliable indicators of status in American society. These three variables are usually interrelated, and they reinforce one another. However, they may be usefully distinguished for purposes of analysis.

EDUCATION

In a highly industrialized nation such as the United States, formal education is a key factor in social mobility. Generations of immigrants have improved their status after reaching the United States through the acquisition of formal education. The situation of blacks has, to some extent, been affected by increasing formal education. Unlike many immigrant groups, however, their advancement has been hampered by the widespread practices of segregation and discrimination which have either denied them access to formal education or relegated them to inferior and inadequate schools. This situation changed somewhat in the 1970s.

Quantity of Education

At the time of emancipation a vast majority (90 percent) of the black people in the United States were illiterate.[2] During slavery it was virtually impossible for the blacks to acquire even the most fundamental tools of reading and writing. During the 1860s, however, blacks made significant strides; by 1870 the illiteracy rate had dropped to 80 percent. In each decade following the Civil War the illiteracy rate among the blacks declined. Yet the differential between blacks and whites has persisted. (See table 4-1). For example, in 1940 the illiteracy rate among blacks was comparable to the rate among white Americans in 1870. Although the decline in black illiteracy has been continuous, the gap between blacks and whites is such that it

TABLE 4-1   Percent of Illiterates in the United States, by Color, 1870–1980*

Year	Total	Nonwhite	White
1870	20.0	79.9	11.5
1880	17.0	70.0	9.4
1890	13.3	56.8	7.7
1900	10.7	44.5	6.2
1910	7.7	30.0	5.0
1920	6.0	23.0	4.0
1930	4.3	16.4	3.0
1940**	2.9	11.5	2.0
1947	2.7	11.0	1.8
1952	2.5	10.2	1.8
1959	2.2	7.5	1.6
1969	1.0	3.6	0.7
1980	0.4	1.6	0.4

*Illiterates are defined as persons unable to both read and write in any language.

**Estimated

Note: Data for 1870 to 1940 are for population 10 years of age and over; data for 1947–1969 are for population 14 years of age and over.

Source: U.S. Department of Labor, Bureau of Labor Statistics, *The Negroes in the United States: Their Economic and Social Situation,* Bulletin No. 1511, 1966, p. 194; U.S. Bureau of the Census, *Statistical Abstract of the United States, 1982–83,* p. 145.

is unlikely that blacks will reach the rate among whites in the near future. In 1980 the illiteracy rate among blacks was 1.6 percent; among whites it was 0.4 percent.

The extent of literacy among black people is a direct result of their enrollment and length of stay in school. In the decade following the Civil War, when most blacks lived on farms, few of their children were enrolled in school. Those who were enrolled attended for only short periods. The schools were overcrowded and the buildings dilapidated; the teachers were most often incompetent, rarely possessing as much as a high school education. This situation improved little with the turn of the century. It is reported that only 58 percent of the black children between the ages of 6 and 14 were enrolled in school as late as 1912. Significant progress has been made in the twentieth century, and the gap between black and white school attendance has continued to narrow. By 1983, 94 percent of blacks and 96 percent of white children between 5 and 15 years of age were enrolled in school.[3]

The rates of literacy and school attendance have increased substantially in recent decades. Similarly, the median number of years of school completed for blacks has increased, and the gap between blacks and whites in this regard has gradually narrowed. By 1983 the median number of years of school completed for blacks was 12.2 compared with 12.6 for white Americans. (See table 4-2.) Black females have the same median number of years of school as males. The small gap between blacks and whites in median number of years of school completed, however, fails to indicate the real difference in educational attainment by these two groups. For example, only 33.9 percent of black students in the United States in 1983 reported completing high school, whereas nearly two-fifths (38.4 percent) of the white students completed high school. At the college level the gap widens still further. Blacks constitute 12 percent of the population but only 8 percent of all college students. Nearly one white American in five (19.5 percent) had completed four or more years of college, compared with only 9.5 percent of blacks. On the other extreme, 7.1 percent of all black people 25 years of age and over had completed less than five years of schooling in 1983, compared with 3 percent of the total American population.

Quality of Education

Data on the extent of literacy, the proportion of school-age children attending school, and the median number of years of school completed indicate that the quantitative differences in education between black and white Americans have narrowed in recent years. However, they indicate little about the differences in the quality of education received by blacks and whites. At the time of the *Brown* vs. *Board of Education* decision of the Supreme Court in 1954, in which the Court declared segregation in

TABLE 4-2 Number of Years of School Completed for Black and White Population, 25 Years of Age and Over, United States, by Sex, 1983

| Race and Sex | Percent of Population Completing | | | | | | | Median School Years Completed |
| | Elementary School | | | High School | | College | | |
	Less Than 5 Years	5–7 Years	8 Years	1–3 Years	4 Years	1–3 Years	4 Years or More	
Total: All races	3.0	5.3	6.8	12.8	37.7	15.6	18.8	12.6
Blacks	7.1	9.6	6.6	19.9	33.9	13.6	9.5	12.2
Male	8.8	9.7	6.3	18.7	32.9	13.6	9.2	12.2
Female	5.8	9.5	6.9	20.8	34.7	13.3	10.0	12.2
Whites	2.4	4.8	6.9	12.1	38.4	15.9	19.5	12.6
Male	2.6	4.8	6.8	11.5	34.3	16.1	24.0	12.7
Female	2.3	4.8	7.1	12.7	42.2	15.7	15.4	12.6

Source: U.S. Bureau of the Census, *Statistical Abstract of the United Staes, 1985*, p. 134.

public education unconstitutional, 68 percent of all blacks still lived in states which maintained segregated schools. Seventeen states and the District of Columbia required segregated schools by law, and four states permitted segregated schools. In many of the remaining states also, black pupils attended segregated schools. These schools were inferior to those attended by white pupils in expenditure per pupil, capital outlay per pupil for schools, length of school year, training of classroom teachers, and number of books in school libraries.

In 1952, for example, Southern states spent an average of $164.83 for the education of one white pupil, compared with $115.08, or 70 percent of that amount, for the education of each black child.[4] The amount of money spent per black pupil varied anywhere from 30 percent of what was spent per white pupil in Mississippi to 85 percent in North Carolina. In the same year the capital outlay per pupil for black schools in southern states was $29.58, or 82 percent of the $36.25 per white pupil.[5]

In 1950 the average number of days in the school year for black pupils in the South was 176, compared with 178 for white pupils. The average number of years of college training attained by black teachers was 3.3, compared with 3.6 for white teachers. The average number of books in school libraries per black pupil enrolled in five southern states was 1.8, compared with 4.7 per white pupil.[6]

These comparative figures serve to indicate the gap in the quality of public elementary and secondary education received by black and white pupils in the South before the 1954 decision of the Supreme Court. It should also be added that prior to the late 1940s and early 1950s the gap between the quality of black education and that received by white pupils was even greater. With increasing pressures for the desegregation of public education, southern states attempted to forestall this eventuality by increasing the support made available for the education of blacks. In the large urban centers where a vast majority of northern blacks were concentrated, the situation differed little insofar as the quality of education was concerned.

Schools in which black children predominate are more likely to be characterized by inadequate facilities.[7] In 1966, for example, 43 percent of black elementary-school pupils in the Northeast attended schools which were at least 40 years old, compared with 18 percent of white pupils. In the United States as a whole, there were an average of thirty-two black pupils per room, compared with twenty-nine white pupils. Twenty-seven percent of all black elementary-school pupils in the United States attended schools without auditoriums, compared with 19 percent of white pupils. Thirty percent of black elementary pupils attended schools without full-time librarians, compared with 22 percent of white pupils of the same level. For black students in secondary schools the differential facilities between their schools and those attended by white pupils were as pronounced as on the elementary level. For example, 80 percent of black secondary-school pupils attended schools equipped with physics laboratories, compared with 94 percent of white secondary pupils.

Since the data on the quality of black education in the South predate the Supreme Court decision of 1954, it might be suspected that the status of black education has changed substantially since that time. However, in the years following the desegregation decision, the changes have not completely altered the pattern of segregated education. A substantial proportion of black pupils continue to attend segregated (and inferior) schools. In the seventeen southern states affected by the decision, it is reported that 84 percent of all black pupils attended integrated schools in 1970.[8] The extent of desegregation varies by both state and geographical region. In the Northeast, for example, 27 percent of all minority pupils attended schools that were 99 to 100 percent minority in 1980. The comparable figures for the Midwest were were 28 percent, the South 14 percent, and the West 10 percent. In large cities outside the South where blacks are concentrated, the schools are becoming more segregated with the exodus of white families to the suburbs. Even in those cities where blacks comprise a numerical minority in the population, they frequently form a majority of pupils in public schools. On the state level Illinois provides a striking example of racial segregation in public education. In 1980 nearly one-half (48.4 percent) of all black public elementary and secondary pupils attended schools that were 99 to 100 percent minority. Throughout the country in 1980, some 17.7 percent of black pupils were enrolled in schools with 99 to 100 percent minority enrollment, while 35.4 percent were enrolled in schools with minority enrollments under 50 percent minority.[9]

The greatest impetus to school desegregation in the South occurred ten years after the Supreme Court decision of 1954, as a result of the Civil Rights Act of 1964. At the time of passage this act only about 1 percent of black pupils enrolled in public schools in the eleven states of the original Confederaccy were attending integraded schools. Title VI of this act authorizes the Department of Health, Education, and Welfare (HEW) to withhold federal funds from school districts maintaining segregated schools. The Office for Civil Rights within HEW is responsible for assuring compliance with the act. While the United States Commission on Civil Rights reported in 1971 that HEW had developed the most comprehensive mechanisms for assuring compliance with the law, it also reported that its performance "has not matched the strength of the compliance mechanisms available to it." Little has been accomplished in the area of northern school desegregation. The commission concluded that HEW was reluctant to utilize the sanction of fund termination to assure compliance with the act.[10] Of equal importance in maintaining racially segregated schools has been the opposition of Republican administrations to school desegregation.

While the data on black pupils attending desegrated schools in the South appear to indicate substantial progress, many virtually all-white private elementary and secondary schools have sprung up throughout that region in an effort to avoid court-ordered desegregation. For example, the number of private elementary and secondary schools increased substantially between 1970 and 1983.

At the college level the quality of black education parallels that of the elementary and secondary levels. Forty-four percent of all blacks pursuing higher education attended predominantly black colleges and universities in the South and Southwest. In the school year 1970–71 there were 111 predominately black colleges and universities in the United States. These included 21 junior colleges, one autonomous medical school, one theological center, and two universities (Atlanta and Howard). Many of these institutions are not accredited by appropriate regional associations or professional accrediting agencies.[11]

In the predominately black colleges and universities, faculty members are less well trained than in predominantly white institutions. For example, in 1965 black students attended colleges with lower proportions of faculty members with earned doctorate degrees than white students. Furthermore, black students are more likely to attend colleges where faculty members are paid substantially lower salaries than they are in colleges with predominantly white student populations.[12]

It is in higher education that blacks have made significant gains in recent years. In 1967, for example, of the black population between 18 and 24 years of age some 297,000 (or 13 perccent in that age category) were enrolled in colleges. Five years later, the number had increased to 540,000 (or 18 percent in that age category). During that period white college enrollment in the same age category declined from 27 percent to 26 percent.[13] This increase in black enrollment resulted from the black rebellions which spread throughout the country in the last half of the 1960s. Administrators of white colleges chose to admit more black students as a means of sharing responsibility for black education and as a means of preserving domestic tranquility, even to the point of altering traditional admissions requirements and providing greater scholarship aid.

According to the Office of Civil Rights of the Department of Education, blacks accounted for 3 percent of students enrolled in four-year institutions in 1972. The figure rose to 10.3 percent in 1976. But that year turned out to be a peak, and by 1982, the latest year for which figures are available, the proportion had declined to 9.6 percent. Thirteen percent of the 18-to-24-year-old population is black. The state of Michigan provides an example of the decline in black enrollment in colleges and universities around the country. In that state, from 1976 to 1984, the number of blacks in four-year public colleges and universities dropped to 16,900 from 19,900, a decline of 18.5 percent.[14]

Most of the new wave of black college students attend predominantly white schools, and as the number of blacks attending college has increased, the number of traditionally black colleges has decreased, especially the black state-supported colleges in the South. Some have become predominantly white, others have emerged with neighboring white schools, and still others have been abolished.[15] The number of predominantly black state colleges has decreased from 35 to 29 in recent years. Three were absorbed by white institutions; three others are now predominantly white. In addition, three others had white enrollments approaching 40 percent in 1971.

As in predominantly black state-supported colleges, private black colleges are experiencing declining enrollments. Unlike many of their white counterparts, these colleges are without endowments, and few have wealthy alumni. Therefore, they depend heavily on student tuition for support, but most of the students are poor. Of the 43 private black four-year colleges in the South, all are experiencing financial difficulties. Prior to the passage of the Higher Education Act of 1965, most black colleges received virtually no federal support. In fiscal year 1970, however, black colleges (public and private) received $123.9 million in federal aid for such programs as student assistance, training grants, operating expenses, and research and development. The total federal appropriation to all colleges was $3,630.4 million, with the lion's share going to wealthy white colleges.[16]

The annexations and mergers of black public colleges, and the financial crises faced by black private colleges have caused concern in the black community. It is felt that the state colleges will lose their identity as black schools and that teachers will lose their jobs, as happened when black public schools were merged with white schools. More important, however, is the fear that the decline in numbers of both public and private black colleges will mean that thousands of black students who are without funds and who lack adequate elementary- and secondary-school preparation will be deprived of college educations.

On the elementary and secondary levels controversy has raged in recent years over the quality of black education. Integrationist-oriented organizations demand complete desegregation of all public schools, for they feel that only through integrated education can black pupils expect to achieve the same quality of education as their white counterparts. Black nationalists, on the other hand, emphasize improving the quality of public schools in the black community instead of busing black pupils to predominantly white schools. In other words, the nationalists and others who share their position, feel that integrated education is not a necessary prerequisite for quality education. While it is true that on the national level black pupils at all levels lag behind white pupils on standardized nonverbal, verbal, reading, mathematics, and general information tests,[17] a debate rages over where the responsibility for this low academic performance lies. Public-school officials and other educators blame the homes from which these children come and refer to the children as "culturally deprived" or "disadvantaged." They claim that because children suffer from economic, cultural, and political disadvantages, they cannot be expected to learn as well as white, middle-class children.[18] The solution, according to this theory, is to integrate public schools so that poor black children will be motivated by middle-class black and white pupils.

Many black educators, however, disagree with this theory, recognizing that the history of public education in the United States demonstrates that generations of white and Asian immigrants have overcome deprivations, including language barriers, and have used public education as the means for achieving social mobility. Black parents recognize that as their children "advance" in public schools, they regress in their performance on standardized tests.[19] Something happens to the educational performance of black pupils once they enter public schools. The parents see effective teaching as the answer to the underachievement of black pupils. Public-school teachers do not teach black pupils with the same degree of diligence as they do middle-class white children. The teachers assume that because the students come from "disadvantaged" homes, they are incapable of learning; consequently, they expect them to fail. Such an attitude is likely to produce the expected results.

Beginning in the late 1960s, in response to the low educational achievement of their children and to white opposition to integrated public schools, black parents initiated a movement for community control of schools. This movement started in New York City in 1968 and spread to other cities. But teachers' unions opposed community control of schools, fearing that those teachers who were not effective would be removed from the schools by black parents. In addition, since many urban public-school districts have black minorities, white administrators and union officials are reluctant to transfer the power that comes with community control of schools to blacks. Therefore, effective school decentralization has not been put to a fair test in most urban areas. Frustrated in their efforts to have their children receive quality public education, many black parents are turning to alternative schools, where their children learn fundamental skills as well as pride in their cultural heritage.

OCCUPATIONAL STATUS

The occupational gap between black and white Americans in the first hundred years since emancipation has remained wide. At the end of the Civil War a vast majority of blacks were employed as either farm laborers or domestic-service workers. By 1890, when data on black occupational status were first collected, nearly 90 percent of black workers were still concentrated in agriculture and domestic-service occupations. Sixty percent of white workers were so employed.[20] Since the beginning of the twentieth century there has been a steady shift among black people away from these occupations, but the shift of white workers has been even greater; thus the occupational gap between black and white has persisted and in some cases widened. For example, in 1980 only 13 percent of white workers were employed as service workers, while 22.6 percent of nonwhite workers were so employed; 4.9 percent of white workers were employed as nonfarm laborers, while 7.6 percent of nonwhite workers were so employed.[21] Although there has been a shift from farm employment for both white and black workers, a greater proportion of white workers than black workers have moved into higher-status occupations. Black workers continue to be concentrated in the lowest-status positions in industry, government, and service occupations.

The greatest change in the occupational status of black people occurred between 1940 and 1970, when federal, state, and municipal government enacted laws forbidding the traditional discriminatory employment practices against blacks. As a result of increasing employment opportunities, significantly greater numbers of blacks were employed in white-collar, skilled occupations. In 1940, 2.6 percent of black workers were employed as clerks and sales workers; in 1980, 21.7 percent were so employed. Among black women, 1.4 percent were employed as clerks and sales workers in 1940 compared with 31 percent in 1980. For black males there was a comparable shift in skilled workers from 4.4 percent in 1940 to 15.2 percent in 1980. In each of these occupational categories, however, blacks are underrepresented. In 1980, 26.5 percent of white workers were employed as clerks and sales workers, compared with 21.7 percent of black workers. (See table 4-3.)

Similar gains for black people from 1940 to 1980 have been reported for professional occupations, but here again blacks are far from being represented in proportions to their numbers in population. As late as 1972, 50 percent of white workers were employed in white-collar occupations while fewer than one-third (29.8 percent) of blacks were so employed. The rate of gain has been such that it is unlikely that the gap between black and white workers will close in the near future. Although the proportion of black professional and technical workers nearly doubled between 1960 and 1980 (from 4.8 percent to 8.2 percent), they are still underrepresented in these high-status, high-paying occupations. The proportion of black workers employed as managers and administrators increased slightly (from 2.6 percent to 4.8 percent) between 1960 and 1980; the proportion of whites in the workforce in these categories in 1980 was twice (9.9 percent) that of blacks. At the other extreme, the proportion of black service workers decreased from 31.7 percent in 1960 to 22.6 percent in 1980, while the proportion of white workers in these

TABLE 4-3 Occupation Distribution of the Civilian Labor-Force Population, 16 Years and Over, for the Black Population of the United States, by Sex, 1980

Occupation	Total population	Black population		
		Both sexes	Men	Women
Civilian labor force (number)	104,449,817	10,582,436	5,330,792	5,251,644
	100.0	100.0	100.0	100.0
Managerial and professional specialty	21.7	13.0	10.8	15.3
Executive, administrative, and managerial	9.9	4.8	5.3	4.4
Professional specialty	11.8	8.2	5.5	10.9
Technical, sales, and administrative support	29.6	24.1	14.4	34.0
Technicians and related support	2.9	2.4	1.8	3.1
Sales	9.8	5.0	3.8	6.3
Administrative support, including clerical	16.8	16.7	8.8	24.6
Services	13.0	22.6	16.8	28.6
Private households	.6	2.4	.2	4.7
Protective services	1.5	1.8	3.0	.6
Services, except protective and household	10.9	18.4	13.6	23.3
Farming, forestry, and fishing	2.9	2.0	3.4	.6
Precision productions, crafts, and repairs	13.0	8.8	15.2	2.3
Operators, fabricators, and laborers	19.1	27.3	37.7	16.8
Machine operators, assemblers, and inspectors	9.7	13.8	14.8	12.7
Transportation and material moving	4.6	5.9	10.7	.9
Handlers, equipment cleaners, helpers, and laborers	4.9	7.6	12.1	3.1
Unemployed, no civilian work experience since 1975	.7	2.1	1.8	2.4

Source: U.S. Bureau of the Census, 1980 Census of Population/EEO Special File.

occupations increased from 9.9 percent to 13 percent in the same period. The differential remains a sizable one.

Although there has been a greater degree of occupational upgrading among black workers than among white workers in the twenty-year period under consideration, marked contrasts in job patterns still persist and are likely to continue, especially in the South, where the gap between black and white occupational status is greatest.[22] Furthermore, black occupational status varies by sex. Black women are more likely to hold high- and low-status occupations than black men.[23] In 1972, for example, 34 percent of all black women were employed in white-collar occupations, while only 14.4 percent of black men were so employed. For whites the comparable figures were 70 percent for women and 55 percent for men. At the bottom of the occupational ladder, 21 percent of black women were employed in service occupations (including private household work), compared with 15 percent for white women.

Black workers continue to be overrepresented in lower-paying, less-skilled jobs and underrepresented in better-paying, higher-skilled occupations. Even when blacks are employed as professionals in private industry their chances for advancement are minimal. Several federal laws, including the Civil Rights Act of 1964 and 1968, not only prohibit discrimination in public and private employment based on race, religion, sex, or national origin, but also require that employers take positive steps to assure that any continuing effects of past discrimination are remedied.[24] Enforcement of these laws has been somewhat less than diligent by the federal agencies involved. For example, a Department of Labor-sponsored study of black professionals in private industry in 1971 found that the salaries of black professionals in private industry reached a plateau after nine years of service, and that very few were employed in supervisory and managerial positions.[25] Of the five thousand black professionals in companies with one hundred or more employees, five hundred were studied. They were all college graduates, having studied science, business administration, engineering, and law. Their median income was $14,389, and the salaries were approximately the same for those with ten years of service as those with fifteen or more. The study concluded that there is an effective ceiling on black advancement in business and a limit on the type of jobs.

Finally, one sociologist predicts a grim future for all black workers in the United States.[26] He sees the black rebellions of the 1960s as a result of the transformation from industrialization to automation in the mid-1950s. This shift, according to his theory, has rendered the black population irrelevant to the American economy, for machines have diminished the need for cheap black labor. Since white America no longer needs the labor of blacks, he feels that black genocide is a possibility. The response of blacks to automation, he maintains, has been to rebel against a society that has cast them aside and in the process stripped them of feelings of self-worth. It is impossible to say with certainty that his prognosis is accurate, but given America's penchant for the use of force to solve problems (real or imagined), coupled with the addiction of its citizens to racism, his prediction could become the ultimate reality for blacks.

A Note on Black People in Government Employment

Black people are overrepresented in the civilian work force of the federal government.[27] In 1985, although they are constituted 12 percent of the total population and approximately 10 percent of the labor force, blacks accounted for 24.1 percent of all federal workers. This difference is largely attributed to the government's hiring policies and the concentration of federal jobs in areas with large black populations. Within the federal government, blacks tend to be concentrated in such agencies as the Government Printing Office, the Federal Services Administration, the Veterans Administration, the Department of Labor, and the Department of Housing and Urban Development, each of which maintains a labor force that is from 20 percent to 40 percent black. In many of the major cities, such as Baltimore, Chicago, Cleveland, Detroit, Los Angeles, New York, Philadelphia, San Francisco, and Washington, D.C., black people account for at least one-fifth of all federal employees.

Although black persons appear to have less difficulty securing employment in the federal government than in private industry, in both instances they occupy a disproportionately large share of the low-paying jobs. In 1971, for example, 28 percent of all black federal employees earned salaries of less than $8065 yearly, and few (4.9 percent) earned in excess of $15,000.[28] The Postal Service, long a stronghold for black employment, recorded nearly one-fifth (19.6 percent) of its lowest-paid employees as black in 1972, while among those in the highest-paid positions only 6.8 percent were black.[29] The pattern persists.

As is generally the case, the proportion of blacks employed by the federal government, their employment status, and (by extension) their earnings, depend on whether they are employed in the South or elsewhere. Within the South they are underrepresented in federal employment, and, when so employed, they are overrepresented in the lowest-paying jobs.

Unemployment Among Black People

In addition to being employed in the lowest-status jobs in government and industry, black Americans are much more likely than white Americans to be unemployed. The unemployment rate among blacks has remained at least twice that of white workers since World War II. (See table 4-4.) Furthermore, if the unemployment rates which have persisted for blacks held for the labor force as a whole, the United States would have been a state of depression since the end of the war. The rate of unemployment for blacks has not dropped below 6.4 percent since 1954. During this period white Americans have frequently enjoyed "unparalleled prosperity," depending on the business cycle. As has been noted by one economist, "What is recession for the white (say, an unemployment rate of 6 percent) is prosperity for the nonwhite. He last saw an unemployment rate below 7.5 percent in 1953—a full decade ago."[30] Even in years of peak employment (some economists define *full employment* as an unemployment rate of 4 percent) the unemployment rate for black persons remains high.

Among black workers unemployment varies by age and sex. Black

TABLE 4-4   Nonwhite and White Unemployment Rates, United States, 1954–84

Year	Nonwhite	White	Ratio of Nonwhite to White
1954	8.8	4.5	2.0
1955	8.0	3.6	2.2
1956	7.5	3.3	2.3
1957	8.0	3.9	2.1
1958	12.6	6.1	2.1
1959	10.7	4.9	2.2
1960	10.2	4.9	2.1
1961	12.4	6.0	2.1
1962	10.9	4.9	2.2
1963	10.8	5.0	2.2
1964	9.6	4.6	2.1
1965	8.1	4.1	2.0
1966	7.3	3.3	2.2
1967	7.4	3.4	2.2
1968	6.7	3.2	2.1
1969	6.4	3.1	2.1
1970	8.2	4.5	1.8
1972	10.0	5.0	2.0
1984	16.0	6.5	2.5

Note: The unemployment rate is the percent of the civilian labor force that is unemployed.

Source: From 1954 to 1959, U.S. Department of Labor, Bureau of Labor Statistics, *The Negroes in the United States: Their Economic and Social Situation*, Bulletin no. 1511, 1966, p. 80. From 1960 to 1972, U.S. Bureau of the Census, *The Social and Economic Status of the Black Population in the United States*, 1972, p. 38; *The State of Black America 1985*, National Urban League, p. ii.

males are sometimes more likely to be unemployed than black females. The pattern is different for white Americans: females are always more likely to be unemployed than males. Among both blacks and whites, younger workers are more likely to be unemployed than older ones. However, all black workers—young or old, male or female—maintain rates of unemployment twice those of white workers. Indeed, the unemployment rate among black teenagers, which virtually always exceeds 20 percent, reached a peak of 48 percent in 1982, a year in which the rate for white teenagers was 20.4 percent and the general white rate was 8.6 percent.[31]

Black Americans are not only twice as likely to be unemployed but are also unemployed for longer periods of time. In 1980, for example, 19 percent of black workers experienced intermittent employment compared with 9.3 percent for white workers.[32]

The disproportionately high rates of black unemployment have been explained as a function of their unfavorable position in the occupational structure; that is, black people are likely to occupy positions that are becoming obsolete. This explanation is no doubt valid in some cases, but it does not explain the disproportionately high rates of unemployment among blacks at all occupational and educational levels. In 1984, for example, only 2.6 percent of white male college graduates were unemployed, while the figure for their black counterparts was 6.3 percent. The same pattern holds for black and white female graduates.[33] The high unemployment rate among blacks, and their tendency to be unemployed for longer periods than white workers, more than anything else, reflects the continuing practice of discrimination against blacks.[34]

One of the most serious aspects of unemployment is that which veterans of America's war of aggression in Vietnam face. Like their black nonveteran counterparts, black veterans of the war are at least twice as likely to be unemployed as white veterans. Furthermore, they experience even higher unemployment rates than black nonveterans.[35] Black veterans between 20 and 29 years of age had unemployment rates ranging anywhere from 11.6 to 13.7 percent between 1970 and 1972. For black nonveterans, the unemployment rates varied between 9.5 and 12 percent. And for white veterans during the same years (last available data), the unemployment rates varied from 6.4 to 8.3 percent.

Black People in Business

The historical development of business enterprise among black people began with the free blacks before the Civil War. However, their business ventures have played an insignificant role in the economy of the United States, and they have not been commensurate with the achievements of blacks in other aspects of American life.[36] Historically, black business ventures have generally been small, single proprietorships and have catered to the segregated black market. With the decline in segregation in recent years, the black businessperson has felt the brunt of changing patterns of race relations. For example, between 1950 and 1960 the total number of black businesspeople declined by nearly one-fourth, from 42,500 to 32,400. The number of black-owned restaurants declined by one-third, and other retail outlets experienced an even greater decline. In addition, there was a decline in the number of black funeral directors and barbers.[37] The gradual decrease in the number of black small-business enterprises reflects, in addition to decreased segregation, a general economic trend in the larger society. Corporations experience greater rates of return than independent business organizations.

Today the black business sector remains small and fragile. However, some progress has been recorded. For example, in a list of the top 100 black businesses published by *Black Enterprise* in 1981, most of those appearing had not existed in 1968. Much of the impetus for the development of the black business sector in the 1970s came from the federal government, but government officials in the 1980s have provided little assistance and have indicated that they are determined to end many programs that play key roles in building an independent black business sector. According to the editor of *Black Enterprise*: "There are now regulations that place a considerable burden on small businesses, and prevent the minority entrepreneur from competing fairly on the open market."[38] At the same time some private business organizations, such as the National Business League and the American Business Council, continue to be strong supporters in advocating black economic development.

Black businesses that continue to market black products have shown the greatest growth, although some others such as energy and technology companies have made gains. Many black-owned businesses could not continue without black support. In 1981 there were more than 40,000 smaller black businesses with paid employees in addition to the major ones on the top 100 list of *Black Enterprise*. Black businesses cover the spectrum from food preparation to magazines to entertainment to computer software. Of the top 100 black businesses, thirteen are oil and energy related, accounting for $359.1 million in sales in 1981. But black business is small compared to white business. In *Fortune* magazine's list of the leading 500 companies in the country in 1980, the smallest company reported $409.6 million in sales, whereas no black-owned business has yet topped the $100 million mark.[39]

The cosmetics business has always been one of the biggest for black people, and most of the major black companies that have made the greatest gains are those that sell products to black consumers. However, four oil companies were among the top ten growth leaders in 1981. And most of the major black business enterprises were formed in the decade between 1960 and 1970. Total sales for the top 100 black businesses amounted to $1.53 billion in 1981. An analysis of these 100 companies shows that 35 are in the Midwest, 28 in the Northeast, 24 in the South, and 13 in the West.[40]

Financial institutions comprise an important segment of the black business sector, not only because they employ people and earn income but also because they form depositories for savings, and their investment decisions are important in black economic development. Black banks and savings and loan associations are crucial to the communities in which they operate. These institutions have had a troubled history, as is indicated by their numbers, assets, and failures.

In 1983 there was a total of 47 black banks in the United States with total assets of $1.55 billion, compared to 37 with $656 million in assets in 1973. This represents a small fraction of the commercial banking industry. Indeed, in 1983 their assets represented .07 percent of the total assets of all commercial banks, and the total number of black banks was only .31 percent of all banks.[41] Furthermore, black-owned banks face low survival rates. For example, over the ten-year period ending in 1983 some 27 percent (roughly one out of four) of black banks in existence in 1973 had disappeared. This rate is considerably higher than for banks as a whole.

The situation for black savings and loan associations is similar to that of black banks. There were 36 such associations in 1983, down from 43 in 1973. These associations had assets of $1,163 billion in 1983 or .15 percent of the assets in all such associations.[42] However, black savings and loan associations have a better survival rate than comparable white associations. Most of the decline occurred in 1982 and 1983 because of high and unstable interest rates.

The life insurance industry has historically been an important one for blacks, but for decades its disposable personal income has declined. Since 1970 its assets have increased at a slower rate than those of commercial banks and savings and loan associations. Major insurance companies (e.g., Prudential) have broadened their fields of operation to include mutual funds, limited partnerships, money-management firms, and regional brokerage houses.[43] In recent years black life insurance companies have faced the problems of continued high unemployment in their traditional lower- and modest-income markets, the aggressive push by mainstream insurance companies to get the business of the black middle- and upper-income customers, and outmoded operating techniques.

At the end of 1983 black life insurance companies were 1.9 percent of the number and held .12 percent of the assets of all life insurance companies. Both percentages declined in the preceding ten years. The total assets of the thirty-eight black life insurance companies were $776 million in 1983, and that growth lagged behind the industry in general.[44] This results from the policies of black insurance companies of serving their traditional market of low-income families while mainstream companies are augmenting their product lines and attempting to reach black middle-income consumers.

While the prospects for black banks and savings and loan associations are bleak, the black insurance companies face even greater difficulties. Many of their services lack mainstream appeal, and their traditional clientele do not have resources to enable them to grow. Their captive market has enabled many black insurance companies to survive, but the prognosis is not good. However, it has been difficult for black insurance companies to enter the mainstream because of the lack of capital and management talent required.

In spite of minor gains, with few exceptions black business accomplishments historically have not been notable, and the future of small business is not promising. The decline of segregation and discrimination lessens the dependence of the black customer on black businesses. Furthermore, there continues to be a decline in retail trade outlets because of competition from large chain stores and supermarkets. Small stores are either purchased by large corporations or forced out of business. The federal government is drastically reducing its support for small-business enterprises. Therefore, the economic outlook for the small entrepreneur is not promising.

INCOME

The continuing pattern of employment discrimination against black people, resulting in their being relegated to the lowest-status occupations, coupled with their low and inferior educational status, is reflected in their earnings. Black family incomes have been and continue to be significantly lower than those for white families. Furthermore, the differential appears to be widening rather than narrowing.[45] Little attention was focused on differential family incomes for blacks and whites prior to World War II, as is reflected in the absence of such data before 1939. Since then, however, black family income has ranged anywhere from 51 percent to 64 percent of white family income. (See table 4-5.) As recently as 1963 black families earned only 53 percent of what white families earned. Although the differential has fluctuated since 1950, the greatest persistent decline in the differential occurred between 1952 and 1955. Since that time the gap has generally widened; blacks did not reach three-fifths of median white family income until 1966, and by 1983 the gap had widened to 56 percent.

The earnings of black families vary with the region of the country in which they live. The gap between black and white families has usually been greater in the South than elsewhere in the United States. But in 1982 the median family income for whites in the South was $23,089; for

TABLE 4-5   Median Family Income in the United States,
             Nonwhites and Whites, 1950–1983

Year	Nonwhite	White	Ratio, Nonwhite to White
1950	$ 1869	$ 3445	0.54
1951	2032	3859	0.53
1952	2338	4114	0.57
1953	2461	4392	0.56
1954	2410	4339	0.56
1955	2549	4605	0.55
1956	2628	4993	0.53
1957	2764	5166	0.54
1958	2711	5300	0.51
1959	3161	5893	0.54
1960	3233	5835	0.55
1961	3191	5981	0.53
1962	3330	6237	0.53
1963	3465	6548	0.53
1964	3839	6858	0.56
1965	3994	7251	0.55
1966	4674	7792	0.60
1967	5094	8234	0.62
1968	5590	8937	0.63
1969	6191	9794	0.63
1970	5516	10236	0.64
1972	7106	11549	0.62
1980	14506	25757	0.56

Note: The median family income for blacks is slightly lower than for nonwhites as a whole.

Source: U.S. Bureau of the Census, *Statistical Abstract of the United States, 1985*, p. 446.

blacks it was $13,044, or 56 percent of the median white family income. In the Northeast black families earned 57 percent of what white families earned. In the North Central states the ratio was 50 percent, and in the West it was 65 percent.[46]

The differential income between blacks and whites varies by sex, residence patterns (farm and nonfarm), and age. Regardless of race, men have higher incomes than women. However, in general the income of black females is closer to that of white females than that of black males is to their white male counterparts.[47] In 1982 black wives who worked full time year-round earned about 67 percent of what black men earned, while white women in the same category earned only 46 percent of what white men earned. Black wives are more likely to work than white wives, and their incomes account for a greater share of the family income. Blacks who work on farms earn significantly less than white farm workers.

In all occupational categories college-educated blacks have incomes closer to those of white college graduates than do blacks who have not completed college. In 1982 black college graduates earned 78 percent of what their white counterparts earned.[48]

A controversy over black economic progress has raged since Daniel Moynihan, the counselor to President Richard Nixon, issued his infamous "benign neglect" memorandum in 1970 after the first full year of the Nixon administration. Moynihan suggested that "the time may have come when the issue of race could benefit from a period of 'benign neglect.' The subject has been too much talked about. The forum has been too much taken over to hysterics, paranoids, and boodlers on all sides." He continued, "We may need a period in which Negro progress continues and racial rhetoric fades. . . . Greater attention to Indians, Mexican-Americans and Puerto Ricans would be useful."[49] This recommendation was made because "in quantitative terms, which are reliable, the American Negro is making extraordinary progress." Regarding the economic status of blacks, he reported that "young Negro families are achieving income parity with young white families. Outside the South, young husband-wife Negro families have 99 percent the income of whites."

As of 1971 the Bureau of the Census reported that young black families living outside the South, in which the head of the household was under 35 years of age, and in which both husband and wife worked, had achieved income parity with their white counterparts.[50] What is generally not recognized, however, is that such families comprised a small fraction (approximately 10 percent) of all black families in the country. The remaining 90 percent lag far behind white families in income. Moreover, the working black wife was the major contributing factor to such income equality. And the earnings of working black wives outside the South were substantially higher than those of white wives. This situation prevailed not because they were paid more but because of a higher proportion of black than white wives worked year round. For those who maintain that recent economic gains made by blacks are "nothing short of revolutionary," it should be pointed out that more than one-third of all blacks were still defined by the government as poor in 1983, and that the percentage is increasing while the white percentage is decreasing. Black people are still the victims of gross economic inequality in the United States, and to exaggerate their minor gains does nothing to improve the situation.

Black earnings are low regardless of where they are employed. At all occupational levels blacks with comparable training and experience can expect to earn less than white workers. In 1982, for example, the mean annual income for black male workers was $11,050 whereas for white workers it was $18,071. The differential between white and black workers persists throughout all occupational categories.[51] It is greatest in private industry and least in federal, state, and local government agencies, where the policy of equal pay for equal work generally prevails. The effects of discrimination in employment are reflected in differential earnings between black and white workers. Fein reports: "The Negro family whose head had some high school earned less than the white with fewer than eight years of schooling; *the Negro who has attended (but not completed) college earns less than the white with only eight years of elementary school;* the Negro college graduate earns but slightly more than does the white high school graduate."[52]

A Note on Poverty Among Blacks

According to the Department of Commerce, one-third (34 percent) of all black people lived in poverty in 1981, as compared with 11 percent of whites. The incidence of poverty is therefore nearly three times as great among blacks as among whites. Throughout the country some 34.4 million families were defined as living below the low-income level. Of these families, 23.5 million were white and 9.7 million were black.[53] Poverty varies with residence, age of household head, number of persons in the family, number of dependent children, region of the country, and family type. The differentially high incidence of poverty among blacks persist throughout each of these characteristics, but among blacks poverty is concentrated in families with female heads (68.5 percent of such families compared with 47.6 percent for white female-headed families). Poor white children outnumber poor black children two to one, but while black children comprise only 15 percent of all children, they equal 32 percent of all poor children.[54]

About one-half of all black people are under 18 years of age. They represent more than one-third of all poor children in the country. About two-thirds of all black families below the poverty level live in the South, although only one-half of all black families live in that region. In the South approximately six out of every ten poor black families live outside metropolitan areas, while outside that region the overwhelming majority of such families (nine out of every ten) reside in metropolitan areas. Children make up 26.8 percent of the total population, but 39.2 percent of all poor people are children. About 13.8 million children, representing 2.2 percent of Americans under the age of 18, were from poor families in 1983. A federal study reported that the number of poor children increased by three million from 1968 to 1983 even though the total number of children decreased by nine million in those years to 62.1 million.[55]

In 1980 the proportion of black families below the poverty level exceeded that of whites regardless of the educational level of the household head. For example, 23 percent of all black married couples were poor, compared with 11.7 of whites in the same category. In addition, black college graduates are twice as likely to be poor as whites with comparable education. In 1983, 36.3 percent of all families with seven or more children were described as being below the poverty level; for blacks it was 60 percent and for whites 26 percent.[56] Furthermore, the proportion of black families below the poverty level in which the male head is employed is greater than in white families. Finally, if the present trend continues, which is likely, increasing numbers of blacks, especially children, will fall below the poverty level.

Two recent reports dramatize the plight of black people in the United States. The Center on Budget and Policy Priorities in its 1984 report, "Falling Behind," demonstrates that in income, poverty, and unemployment, blacks are facing serious problems under the Reagan administration.[57] Some of the center's findings: Blacks in every income stratum, from poorest to the most affluent, lost ground and had less disposable income in 1984 than in 1980 (after adjusting for inflation). From 1980 to 1983, the income of the typical black family fell by 5.3 percent. No other population group lost so heavily. In 1982 the after-tax income of black Americans was $3.1 billion lower than it had been in 1980 (after adjusting for inflation). Most blacks are poor, and the poorest 20 percent of all families in the United States received just 4.7 percent of the national income, while the wealthiest 20 percent received 42.7 percent of the national income, nearly nine times as much.

Poverty among blacks has grown significantly worse since 1980. The gap between black poverty and white poverty has widened substantially. Among children under the age of 6, half (49.5 percent) of all black children are poor. Of the Americans who have fallen into poverty since 1980, 22 percent are black. Since 1980 blacks have been nearly twice as likely as other Americans to become poor. From 1980 to 1983, white poverty rose from 10.2 percent to 12.1 percent, meaning that an additional 1.9 percent of the white population fell into poverty during this period. For blacks, however, the poverty rate rose from 32.5 percent to 35.7 percent.

Finally, the *New York Times* reported in 1985 that because of racial discrimination, black professionals were leaving mainstream white-dominated companies to pursue self-employment or careers in black-owned companies.[58] They had become disenchanted with racial barriers blocking their success. As one black professional put it, "When you're black in a white corporation, you know you're black in a white corporation. And no matter how well you do in your position, there is a limit to how far you'll go and how much you'll earn the next year." Many of the black professionals attribute their plight to the policies of the Reagan administration in easing affirmative-action guidelines.

•   •   •

Black Americans are overrepresented in the lowest socioeconomic-status category in society. In the first one hundred years after emancipation, blacks lagged behind white Americans in education, occupational status, and income. Significant gains have been made in each of these categories, especially since World War II, but the gap is such that many decades, and perhaps centuries, will be required before black people can be expected to occupy a status comparable to that of white Americans.

Education, occupation, and income are interrelated as status variables. Occupation is generally determined by educational background, and occupation determines income. As long as black people are relegated to inferior education, the likelihood of their improving their level of living is minimal. In addition, blacks face problems which white Americans are spared. With blacks, simply improving one's educational status is not necessarily a means to social mobility. Indeed, within the context of American society race plays the crucial role in all aspects of life. Once one is identifiable as black, he or she is not simply, say, a college graduate, aged 23, who is trained as an engineer and who is eligible for a beginning salary of $35,000. Being black takes precedence over whatever other attributes he or she might possess.

One hundred years after emancipation racism is still the dominant force in American life insofar as attitudes and behavior toward black citizens are concerned. Changes in the status of blacks have occurred in the last twenty years, but the almost total lack of any significant change in the first hundred years after emancipation has had the effect of compounding the problem. Black infants born in the 1980s are likely to experience less difficulty becoming middle-class Americans than their ancestors born in the 1870s or their parents born in the 1950s, but the ease with which they achieve this status will not depend solely on their educational achievement, occupation, or income. It will depend to a great extent on the willingness of their fellow white citizens to accord them the rights which the whites take for granted for themselves and on the willingness of the government to assume responsibilities toward them in the same way that it makes demands upon them. Increasingly the economic struggle of black people in the United States is, literally, one for survival.

This situation attains in the United States because racism sustains and reinforces the privileges that white Americans enjoy, thereby maintaining white dominance and black oppression. If one group enjoys privileges denied another, the likelihood is that the dominant group will strive to preserve its position at all costs.

SELECTED BIBLIOGRAPHY

ALLEN, ROBERT L. *Black Awakening in Capitalist America.* New York: Doubleday & Co., 1970.
ASHMORE, HARRY S. *The Negro and the Schools.* Chapel Hill: University of North Carolina Press, 1954.

BALLARD, ALLEN B. *The Education of Black Folk.* New York: Harper & Row, Publishers, 1973.

BRIMMER, ANDREW F. "The Negro in the National Economy." In *The American Negro Reference Book.* Edited by John P. Davis. Englewood Cliffs, N.J.: Prentice-Hall, 1966.

BROOM, LEONARD, and NORVAL GLENN. *Transformation of the Negro American.* New York: Harper & Row, Publishers, 1965.

CLARK, KENNETH. *Dark Ghetto.* New York: Harper & Row, Publishers, 1965.

DRAKE, ST. CLAIR, and HORACE CAYTON. *Black Metropolis.* New York: Harcourt, Brace & Co., 1945.

EDWARDS, G. FRANKLIN. *The Negro Professional Class.* New York: Free Press, 1959.

FEIN, RASHI. "An Economic and Social Profile of the Negro American." In *The Negro American.* Edited by Talcott Parsons and Kenneth Clark. Boston: Houghton Mifflin Co., 1966.

FRAZIER, E. FRANKLIN. *The Negro in the United States.* New York: Macmillan Co., 1957.

KOZOL, JONATHAN. *Death at an Early Age: The Destruction of the Hearts and Minds of Negro Children in the Boston Public Schools.* Boston: Houghton Mifflin Co., 1967.

The Negro Handbook. Chicago: Johnson Publishing Co., 1966.

PINKNEY, ALPHONSO. *The Myth of Black Progress.* New York and London: Cambridge University Press, 1984.

SOWELL, THOMAS. *Black Education: Myths and Tragedies.* New York: David McKay Co., 1972.

The State of Black America 1985. Washington, D.C.: National Urban League, 1985.

TABB, WILLIAM. *The Political Economy of the Black Ghetto.* New York: W. W. Norton & Co., 1970.

U.S. BUREAU OF THE CENSUS. *The Social and Economic Status of the Black Population in the United States, 1972.* Washington, D.C.: Government Printing Office, 1973.

U.S. BUREAU OF THE CENSUS. *Statistical Abstract of the United States, 1985.* Washington, D.C.: Government Printing Office, 1985.

U.S. COMMISSION ON CIVIL RIGHTS. *Racial Isolation in the Public Schools.* Washington, D.C.: Government Printing Office, 1967.

U.S. COMMISSION ON CIVIL RIGHTS. *Unemployment and Underemployment among Blacks, Hispanics, and Women.* Washington, D.C.: U.S. Commission on Civil Rights, 1982.

U.S. DEPARTMENT OF EDUCATION. *Equality of Educational Opportunity.* Washington, D.C.: Government Printing Office, 1966.

WILLHELM, SIDNEY. *Who Needs the Negro?* Cambridge, Mass.: Schenkman Publishing Co., 1970.

NOTES

[1]Data on the black population in the United States are sometimes entered as "Negro" and sometimes combined with other "nonwhite" minorities. Since blacks have made up at least 94 percent of the nonwhite population since the first census, "nonwhite" and "Negro" are frequently used interchangeably.

[2]U.S. Department of Labor, Bureau of Labor Statistics, "A Century of Change: Negroes in the U.S. Economy, 1860–1960," *Monthly Labor Review* (December 1962), p. 1361.

[3]U.S. Bureau of the Census, *Statistical Abstract of the United States, 1985* (Washington, D.C.: Government Printing Office, 1985), p. 132.

[4]Harry S. Ashmore, *The Negro and the Schools* (Chapel Hill: University of North Carolina Press, 1954), p. 153.

[5]Ibid., p. 156.

[6]Ibid., pp. 157–60.

[7]U.S. Department of Health, Education, and Welfare, Office of Education, *Equality of Educational Opportunity* (Washington, D.C.: Government Printing Office, 1966). pp. 10–13. These are the most recent data available.

[8]*Statistical Abstract, 1972,* p.118.

[9]*Statistical Abstract, 1985.* p. 139.

[10]United States Commission on Civil Rights, *The Federal Civil Rights Effort: One Year Later* (Washington, D.C.: Government Printing Office, 1972), pp. 92–104.

[11]U.S. Department of Health, Education, and Welfare, Office of Education, *Federal Agencies and Black Colleges* (Washington, D.C.: Government Printing Office, 1972), pp. 82–85.

[12]U.S. Department of Health, Education, and Welfare, Office of Education, *Equality of Educational Opportunity*, p. 26.

[13]U.S. Bureau of the Census, *The Social and Economic Status of the Black Population in the United States, 1972* (Washington, D.C.: Government Printing Office, 1973), p. 14.

[14]Reported in the *New York Times*, October 27, 1985, p. 1.

[15]Paul Delaney, "Black State Colleges Are Found Periled; Integration a Factor," *New York Times*, November 26, 1971, p. 1.

[16]U.S. Department of Health, Education, and Welfare, Office of Education, *Federal Agencies and Black Colleges*, p. 5.

[17]*Statistical Abstract, 1972*, p. 121.

[18]U.S. Department of Health, Education, and Welfare, Office of Education, *Equality of Educational Opportunity*, pp. 14–21; U.S. Commission on Civil Rights, *Racial Isolation in the Public Schools* (Washington, D.C.: Government Printing Office, 1967), pp. 77–86.

[19]Kenneth Clark, *Dark Ghetto* (New York: Harper & Row, 1965), p. 120.

[20]U.S. Department of Labor, Bureau of Labor Statistics, "A Century of Change," p. 1360.

[21]U.S. Bureau of the Census, *America's Black Population: 1970 to 1982: A Statistical View* (Washington, D.C.: Government Printing Office, 1983), p. 11. Note: clerical and sales include administrative support; skilled workers include precision production, crafts, and repairs.

[22]Jack P. Gibbs. "Occupational Differentiation of Negroes and Whites in the United States," *Social Forces* 44 (December 1965), 159–65.

[23]U.S. Bureau of the Census, *Characteristics of the Population: General Social and Economic Characteristics, United States Summary, 1981*, table 163.

[24]U.S. Commission on Civil Rights, *Equal Employment Opportunity under Federal Law* (Washington, D.C.: Government Printing Office, 1971).

[25]*New York Times*, September 11, 1973, p. 21.

[26]Sidney M. Willhelm, *Who Needs The Negro?* (Cambridge, Mass.: Schenkman, 1970).

[27]*Statistical Abstract, 1985*, p. 326.

[28]*Statistical Abstract, 1972*, p. 401.

[29]U.S. Bureau of the Census, *Status of the Black Population 1972*, p. 56.

[30]Rashi Fein, "An Economic and Social Profile of the Negro American," *The Negro American*, ed. Talcott Parsons and Kenneth Clark (Boston: Houghton Mifflin, 1966), p. 114.

[31]U.S. Bureau of the Census, *America's Black Population: 1970 to 1982: A Statistical View*, p. 9.

[32]U.S. Commission on Civil Rights, *Unemployment and Underemployment among Blacks, Hispanics, and Women* (Washington, D.C.: U.S. Commission on Civil Rights, 1982), p. 5.

[33]*Statistical Abstract, 1985*, p. 407.

[34]Ralph Turner, "Foci of Discrimination in the Employment of Nonwhites," *American Journal of Sociology* 58 (November 1952), 247–56.

[35]U.S. Bureau of the Census, *Status of the Black Population 1972*, p. 42.

[36]E. Franklin Frazier, *The Negro in the United States* (New York: Macmillan, 1957), pp. 387–93; Gunnar Myrdal, *An American Dilemma* (New York: Harper, 1944), pp. 307–14.

[37]*The Negro Handbook* (Chicago: Johnson, 1966), pp. 214–15.

[38]*Black Enterprise*, June 1981, p. 15.

[39]Ibid., p. 117.

[40]Ibid., p. 118.

[41]William D. Bradford, "The Potential and Problems of Black Financial Institutions," in *The State of Black America 1985* (Washington, D.C.: National Urban League, 1985), pp. 130–32.

[42]Ibid., pp. 133–34.

[43]Ibid., p. 135.

[44]Ibid., pp. 136–37.

[45]James A. Geshwender, "Social Structure and the Negro Revolt: An Examination of Some Hypotheses," *Social Forces* 43 (December 1964), 248–56.

[46]*Statistical Abstract, 1985*, p. 447.

[47]Ibid., p. 452.

[48]Ibid., p. 447.

[49]Daniel P. Moynihan, "Memorandum for the President," *New York Times*, March 1, 1970, p. 69.

[50]U.S. Bureau of the Census, *Status of the Black Population 1972*, pp. 1–2.

[51]*Statistical Abstract, 1985*, p. 453.

[52]Fein, "Profile of the Negro American," p. 120 (italics in the original).

[53]The low-income threshold for a nonfarm family of four was $10,178 in 1983. *Statistical Abstract, 1985*, p. 429.

[54]Reported in the *New York Times*, October 20, 1985.

[55]From the Congressional Budget Office. Reported in the *New York Times*, May 23, 1985.

[56]*Statistical Abstract, 1985*, p. 458.

[57]*Falling Behind: A Report on How Blacks Have Fared under the Reagan Policies* (Washington, D.C.: Center on Budget and Policy Priorities, 1984).

[58]Jonathan P. Hicks, "Black Professionals Refashion Their Careers," *New York Times*, November 29, 1985, p. 1.

CHAPTER FIVE
SOCIAL INSTITUTIONS

The institutional life of the black community in the United States emerged and developed as a result of the peculiar interaction of black and white Americans through the years. Few aspects of institutional life in Africa survived the transfer of slaves to North America. With few exceptions, the distinctive features of black life in the United States today stem from the historical, social, and economic forces which these people have encountered since their arrival in North America. Their social institutions are a reflection of life in a racist society.

This chapter focuses on three social institutions: family life, politics, and religion. Other distinctive social institutions are discussed in appropriate sections of other chapters.

THE FAMILY

The organization and behavior patterns of the black family in the United States results mainly from economic and social conditions which blacks have encountered. Few survivals of the original African family system remain. From the breakup of the African family during slavery to the overwhelming urbanization of black people in the 1980s, family life has been in a constant process of change, adapting to economic and social forces emanating from the larger society.

Developmental Processes

The family system which developed among black people during slavery was one with few of the characteristics that were normal to the white

American family of the time. The very nature of slavery as an economic institution, as well as the attitudes which led to the institutionalization of Afro-American slavery militated against black family stability. Associations between male and female slaves were frequently for the sole purpose of satisfying sexual desires. Slaveholders could, and often did, mate their slaves to produce additional property. Male slaves were frequently used as stallions; in such cases, no bonds of affection were likely to develop between them and female slaves. Furthermore, since slaves were the property of slaveholders, any family relationships which might develop could be, and frequently were, dissolved through the sale of one of the parties. Any offspring to such a union usually remained with the mother, while the father continued his sexual exploits on a new plantation.

Slave mothers frequently were affectionate and devoted to their offspring, but both the separation of the father and the presence of the slaveholder as a promiscuous role model led to the matricentric family, a development which has to some extent persisted to the present time. Children rarely saw their fathers, and mothers assumed responsibility for parental affection and care. When separated from her children, the slave mother often visited them at night. The mother, then, was the dominant and important figure in the black slave family.

Because of the precariousness of their status—economically, socially, and legally—and because of their slave heritage, with its disregard for stable family life, blacks who were free before the Civil War were unable to develop stable family relations.[1] Family disorganization, including sexual promiscuity, was widespread. However, many of the mulatto children born to black women were kept by their mothers and accorded care despite severe hardships. Among the more economically secure free blacks, family relations attained a high degree of stability. Many of the properous mulattoes patterned their families after the middle- and upper-class white families.

The Civil War and emancipation had a disrupting effect on whatever degree of stability slave families had achieved. Marriage as a formal and legal relationship between males and females was not allowed to become a part of the mores among most slaves. However, during slavery some stable families of husband, wife, and children did develop. With the complete uprooting of the social order in the South, family instability was but one element in the widespread social disorganization found among the ex-slaves. In the exodus from the plantations and in the general aimless wandering which accompanied freedom, many black mothers left their children behind. Yet many others refused to part from their children, and reports testify to the sacrifices which many of them made to keep their children.[2]

Promiscuous sexual relations and frequent changing of partners became the rule among ex-slaves, especially among those who experienced difficulties adjusting in an era largely characterized by anomie. Religious leaders, state legislatures, military authorities, the Freedmen's Bureau, missionary schools, and the mass media all joined the effort to impose institutional marriage and family norms on the freedmen.[3] These efforts succeeded in some cases, but in others official monogamous marriage and stable family relations required a difficult form of self-discipline. Nevertheless, by the end of the Reconstruction, blacks had come to accept many of the family patterns of the larger society.

The restoration of white supremacy in the South following the Reconstruction imposed economic and social hardships on the black people. It became virtually impossible for the black man to assume a position of dominance or of equality with the black female. Economic exploitation, unemployment, and social subordination of black males in the larger society served to render them ineffectual as husbands and fathers. The appearance of Jim Crow laws toward the end of the nineteenth century further humiliated the black male; to a great extent these laws were geared toward keeping him "in his place" (i.e., away from the white female). Furthermore, with the widespread urbanization of the blacks after 1900, family life was again disrupted. The social norms which made for family stability in the rural South were without force in the urban slums. Among the lower-income blacks, social disorganization was manifested in broken families and children born out of wedlock. On the other hand, a growing middle class among urban blacks was characterized by stable family relations and rigid adherence to the norms governing white, middle-class families.

The Family in the 1980s:
Demographic Characteristics

As of March 1983 there were approximately 6,530,000 black families in the United States. Of these families 53 percent were husband-wife families, 42 percent were headed by females with no husband present, and 5 percent were headed by males with no wife present.[4] Slightly more than one-half of black families were composed of both husband and wife. Of the 53,407,000 white families in the country at the same time, 87 percent were husband-wife families, 10.5 percent were headed by females, and 2.6 percent were headed by males. For black families the proportion with both husband and wife present has steadily decreased in recent years. In 1970, 64 percent of all black families were husband-wife families, in 1983, 53 percent were, representing a decline of 15 percent in 13 years. Compared to white female heads of families, black women are more likely to have their marriages disrupted through separation (19.3 percent vs. 3.2 percent) and through divorce than white women. In 1981, 18 percent of black women household heads were divorced, compared with 11 percent for white women. Also, black women who are heads of families are less likely than white women to be widowed (19.5 percent for blacks, 30 percent for whites) as a result of the longer life expectancy among white women.

Black families are larger than white families. The average size of the American family in 1983 was 3.26 persons.[5] For black families it was 3.7 persons and for white families it was 3.2 persons. Sixty percent of all black families included children under 18 years of age, compared with only 50 percent for all families. Furthermore, black families are more likely to include other relatives and unrelated individuals than are white families. That is, black families more closely approach the extended-family pattern than do white families and are more likely to be augmented by unrelated individuals.[6] While the majority of black families are nuclear families of husband, wife, and children, nearly one-fourth are extended families, and one-tenth are augmented families.

In some cases black families are made up of two or more nuclear families in the same household. This extended-family arrangement is called a subfamily. In 1970, 6 percent of all black families were subfamilies, compared with only 2 percent for white families.[7] Allthough black families are larger, they earn significantly less than white families do. In 1982 the median income for black familes was $13,599, or 55 percent of the $24,603 median income for white families. This difference in family income existed despite the greater proportion of working wives in black families than in white families. Some 60 percent of black wives worked, compared with 49 percent of white wives.

Regionally, black families in the United States are about evenly divided between the southern and nonsouthern states, but within these regions some differences occur. Few black families outside the south (approximately 1.4 percent) live on farms, whereas in the South about 3.3 percent live on farms. The black family is larger in the South than outside that region and includes more dependent children.

Black families are less likely than white families to own their own homes. In 1983, for example, 45 percent of all black families owned their homes; 68 percent of white families were homeowners.[8] Black home ownership is greatest in the South (51.1 percent), followed by the North Central region (43.4 percent), and the West (39.6 percent). In the Northeast it is lowest (32.7 percent).

Because black families earn less than white families, they are required to spend a larger percentage of their earnings for basic needs— food, shelter, and clothing. Black and white families spend approximately the same proportions of their incomes for shelter (including fuel, light, refrigeration, and water) and for clothing. Furthermore, black families live in more congested housing than white families. In 1980 the average number of black persons per occupied housing unit was 3.07; for whites it was 2.67 persons. Whether they own or rent their places of residence, black families are more likely than white families to live in housing units lacking some or all plumbing facilities.[9] In 1980, 5 percent of all black families lived in housing lacking complete plumbing facilities, compared with 1 percent of white families. In short, black families are required to pay a greater portion of their income than white families for inferior housing.

In an affluent society like the United States certain household appliances and equipment are taken for granted by the vast majority of citizens. But as is the case in every other area, blacks lag behind whites in this regard. In 1980, 2 percent of black and white households had one bedroom. Only 2 percent of white households had no bathrooms, while 6 percent of black households fell into this category. Four percent of black households had no kitchen facilities, while for whites the figure was 1 percent. Telephones are almost universal in America households, but 16 percent of homes occupied by blacks had no telephones while only 5 percent of white households lacked telephones.[10] Finally, although room heaters cause many fires resulting in deaths, 14 percent of all black households had such heaters, compared with 6 percent of white households.

Family Stability

The economic and social conditions under which black Americans have been forced to live have adversely affected their family lives. The legacy of slavery, widespread poverty, racial segregation and discrimination, and rapid urbanization have led to "family disorganization" among blacks. This is usually said to characterize lower-class black families, for their lifestyle often differs from that of middle-class white families. Some evidence indicates that when black people achieve middle-class status, family stability becomes even more important than it is among the white middle class.[11] But a majority of black people are found in the lowest socioeconomic-status positions in the society.

Perhaps no institution in the black community has been more distorted and misunderstood than the black family. As late as March 1965, the Office of Policy Planning and Research of the Department of Labor issued a controversial report, compiled by Daniel P. Moynihan, assistant secretary of labor, entitled *The Negro Family: The Case for National Action.* In this report Moynihan declared: "At the heart of the deterioration of the fabric of Negro society is the deterioration of the Negro family. It is the fundamental source of weakness of the Negro community at the present time."[12] Such a charge was supported by the following allegations: (1) "nearly a quarter of urban Negro marriages are dissolved," (2) "nearly one-quarter of Negro births are now illegitimate;" (3) "almost one-fourth of Negro families are headed by females;" and (4) "the breakdown of the

Negro family has led to a startling increase in welfare dependency." Following its publication this report was criticized by black civil rights leaders and social scientists.[13] There are many criticisms to be made of Moynihan's formulation as well as his assumption that American blacks are themselves to blame for conditions forced on them by the society. In June 1965 President Lyndon Johnson announced in a commencement address at Howard University that he would convene in the fall "a White House conference of scholars, and experts, and outstanding Negro leaders—men of both races—and officials of government at every level. This White House conference's theme and title will be 'To Fulfill These Rights.' " That the so-called breakdown of the black family, which Moynihan (who assisted in drafting the speech) had characterized as a "tangle of pathology," would be the theme of the conference was clear from the president's comments in the speech: "The family is the cornerstone of our society. . . . When the family collapses it is the children that are usually damaged. When this happens on a massive scale the community itself is crippled."[14] Angered by the age-old American tactic of "blaming the victim," black civil rights leaders and educators forced the scaling down of the White House conference to a planning meeting for a larger one to be held the following spring. When the conference finally met, those in attendance seized the opportunity to criticize what had become known as the Moynihan Report.

It cannot be denied that the black family has shown an amazing ability to achieve and maintain a remarkable degree of stability in spite of the overwhelming odds of white racist oppression. If the black family somehow managed to survive the brutality of slavery, the total disruption of the post-Civil War years, and the degradation of institutionalized white supremacy, it is likely that in an era of increasing black pride it is stronger than ever.

Examination of Moynihan's indicators of black family "deterioration" quickly explains the anger expressed by black leaders. If the high rate of dissolution of marriages among urban blacks indicates black family breakdown, then the urban American white family is also breaking down. The marriage rate among Americans in 1983 was approximately 10.5 per 1000 population, and the divorce rate was 5.0 per 1000 population.[15] While black families are more likely to be dissolved through separation, the divorce rate is significantly higher for blacks than for whites. But these data hardly tell the whole story. In many black families the husband and father technically leaves the household so that the wife and mother can become eligible for public assistance.[16] These marriages are then recorded as dissolved. Thus the family can supplement its meager income.

The question of children born out of wedlock has concerned almost all scholars who write about the black family. In 1967 it was estimated that 9 percent of all live births in the United States were out-of-wedlock births.

The rate for blacks is said to be seven times that of whites.[17] These data are questionable. White out-of-wedlock births frequently occur in private hospitals in which the mother is attended by sympathetic physicians. Most black babies are born in public hospitals, where they are more likely to be recorded as "illegitimate." These different circumstances are likely to lead to significant differentials in reporting.

Childbirth outside of marriage is invariably seen by Americans as a function of moral laxity. Although one of the norms of the society prohibits sexual intercourse prior to marriage, a report of the Department of Health, Education, and Welfare estimates that one-third of all firstborn children in the United States between 1964 and 1968 were conceived out of wedlock.[18] In most cases marriages were hastily arranged before the birth, but the marriage partners had still violated the societal taboo on premarital sexual intercourse. With such high figures it is clear that the proportion of blacks involved could have been responsible for only a fraction of these premarital pregnancies. Furthermore, studies show that a high proportion of black children who are born out of wedlock are "legitimized" by the subsequent marriage of the natural parents.[19] In other words, cultural variation operates to impel white parents to "legitimize" the prospective offspring before birth, while among blacks it is more likely to happen after birth.

Furthermore, black unwed expectant mothers are less likely than whites to terminate pregnancy through abortion. When abortion was illegal in the United States, it was estimated that nearly two million such operations were performed yearly and that white women accounted for approximately 90 percent of them. The stigma attached to children born out of wedlock has never been as pervasive among blacks as among whites.[20] Bernard concluded after summarizing studies of premarital pregnancies that while black women do not reject the societal taboo on premarital pregnancies, out-of-wedlock birth among blacks is "not accepted—let alone welcomed," even in low-income families. For many it is a traumatic experience.[21] Once the baby is born, it is likely to be seen as having a right to live in the family and the community without being stigmatized. Such babies are usually kept within the mother's family, while in white families they are more likely to be offered for adoption.

Moynihan's third indicator of black family "deterioration" is the high proportion of black families headed by females. According to the Bureau of the Census, in 1973 more than one-third of all black famiies (34.6 percent) were headed by females, in contrast to about one-tenth of white families (9.6 percent).[22] In order to survive in a hostile atmosphere black families have historically been forced to develop a network of informal arrangements. One of these is the quasi-extended family pattern characteristic of many of the world's people. Black families are frequently headed by females because such societal pressures as employment discrimination against black men make it difficult for them to support their families. When the black husband leaves the family, the children are frequently left in a household in which there are many adults—aunts, uncles, and grandparents. (Such an atmosphere might be said to be more wholesome than the small isolated nuclear family.)

The effects of so-called family disorganization on the personalities of children have been the subject of many studies.[23] Children from homes in which the father is absent are said to seek immediate gratification far more than children with the fathers present in the home. This inability to defer gratification has been alleged to be correlated with immature, neurotic, and criminal behavior. Furthermore, such children are reported to experience difficulty in distinguishing sex roles, a condition which supposedly manifests itself in femininity among males, in delayed marriage or divorce, and in pseudomasculine toughness. Finally, it has been suggested that families without fathers are more likely to produce schizophrenic children than families in which the father is present.

Many of these studies employ dubious methodology or draw unwarranted conclusions from the data. For example, one study said that children from homes in which the father was absent tended to seek more immediate gratification than those from homes in which the father was present; conclusions were based on whether the children chose to receive a small candy bar immediately or a large bar a week later. Those from father-absent families were more likely to choose the small candy bar rather than wait, while those from families in which the father was present were more inclined to wait for the larger candy bar.[24] Whether this represents an accurate measure of ability to delay gratification is open to question, as is the assertion that such behavior is an important factor in criminal, immature, and neurotic behavior. Another study maintained that black males from lower-class, father-absent homes scored higher on measures of femininity than white males from comparable class backgrounds but from father-present families. This conclusion was arrived at because black men were more likely than whites to agree with such statements as "I would like to be a singer."[25] Clearly this method of reaching conclusions says more about those administering the test and interpreting the results than about the subjects.

In still another study, the researcher matched twenty-one adult black males whose fathers had been absent during early childhood with twenty-one black men who possessed similar characteristics but whose fathers were present during their early childhoods. When asked whether they felt they had been victims of discrimination, 48 percent of those from father-absent families in childhood responded affirmatively, compared with 29 percent whose fathers were present during childhood.[26] The interpretation given to this finding is that adult males from father-absent families during childhood are more inclined to feel that they were "victimized" during childhood than their counterparts from father-present families. It seems that these data were misinterpreted—any adult black male who does not know that he has been a victim of discrimination at some point in his life is clearly living in a fantasy world.

If the so-called breakdown of the black family has led to an increase in welfare dependency, as Moynihan maintained, it says more about American racism than about black people. At the time of the report the government of the United States was beginning the expensive military buildup of Indochina, one of its many wars of aggression which cost the taxpayers $1000 billion between 1946 and 1969, a sum far in excess of that spent on social welfare programs. Furthermore, in 1969, 90 percent of all black families receiving Aid to Families with Dependent Children (AFDC) were those in which the father was absent, compared to 73 percent of all white recipients. On the other hand, in black families with the father present only 11 percent received AFDC, in contrast to 24 percent for white families with the father present.[27]

There are many problems facing the black family today. The divorce rate among blacks increased threefold in twenty years. The increasingly high rates of unemployment and underemployment do not lend themselves to family stability. And in recent years there has been an increase in the number of families headed by single women. By 1983, 55 percent of black babies were born to unmarried mothers, a significant proportion of them teenagers.[28] Some researchers maintain that these problems are the cause of widespread poverty in black families while others attribute the problems to poverty itself. But most agree that there is a correlation between the two. It is undeniable that families headed by females tend to be poorer that two-parent families. And working women earn less than their male counterparts.

The Reagan administration attributes these problems to the welfare system, which it argues has led families to split up and has created a state of welfare dependency. It encourages reductions in government spending, forcing individuals receiving welfare to work (while reducing child-care facilities), and forcing the fathers of these children to support them. On the other hand, more humane social analysts attribute the problems to the long history of discrimination against blacks in the United States, bringing about widespread unemployment. They would increase government-support programs to a level practiced by governments in most Western industrialized countries.

Furthermore, many black scholars feel that the growth of poor, female-headed households is a direct result of the racism of the society. Black males face frustrations because they feel the cards are stacked against them and rather than trying against the odds of failing, it is better not to try at all. "In a society where the male is supposed to be the breadwinner," one psychiatrist said, "something that is still deep in our psychology, it's a tremendous psychological burden when you know you don't have a snowball's chance in hell of taking care of your family. One of the defenses is to not care, to not do, not try."[29] Males often seek to prove their adequacy and adulthood as males by producing a baby, and females often seek to prove their worth by producing a child.

One of the primary reasons that more black children live in single-parent families is that black teenage pregnancies have been increasing rapidly in recent years. In 1980 about 272,000 births occurred to unmarried women below the age of 20. About 134,000 of these were to blacks and 131,000 to whites. And although blacks accounted for only 28 percent of all adolescent births, they accounted for nearly half of nonmarital births.[30] The National Urban League reports that in 1982 "one out of every four black babies was to a female 19 years of age or younger and nearly 90 percent of these women and girls were unmarried."[31] Furthermore, there were nearly 150,000 babies born to black, teenaged mothers in 1982 alone. The League estimates that at this rate by 1988 another one million babies will be born to teenaged mothers.

The Alan Guttmacher Institute of New York reports that teenage pregnancy is not limited to blacks, but a disproportionate number become pregnant. In 1981 there were 1.3 million children living with teenage mothers, about half of whom were unmarried. An additional 1.6 million children under age 5 were living with mothers who were teenagers when they gave birth.[32] Adolescent births represented 26 percent of all births among blacks, compared to less than 14 percent among whites. About 46 percent of births among black adolescents were to girls under 18, compared to 34 percent among white adolescents. The teen birthrate for blacks was two times higher than for whites. Furthermore, pregnant white teenagers are four times as likely as blacks to marry before their babies are born.

A cross-cultural study of teenage pregnancy was conducted by the Guttmacher Institute in 1981. Although the study covered thirty-seven countries, it was focused on five countries in addition to the United States: Canada, England, France, the Netherlands, and Sweden. It was found that the rates of adolescent pregnancy were considerably higher in the United States than in these countries, although the incidence of sexual activity was for the most part not very different; in some cases it was actually higher in other countries. In addition to teenage pregnancy, the United States had the highest rates of teenage birth and abortion. And the rates are increasing yearly.[33] In the United States the study found that "the pregnancy rates among black teenagers are sufficiently higher than those among whites to influence the rates of the total adolescent population, even though in 1980, black teenagers represented only about 14 percent of all 15–19 year olds." It concluded that "teenage pregnancy rates are lower in countries where there is greater availability of contraceptive services and of sex education; levels of adolescent sexual activity in the United States are not very different from those in countries with much lower teenage pregnancy rates. Although the teenage pregnancy rate of American blacks is much higher than that of whites, this difference does not explain the gap between the pregnancy rates in the United States and the other countries."

It would be a mistake to minimize the problems faced by black families in the United States, for there are many. However, from the breakup of the African family during slavery to the overwhelming urbanization of blacks in the twentieth century, the black family has demonstrated an amazing degree of resilience, adapting to the social and economic forces emanating from the larger society. The black family is a complex social institution, and its members must not be blamed for the problems imposed by the larger society.

Patterns of Family Life

In many ways black family life in the United States differs from white family life. It is often maintained that in the black family dominance is vested in the female, while in white families dominance is vested in the male or is shared by the husband and wife. In the vast majority of black families, as in white families, dominance is shared between the mother and the father (egalitarian pattern) or is vested in the father (patriarchal pattern).[34] Although about two-fifths of all black families are headed by females, they represent a minority. These are the poorest families in the society; as soon as blacks achieve middle-class status, their family patterns become similar to those of economically comparable white families. Consequently, the major differences in patterns of family life between blacks and whites result from economic factors.

One of the chief societal functions of the family is the socialization of offspring. In the case of black parents this role becomes more difficult, for theirs is not simply a task of instilling skills, knowledge, attitudes, and values; they must also socialize their offspring into the peculiar status of being black in a racist society. Child-rearing practices constitute crucial aspects of the socialization process. In the 1940s Davis and Havighurst conducted a study of racial and class differences in child-rearing practices. They reported that few differences existed when black and white families occupied similar social-class positions.[35] Subsequent studies report findings inconsistent with these.[36] One similar study, however, reports that black mothers are less likely to expose themselves to child-rearing literature than are white mothers, regardless of social class position, but that black mothers who are so exposed express more favorable attitudes toward child-rearing than do white mothers.[37] Although contradictory findings are reported, considerable evidence indicates that middle-class black parents are more like middle-class white parents in their child-rearing practices than they are like lower-class black parents.

In an effort to counteract the proliferation of books characterizing the black family as pathological, several black social scientists have published studies which attempt to present the black family as an institution characterized by both strengths and weaknesses.[38] In general, these studies posit that an examination of the strengths of black families is a necessary antidote to past and present preoccupation with their weaknesses. Historically, the black family has been presented in American scholarship as a "matriarchal" institution so unstable that it is responsible for many of the problems faced by blacks in the United States.

Robert Hill has enumerated some of the strengths of black families.[39] He sees certain characteristics of black families that contribute to their survival, development, and stability: strong kinship bonds, strong work orientation, adaptability of family roles, strong achievement orientation, and strong religious orientation. In black families kinship relations are strong, minors and the elderly are absorbed in the family, and informal adoption is relatively commonplace. Contrary to popular stereotypes, black families place a strong emphasis on work, as is evidenced by the number of families with two or more wage earners. When blacks refuse to work it is because they are relegated to the lowest-paid jobs.

Although most black families are two-parent families in which decision making is shared, it is often necessary for each member of the family to temporarily assume the roles of others, as when both parents work or when a key member is absent for some unexpected reason. Another of the strengths of black families is their high achievement orientation, even among the poor. Indeed, black parents maintain higher aspirations for their children than white parents do and black youths have higher educational and occupational aspirations than their white counterparts.[40] Finally, a strong religious orientation has served as a survival mechanism for black families throughout a long and difficult history.

Any social institution in a society with as many contradictions, inconsistencies, and prejudices as exist in the United States is likely to face problems. And the black family has its share of these problems. In a period of rapid social change, as is characteristic of American society, much can be learned from the black family, an institution which has maintained a reasonable degree of stability through a long series of crises.

POLITICS

With rare exceptions, black Americans have played a minor role in the political life of the United States, both in the electoral process and in public office. Historically, black people have been heavily concentrated in the South, where various techniques have been used to keep them from voting. Except during the period of Radical Reconstruction, the South succeeded in virtually disfranchising its many blacks. In 1898, for example, a senator from South Carolina boldly declared from the floor of the Senate that his state had virtually eliminated black people from voting. "We have done our best. We have scratched our heads to find out how we could eliminate the last one of them. We stuffed ballot boxes. We shot them. We are not ashamed of it."[41] Because of increasing pressure for greater civil rights, and because of additional civil rights legislation ensuring their voting rights, black people are becoming more active in American political life.

Historical Trends

Black people have been active in varying degrees in the political life of the United States since the beginnings of the Radical Reconstruction. On the national level, three blacks served in the 41st Congress (1869–1871), two in the House of Representatives and one in the Senate.[42] With the exception of the 50th Congress (1887–89), blacks served in every U. S. Congress from 1869 to 1901. The largest number—seven—served in the 43rd and 44th Congresses. All these congressman represented southern states, and by the turn of the twentieth century, blacks had been effectively disfranchised in that region. The last black man from the South to serve was a representative from North Carolina whose service ended in 1901.

No blacks served in the national Congress from the 57th Congress (1901–03) through the 71st Congress (1929–31), but the widespread migration of black people northward and the availability of the franchise to them resulted in the election to the 72nd Congress of the first black from the North. Since that time one or more blacks have served in every Congress. With the concentration of black people in large urban centers, as a result of residential segregation, the number of blacks in Congress has gradually increased. The first black senator (from Massachusetts) since 1881 was elected to the 93rd Congress (1973–74).

Although black Americans have frequently constituted a majority in the population of several political subdivisions in the South, since the Reconstruction they have held little, if any, political power. On the state and local level blacks held important offices during the Reconstruction. During this period they were elected or appointed to such public offices as supreme court justice, lieutenant governor, secretary of state, state treasurer, superintendent of public instruction, and virtually every other public office except that of governor. In the state constitutional conventions, blacks were well represented, especially in South Carolina, Louisiana, Florida, and Virginia. At no time, however, can it be said that they effectively controlled the affairs of any state.

Beginning with the elections for the constitutional conventions in 1867, black people in the South voted in large numbers. At that time the total black vote exceeded the vote of white southerners.[43] Throughout the Radical Reconstruction blacks actively exercised the franchise. With the restoration of white supremacy in 1877, the gains registered in this period gradually disappeared. The Populist movement in the 1890s witnessed a resurgence of black voting, but it was short lived. By the turn of the twentieth century, through a series of devices, some legal and some illegal, the South had effectively disfranchised most of its black citizens.[44] At that time so few black people lived outside the South that their voting strength was insignificant.

With the wholesale disfranchisement of black people in the South after 1900, they were hardly represented in public office in that region during the first half of the twentieth century. With increased voting guarantees, especially the Voting Rights Act of 1965, blacks have been elected to public office at various levels—from state senator to local boards of education and, in several cases, to county sheriff—since the rise of the civil rights movement.

In the North the concentration of black people in urban areas is a relatively recent development. In the second half of the twentieth century, increasingly large numbers of blacks have held elective and appointive offices at various levels, from state senator to mayor to judges of various levels, including the U.S. Supreme Court.

With the internal redistribution of black people in the twentieth century, northern cities became the center of black political behavior. Black voters are frequently cultivated by white politicians because in certain "decisive" states black voters hold the balance of power—their voters have determined the outcome of elections.[45] In the South, especially since the passage of the Civil Rights Act of 1964 and the Voting Rights Act of 1965, black people have been registered and voting in increasing numbers. This increased participation in elections was made evident by the election returns in 1984, when black people were elected to state legislatures and local offices throughout the South, although still not nearly in proportion to their number in the population.

Voting Rights

The right to vote is one of the basic civil rights guaranteed to citizens by the Constitution of the United States. Yet hardly any aspect of the black's quest for equality has met with greater resistance in the South than the right to vote. Several judicial decrees and legislative acts have not succeeded in fully translating this constitutional guarantee into a reality for millions of black citizens of the United States.[46] With emancipation, two amendments, the Fourteenth and Fifteenth, were written into the

Constitution especially to protect the voting rights of the newly freed slaves. These amendments specifically directed states to guarantee voting rights to black citizens.

Three civil rights acts were enacted between 1866 and 1875 as a means of assuring equality of treatment (including the right to vote) to America's blacks. These acts—the Civil Rights Act of 1866, the Civil Rights Act of 1870, and the Civil Rights Act of 1875—together with constitutional guarantees, served to permit black people in the South to exercise the right to vote with relative ease during the Reconstruction. After the Reconstruction, however, several states adopted so-called grandfather clauses, which restricted registration and voting to persons who had voted prior to emancipation. This practice was finally declared unconstitutional by the Supreme Court in 1915.[47] With this defeat southerners adopted the "white primary," in which the Democratic party prohibited blacks from participating in primary elections in nine states. When the white primary was outlawed, many southern states resorted to the gerrymander as a means of disfranchising blacks. In a long series of cases the Supreme Court eventually curbed this practice also.

In addition to the above techniques, the poll tax, property, educational, and "character" requirements were used to keep black citizens from voting. Perhaps the most effective means of disfranchising blacks, however, were those of intimidation and violence.[48]

Because of the difficulties encountered by black people attempting to vote in the South, special legislation was again enacted in the 1950s and 1960s. The Civil Rights Act of 1957 attempted to guarantee that any black so desiring could vote. The federal government, through the Justice Department, was empowered to institute lawsuits to ensure blacks the right to vote. The Civil Rights Act of 1960 empowered the attorney general ultimately to certify blacks as qualified voters in areas where they had been kept from voting through discrimination. And the Civil Rights Act of 1964 included voting rights guarantees. One important aspect of this act is the provision that a sixth-grade education is a presumption of literacy for voting purposes.

In spite of the Constitution, the nineteenth-century civil rights acts, the judicial ruling of the Supreme Court, and the twentieth-century civil rights acts, black Americans have continued to experience difficulties in voting throughout the Deep South. After the Civil Rights Act of 1964, civil rights organizations were urged to discontinue direct-action protests and to concentrate on voter registration among black people. It was felt that the most effective means of achieving their goals was through registering blacks to vote. When large-scale attempts were made to register black people in the South, voting registrars again utilized various techniques to keep them from voting. Acts of violence (so characteristic in the South) met voter-registration workers and black people attempting to vote. Civil rights workers and the leaders of civil rights organizations urged the enactment of new legislation to guarantee southern blacks the right to vote. As a result of these pressures, the Voting Rights Act of 1965 was enacted by Congress and signed into law on August 6. This act contains many provisions designed to assure black people that devices previously employed to disfranchise them would no longer serve this purpose. For example, literacy as a qualification for voting was suspended, and voter registration may be supervised by federal officials in political subdivisions where a pattern of discrimination is discerned.

Although intimidation and threats will no doubt continue to deter many eligible black voters, a long series of legislative acts and judicial rulings, over a period of more than one hundred years, has finally established, in principle, the right of black people to vote.

Political Organization and Behavior

The second half of the twentieth century has seen the growth of greater cohesiveness in the black community than has existed since emancipation as a direct result of increasing identification among black people and the demand for greater civil rights. The black community nowhere represents a completely unified force, however. Clearly some communities are better organized than others. The Atlanta, Georgia, black subcommunity, for example, is described by Hunter as a community with a high degree of social organization.[49] The black leadership of Atlanta followed the pattern of leadership in the larger community. However, the black community exerted less influence on policy decisions in the larger community than other associational groupings, such as organized labor or the Jewish subcommunity. Other subcommunities were represented on policy-making committees in the larger community, but the black subcommunity was not represented: " . . . the [black] subcommunity . . . stands alone in its isolation from the sources of power as no other unit within the metropolitan area. Its channels of communication in most of its power relations with the larger community are partially blocked, if not totally closed." Because of the larger number of blacks, and because of the relatively high proportion of middle-class blacks, there was a high degree of civic participation among Atlanta's blacks. Even there, however, they were powerless to influence basic community decisions.[50]

As a political force, black people lack the organization necessary for effective action. In many urban areas the black community has enough numerical strength to organize effective civic action, but its members have relied on the courts and direct-action demonstrations to gain political ends. Several factors account for this lack of conventional political behavior among black people.[51] They are overrepresented in the lower class, and lower-class people are less likely to participate in political activities. In addition to the general tendency of lower-class people to shun political activity, economic problems are widespread among lower-class blacks. Their lives are such that the personal problems of employment and maintenance are so pervasive as to rule out politics. In addition, lower-class blacks lack a sense of identification with their communities.

Within the black community there has been a tendency for middle-class blacks to avoid associations with the lower class.[52] Since the middle class characteristically assumes positions of political leadership in the community, the antipathy which middle-class blacks maintain toward the lower class renders cooperation difficult. Furthermore, the middle class and the lower class represent divergent values. Most middle-class blacks occupy this status as a result of social mobility, and they are eager to forget their lower-class heritage.

Few individuals in the black community possess the requisite wealth for large-scale political undertakings. The middle class is usually made up of professionals, and few black businesses are of such magnitude as to provide their owners with the wealth required for political leadership. Even civic and civil rights organizations within the black community are usually lacking in membership and funds. Rarely are they maintained by the residents of the community.

The structure of the black community, then, is such that widespread conventional political activity has been lacking. Black leaders have tended to rely on the courts and demonstrations to achieve political ends. There is some evidence, however, of a trend toward conventional political behavior on the part of blacks.[53] There is increasing recognition that the problems confronting blacks—in employment, in education, and in housing—are of such magnitude that it is unlikely that they can be solved simply by achieving full constitutional rights.

In recent years black citizens have registered to vote in increasing numbers in the South, and they have elected blacks to political offices throughout the United States. For example, the Bureau of the Census reported that 58.5 percent of eligible black voters in the South were registered for the election of 1984, compared to 66.5 percent registration among whites.[54] When they vote, blacks usually exert a "liberalizing" influence on an election. It is often said that the black voter votes "race" first. The character of American society being what it is, a vote on an issue beneficial to blacks or for a politician who campaigns on behalf of blacks is likely to exert a liberalizing influence, especially in the South. Blacks will likely continue to vote for issues and politicians who serve their interests and against those who do not.[55]

Changes are occurring in the nature of black leadership.[56] Traditionally, the black leader—usualy moderate and often a minister—was acceptable to the larger (i.e., white) community. However, blacks are now demanding that their leaders be responsible to the black community. The more militant they are, especially on race issues, the greater their likelihood of receiving community support.

Public Officials

When Congress convened in January 1984, its twenty black members represented the largest number of black Americans in Congress since Reconstruction. Many other blacks held elective or appointive offices on the national level. By March 1984 more than 5654 blacks held positions to which they had been elected, an increase of more than twice the number in such positions in 1973. In addition to those in Congress, these positions included state, county, and municipal officials.[57] Also, black judges were serving on the U.S. Court of Appeals, the Customs Court, U.S. district courts, and the U.S. Supreme Court. Several dozen blacks were serving as ambassadors and Foreign Service officers.

In 1984 the number of blacks holding elective or appointive offices in state, county, and municipal agencies throughout the country increased sharply, especially in the South. By the November 1984 elections 3498 blacks in the South had been elected to public office. The South was followed by the Midwest with 1137, the Northeast with 688, and the West with 331. Louisiana led all states in the South with 438, followed by Mississippi with 430, Alabama with 314, Georgia with 301, and Arkansas with 296. Several other southern states had at least 200 black elected officials. These black public officials included 4 members of Congress, more than 200 state senators and representatives, 2240 city and county officials, 322 law-enforcement officials (including judges), and 730 school officials.

All 20 members of Congress in 1984 were members of the Congressional Black Caucus, which had originated in 1969 with 9 members.[58] No black person has served in the Senate since the defeat of the black senator from Massachusetts in 1979. In 1984 all but 5 of the black members of Congress represented districts that were predominantly black. States in the Midwest had 9 black persons in Congress; those in the Northeast, South, and West had 4 black Representatives each, counting the one nonvoting member from the District of Columbia. All were members of the Democratic party.

In the Congress the blacks chaired 5 Standing Committees: Budget, Education and Labor, Standards of Official Conduct, Small Business, and the District of Columbia Committee. They also chair 16 subcommittees and 2 select committees (Hunger and Narcotics Abuse and Control).[59]

Throughout the country in 1984, black elected officials held 15 executive and 385 legislative positions. Of the 15 executives 4 were administrators, and 11 were members of state education boards. One administrator and 8 education officials served in the U.S. Virgin Islands.

In 1984 blacks accounted for 5 percent of all state legislators in the country; Alabama led with 17.1 percent, Massachusetts had 12.8 percent, South Carolina 12.4 percent, and Michigan and Mississippi 11.5 percent each. The states with the largest numbers of black legislators were Georgia with 25 and Alabama and Maryland with 24 each. Illinois, with 6, had the largest number of black senators, and there were 13 in the Virgin Islands.

There were 5 black substate regional officials (members of intergovernmental agencies that administer activities involving two or more municipalities) in 1984: 3 in California, 2 in Illinois, and 1 in North Carolina. Organized county governments can be found in forty-eight states—all except Connecticut and Rhode Island. These county governments elect officials, including members of governing bodies, commissions, judges, tax collectors, and several other offices. In 1984 there were 518 black county officials, comprising 9 percent of all black elected officials. Louisiana had the largest number of these black officials.

On the municipal level there are mayors, members of municipal boards, neighborhood advisory commissions and others. In 1984 municipal officials made up the largest number of black elected officials—2735, or 48 percent. There were more than 225 black mayors in 1984, 28 of whom administer cities with more than 50,000 inhabitants. Many of the largest cities in the country had black mayors. Some examples: Chicago, Los Angeles, Philadelphia, Detroit, Washington, D.C., Atlanta, New Orleans, Oakland, Calif., Richmond, Va., Birmingham, Ala., Newark, N.J., and Charlotte, N.C. These black mayors usually succeeded white politicians who had left the cities plagued with a variety of problems. And with the complex nature of relations between municipal and state governments and the federal government, the tasks confronting newly elected black mayors have been formidable. Other black municipal officials included 2056 members of governing bodies, 67 members of municipal boards, 234 advisory neighborhood commissions, and some 123 other officials.

There are more than 600 black officials in judicial and law-enforcement positions, including some 345 judges, 230 constables and magistrates, 34 police chiefs, sheriffs, and marshalls, and 26 other judicial and law-enforcement officials. On the assumption that blacks commit a disproportionately high number of crimes, many of the largest cities have appointed black chiefs of police. Many judges are appointed and are not included in these data.

Education, like law enforcement, is an area where many blacks are either appointed or elected. No doubt this is the case because in many cities in the country, both large and small, black pupils predominate in public schools. Consequently, in 1984 education officials comprised 25 percent of all black elected officials, making for a total of 1363 persons in such positions. These officials served at state, county, and municipal levels, including 11 members of state education agencies, 45 members of university and college boards, and 1300 local school board members.

Females comprised 22 percent of all black elected officials. There were two U.S. representatives, 75 state legislators, 14 regional officials, 64 county officials, 602 municipal officials, 78 judges and law-enforcement officials, and 424 education officials. The largest number was in the South (53.7 percent), but the states with the largest numbers were outside that region: Michigan had 92, New York 87, Illinois 75, California and Mississippi 71 each, and the District of Columbia 113.

In general, black Americans hold disproportionately few elective and appointive offices—about 1.2 percent of the nation's total. The pattern varies with the region of the country, and in recent years the greatest amount of political activity has taken place in the South. In that region black political activity has had a significant impact, especially in decreasing the extent of routine violence against blacks characteristic of the South. In addition, black elected officials have often been able to attract much needed industries to the areas they control. Outside the Deep South, with the exodus of whites to the suburbs it is likely that cities such as Baltimore, Detroit, and St. Louis, all of which are 40 percent to 50 percent black, will become predominantly black. They, too, will probably be controlled by blacks in the near future. While such transfers of power from whites to blacks are not likely to alter the plight of black people in these cities significantly, they will have more honest governments, and the election of black officials will contribute to the growing spread of black solidarity and race pride.

Although blacks hold a disproportionately small share of the elective and appointive offices in the United States, they have had some national impact. With the ascendancy of black nationalist sentiment, black politicians have organized themselves into caucuses, from the municipal to the national level. Perhaps the best known of these groups in the Congressional Black Caucus. This group was organized in 1969 "to put the black perspective into legislation," according to its chairman.[60] One of its first acts was to request a meeting with the president in 1970 to present a document outlining its perception of how the black community viewed his legislative proposals. When the request was ignored, members of the caucus boycotted the president's State of the Union address and drafted a list of sixty-one recommendations to which the president should give urgent consideration.[61] These recommendations covered such areas as employment rights, welfare reform, housing and urban development, justice and civil rights, and foreign policy.

The effectiveness of black elected officials, especially in urban areas, has been threatened by a movement toward metropolitan or regional government, already in existence in several localities.[62] This approach takes two forms: city-county consolidation and regional planning-and-development commissions. Both are seen as threats to black control in cities with a majority. However, with increasing black political sophistication such movements will not proceed unchecked.

All evidence indicates that black people are an emerging political force in American society. They are likely to vote in increasing numbers and to elect more and more blacks to political office. Such political activity is important in the black's quest for equality. However, many of the problems faced by black people are not amenable to political solutions. Therefore conventional political behavior is likely to prove ineffective in dealing with many of the problems encountered by black people. They have been virtually ignored as citizens for so long that any solutions to the many problems they face in American society are likely to require radical social action on many fronts.[63]

RELIGION

Religion has traditionally played an important role in the life of black Americans. The character of their religion is a reflection of their precarious status in the larger society. Denied the opportunity to participate as equals in the religious life and other institutions of the larger society, black people organized their own religious denominations as a means of coping with the social isolation they encountered. Although their religious institutions contain the same basic elements as white Protestantism, it is especially in their religion that some elements of their African heritage are to be found.[64]

Developmental History

The first black people to settle permanently in what is now the United States were systematically stripped of their traditional culture, including their religious practices. In contrast to those who settled in the Caribbean and South America, the slaves did not establish their traditional cults in North America. Slaveholders succeeded in forcing slaves to abandon the outward manifestations of their "heathen" religions. Few of the slaves had been converted to Christianity before their arrival in North America, and throughout much of the slavery era many slaveholders opposed religious instruction for slaves. African slaves had been baptized since their first importation, but ". . . it was not until the opening of the eighteenth century that a systematic attempt was made on the part of the Church of England to Christianize Negroes in America."[65] These efforts were carried out by the Society for the Propagation of the Gospel in Foreign Parts, which was chartered in England in 1701. Soon afterward white Baptist and Methodist ministers and missionaries began proselytizing among the slaves. The slaves responded considerably more enthusiastically to these efforts than they had to those from ministers and missionaries of the Church of England. Frazier sees the uneducated and emotional appeals of the Baptists and Methodists as fulfilling a special need of the slaves.[66]

On many plantations slaves were allowed to worship in white churches, often seated in the gallery but sometimes in a separate section on the main floor. In such cases the services were invariably conducted by white ministers, but there were occasionally black ministers among the slaves. Black ministers were viewed by slaveholders with distrust, especially after the rebellion of Nat Turner, who was himself a minister. But black ministers were tolerated as long as they confined themselves to sermons in which they instilled in the slaves acceptance of their status. As Myrdal has written, "Undoubtedly the great bulk of the Southern Negro preachers advocated complete acceptance of slave status."[67] By the time of emancipation a significant proportion of the slaves had been converted to Christianity, and their religious practices provided an outlet for the frustration resulting from their status. Furthermore, religion gave them a basis of social cohesion for the first time since their arrival in the New World.

The religious life of the free blacks during the slavery era differed from that of the slaves. At first black people in the North and South attended services along with white worshipers. And in both regions black ministers served mixed black-white congregations as well as all-black congregations. Several black ministers achieved widespread distinction as orators and preached to predominantly white congregations. The separate black church was established in the 1770s because of increasing tension resulting from blacks' attendance at predominantly white churches.[68] By the turn of the nineteenth century free blacks had established both Methodist and Protestant Episcopal churches. Baptist churches, independent of white churches, were also organized during this time. In the North the churches of the free blacks assisted their counterparts in the South in two ways: Northern black churches were frequently centers of Abolitionist activity, and they aided runaway slaves by serving as stations in the Underground Railroad.

During Reconstruction the black church provided a source of social organization and social control in a time of social disruption for the newly freed slaves. There were initial conflicts between the freedmen and those blacks who had been free before the Civil War, but these were short lived. Perhaps the most important role of the black church in this period was played in political life.[69] Since blacks in the South enjoyed civil rights on a wide scale, many of the politicians of this period were recruited from among religious leaders. They served in state legislatures, in the Freedmen's Bureau, and in many federal appointive positions. Two of the twenty blacks elected to the federal House of Representatives between 1869 and 1901 were ministers, as was one of the two senators.

The restoration of white supremacy in the South served to strip these leaders of their political power in the larger community, and many of them became leaders in education and other community institutions serving black people. The black church as a separate institution was the primary source of social life among black people. The ministry was the main source of leadership, and it was through the ministry that the black community maintained contact with the larger community. As Myrdal has written,

> In practically all rural areas, and in many urban ones, the preacher stood out as the acknowledged local leader of the Negroes. His function became to transmit the whites' wishes to the Negroes and to beg the whites for favors for his people. He became—in our terminology—the typical accommodating Negro leader. To this degree the Negro church perpetuated the traditions of slavery.[70]

The frustrations inherent in the lives of black Americans made some form of outlet essential. The character of black religion (concerned with other-worldly matters) meant that it posed no serious threat to established patterns of white supremacy. Therefore, religious activity among blacks was not only tolerated but encouraged. The minister could be trusted, and the church contained the black masses.

In the North, where white supremacy was less well institutionalized, the black church remained somewhat more independent. Unlike their southern counterparts, northern black ministers were more responsive to the needs of their followers than to the white community. Therefore, they were more likely to become involved in the politics of the larger community and frequently became leaders in opposition to segregation and discrimination against blacks. Furthermore, within the black community they engaged in social service work. On the whole, however, the black church in the North was not a militant force for social change.

With the widespread urbanization of black people that began in the second decade of the twentieth century, the focus of black life shifted from the rural South to the cities in the South and elsewhere. This radical change, like that brought about by emancipation, had a disrupting effect on the lives of black people. The uprooted masses flocked to cities, and again the church provided a basis for social organization. But within the urban environment the black church, like religious institutions in the larger society, addressed itself to problems facing its members and de-emphasized its other-worldly outlook. At the same time the established urban black church gradually became less emotional in its services. Because of the widespread social disorganization accompanying the urbanization of blacks, many of them continued to feel the need for outlets from the frustrations they faced. Therefore they sought refuge in "store-front" churches, many of which were peripherally affiliated with the more institutional denominations, or in the many cults which developed.[71] The black church continued to be the primary source of social cohesion, but it did not play an important role in the endeavors of black people to achieve greater civil rights during the first half of the twentieth century.

With the greater emphasis on civil rights at midcentury, the black church became one of the prime agencies advocating social change in race relations. Black ministers became leaders in the civil rights movement, and the movement has to a large extent continued to have a religious base. Since religion had always been the only well-organized institution within the black community, such a development was inevitable.

Religious Affiliation

The lack of participation by blacks in the organized religious life of American society in general reflects their lack of acceptance by the larger society. In some respects the Christian church is one of America's most segregated institutions. The major black churches are undergoing some transformation, however, and black people are gradually being accepted into membership in predominantly white churches.

It is impossible to specify the exact membership of any major religious denomination at any time because the census does not collect this information at its regular enumerations. Therefore, it is necessary to rely on data provided by the religious organizations. It is estimated that 44 percent of the total black population are church members.[72] Although there are thirty different black denominations, 7 out of every 8 black church members are Baptists or Methodists. Black Christians are concentrated in six predominantly black denominations. Of these, the National Baptist Convention, U.S.A., claiming 5.5 million members, is the largest. Its membership, as large as the other five combined, is distributed among more than 26,000 member churches with a total of 27,000 ministers. The National Baptists Convention of America, the second largest predominantly black denomination, reported 2.6 million members in 1980. This group listed 11,400 churches and 28,500 ministers. The Progressive National Baptist Convention, Incorporated, the third of the major Baptist denominations, reported 522,000 members, 655 churches, and 863 ministers in 1980. These three Baptist denominations combined (approximately 8.6 million members) represent more than half of the black church members in the United States, including the members of the predominantly white denominations.

Following Baptists, Methodists rank second among the predominantly black denominations. The African Methodist Episcopal Church, with 1.9 million members, 3050 churches, and 3938 ministers in 1980, was the largest of the Methodist denominations. The African Methodist Episcopal Zion Church, with 1.1 million members, 6020 churches, and 3938 ministers in 1980 ranked second. The Christian Methodist Episcopal Church, with 500,000 members, 2598 churches, and 2,200 ministers, ranked third in size.

Black Christians who are not members of the six major denominations but who worship in black churches are concentrated in some twenty-four separate denominations. Some of these, such as Christ's Sanctified Holy Church with a membership of 600, are small. Others, such as the Church of God in Christ, have a membership of 400,000.

In addition to the black denominations, several of the predominantly white religious groups and denominations have sizable black memberships. Of these, the Roman Catholic Church reported the largest black membership. In 1980 the Roman Catholic Church reported a black membership of 1.3 million out of a total membership of more than 45 million. Black Catholics are found in more than 500 parishes served by more than 800 priests. The Methodist Church reported 374,000 black members out of a total membership of more than 10 million in 1980. The American Baptist Convention reported 200,000 black members out of a total membership of 1.5 million. The Seventh-Day Adventists reported 168,000 black members out of a total of 371,000 members in 1980, giving it the highest proportion of black members of any predominantly white religious group in the United States. Other denominations, such as the Christian Churches (Disciples of Christ), the Protestant Episcopal Church, the Congregational Christian Churches, the United Church of Christ, and the United Presbyterian Church in the United States of America, include blacks as members, but except for the Congregational Christian Churches with approximately one-third blacks in its membership, the proportion of black members is small.

Black people tend to worship with other blacks. A vast majority are members of black denominations of the Christian church, and even when they hold membership in predominantly white religious groups or denominations, the likelihood is that they worship in segregated black churches.

In the second decade of the twentieth century cults, such as the Holiness churches, and non-Christian religions attracted many black migrants to cities. More recently urban black people have flocked to the Muslim Mission (formerly Nation of Islam), popularly known as the Black Muslims. There are several Islamic groups in the black community, but the Nation of Islam, with an estimated membership of thousands and temples in every major city in the country, is not only the largest but also the fastest growing. It is impossible to estimate accurately the membership of these religious groups, but they thrive in black residential sections of large cities throughout the United States.

Structure and Patterns

Since black religion in America, like other aspects of black life, is highly segregated, it might be expected to differ in some regards from religion in the larger society. The black church runs the gamut from the separationist sects and cults in large urban centers, which appeal to the poor and use emotionalism as an important part of the services, to the upper-class Protestant churches represented by the Congregationalist, Episcopal, and Presbyterian denominations, which are totally devoid of emotionalism in their services. Regardless of the type of service, black people are more likely to be affiliated with some form of church than are white Americans. Myrdal reports that in the 1930s, 44 percent of the black population were members of churches, compared with 42 percent of the white population.[73] This figure probably represented an underenumeration among blacks, because they are more likely than whites to attend services at store-front churches and to be members of small religious cults and sects whose memberships are rarely reported in church statistics.

The black community is noted for the number of churches it includes. Drake and Cayton enumerated some 500 churches in Chicago that served some 200,000 members. These churches represented more than thirty denominations. Seventy-five percent of these churches were storefront churches or "house churches" with an average membership of fewer than 25 persons.[74] A study of central Harlem in the 1960s enumerated 418 church buildings. Of this number only 122 were housed in conventional church buildings; 232 were located either in store fronts or in residential buildings; the remainder were located in large meeting halls, private homes, or social agencies.[75]

Among conventional black Protestants, religious services follow a pattern similar to that of white Protestant churches. In general, few innovations have been made in the services. The choir sings alone or is joined by the congregation in the singing of hymns; music is supplied by an organ (a piano in small churches); prayer is recited by the minister; the sermon (the center of the service) is delivered by the minister; and the collection, an essential part of the service, frequently consumes a significant proportion of the time allocated to the service.[76] In some Baptist and Methodist churches the services frequently assume a more emotional tone than in other Protestant denominations. There are frequent responses to the sermon on the part of the congregation. These responses take the form of "yes" or "Amen." Such practices are characteristic of churches which cater to the poor because middle-class Baptists and Methodists avoid outward displays of emotionalism. As Baptist and Methodist churches have altered the content of their services, some of their members have turned to storefront churches and Holiness sects: ". . . the popular Protestant denominations (Methodist and Baptist) do not generally meet the emotional, psycho-

logical, and economic needs of traditionalists and/or submerged socioeconomic groups; consequently there has been a striking attraction of some
groups who are not adjusted to religious and social change to faiths which
emphasize emotion and sometimes economic provision."[77]

A small minority of blacks are members of such predominantly
white denominations as the Congregational, Episcopal, and Presbyterian
churches. Such black membership is drawn from the middle and upper
classes. Similarly, what Frazier calls "a small intellectual fringe among
middle-class Negroes" has affiliated with the Unitarian Church. He sees
these affiliations on the part of blacks as attempts to enhance their professional and social status and to lose their racial identity.[78]

The Roman Catholic Church in America is predominantly a white
church. However, it has never been so segregated in its services as Protestant churches are.[79] In many areas of the South the Roman Catholic
Church is the only church which black people have traditionally attended
with white worshipers. Because of its rigid hierarchical structure, the Catholic Church has the advantage over Protestant churches in that integration can be imposed from the top of the organization. Catholic schools
and other facilities in the South were among the first to desegregate their
facilities, although not without strong resistance from Catholic laymen.
Because of its racial attitudes regarding religious services, the Catholic
Church has tripled its black membership in less than three decades.[80]

The typical urban, Protestant, black church attempts to serve its
members as well as God. The 11 A.M. Sunday service is usually the main
event of the day, although many of the churches conduct Sunday evening
services as well. Sunday school is maintained for children, and a variety of
other services, such as special rallies, women's day, and children's day are
conducted during the week. There are numerous men's and women's
organizations associated with the church. The church building may be
used for a variety of functions, including meetings for community organizations, social events, concerts, and mass meetings. In many ways the
black church building serves as a community center for social and civic
activities.

Rural churches in the South and the many urban sects differ somewhat. The rural church remains more conservative and other-worldly
than its urban counterpart. It is more emotional in its services, and the
members participate more freely. Frazier describes a typical rural service
as follows:

> After the congregation has assembled, someone—usually a deacon or a
> prominent member—"raises a hymn," that is, begins singing. The noise dies
> down, and, as the singer's voice grows in volume, the congregation joins in
> the singing. The singing is followed by a prayer by a deacon, which is
> approved by "Amens" on the part of the congregation. Then follow more
> spontaneous singing and prayer. After this comes the sermon, which is

characterized by much dramatization on the part of the minister. Members of the audience express their approvals by "Amens," groans, and such expressions as "Preach it," "Yes, Lord." As a minister reaches the climax, "shouting" or a form of ecstatic dancing begins. The contagion often spreads until most of the congregation is "shouting." As the "shouting" dies down, someone—very likely the minister, who has not lost control of the services—"raises a hymn." Afterward the minister turns to such practical matters as collection and announcements concerning future services.[81]

Rural black churches in the South are usually small, wood structures. They are unpretentious and are frequently dilapidated. Ministers lack formal religious training, and in the 1930s a vast majority had completed no more formal education than grammar school.[82] Their sermons are usually other-worldly in their content, having no relevance to the day-to-day lives of their worshipers. Nevertheless, the rural church is perhaps the outstanding social institution among rural blacks. It serves as a means of escape from the harsh lives they lead. Furthermore, it is the medium through which the community maintains its social cohesion.

Store-front churches in cities do not differ significantly in their services from the rural church. Some of the cults to which many blacks have flocked seek to "purify" Christianity by requiring their members to reject "sinful" activities, such as drinking alcoholic beverages, dancing, playing cards, and swearing. Perhaps the best known of the Holiness sects are the Father Divine Peace Mission Movement and the Unified House of Prayer for All People, founded by Bishop Charles Emanuel Grace. Other cults have rejected Christianity and are linked to the non-Christian religions of the world. These churches include the Church of God (or Black Jews), the Moorish Science Temple of America, and, more recently, the Muslim Mission. These cults represent a radical departure from Christianity, and services are frequently conducted in languages other than English, such as Hebrew and Arabic.

The Church and Civil Rights

The Montgomery Bus Boycott, originating in 1955, signaled the beginning, in modern times, of mass direct action on the part of black people to improve their status in the United States.[83] The bus boycott was organized and led by the late Martin Luther King, Jr., a Baptist minister who had become the acknowledged leader of the movement for greater civil rights for America's blacks. It is unlikely that the success of this act of mass protest could have been achieved without the involvement of the black church. Since the Civil War the black church has been the most cohesive social institution in the black community. Therefore it was inevitable that the church would play a dominant role in any emerging movement for greater civil rights. Historically, the black church played an insignificant role in matters pertaining to civil rights, concentrating rather

on other-worldly matters in adherence to the norm of the larger society—
that the church should not involve itself in politics. Radical social action is
not alien to black religion, however. Three of the most famous of the
slave insurrections were led by black ministers: Gabriel Prosser, Nat
Turner, and Denmark Vesey. But the discrepancy between Christian
teachings and American social practices thrust the black church into the
forefront of the black rebellion against segregation and discrimination.

Since the Montgomery Bus Boycott, the civil rights movement has
changed strategy on occasion, but has remained an essentially religious
movement. Moreover, it has belatedly involved white religious leaders and
laypeople as well as blacks. Initially the civil rights movement was strongly
tied to such Christian precepts as love of one's adversary and nonviolent
resistance. Response on the part of many white Americans, especially in
the South, has led many black people to question the wisdom of these
techniques. Although until his assassination in April 1968 Martin Luther
King remained the undisputed leader of the black protest movement, his
strategy had been questioned.[84] For example, during the summer of
1964, in Mississippi alone, white Christians bombed or burned thirty-four
black churches. These churches had long been sanctuaries in which blacks
could be immune to outside intrusion. These and hundreds of similar acts
of violence, including the murder of ministers, have led black people to
question the notion that nonviolence and love disarm one's adversary.

Civil rights protest meetings, voter-registration drives, mass-action
demonstrations, and "freedom schools" were held in churches, and black
ministers continued to play a dominant role in civil rights activities. The
role of the black church in the protest movement has accounted for much
of the movement's early success in breaking down barriers of segregation
in the South. The protest movement had its origins in religion.[85] Black
ministers continue to occupy leadership positions in civil rights activities.
Furthermore, because of its religious orientation, thousands of white religious leaders and laymen were impelled to align themselves with the black
protest movement.[86] Hundreds of white clergymen were arrested in civil
rights demonstrations, and during the civil rights march from Selma to
Montgomery, Alabama, in March 1965, leaders of each of the major
religious organizations were either present or represented, as a means of
demonstrating their support. In recent years the leaders of each of the
national organizations representing the three major religious groups in
the United States—Protestants, Catholics, and Jews—have appealed to
their followers to discontinue practices of segregation and discrimination
in religious worship, education, employment, and housing and to adopt
attitudes of love and brotherhood toward blacks.

For his civil rights leadership and accomplishments, Martin Luther
King became an internationally known and respected personality, receiving the Nobel Prize for Peace in 1964. In the United States his birthday

became a national holiday in 1985. One of his associates, the Reverend Jesse Jackson, became the first viable black presidential candidate, running for the Democratic nomination in 1984. He has since become an important figure in international affairs and is considered to be the most important black political leader in the United States.

Both the role of the black church in civil rights protest activities and the religiousness of black people have been noted. The question of the link between these two elements might be raised. That is, does religion serve as a deterrent or motivation for civil rights activities? In a nationwide survey of black people an attempt was made to answer this question.[87] In general it was found that greater religious involvement was accompanied by diminished militancy in civil rights. Furthermore, blacks who were members of predominantly black denominations, such as Baptists and Methodists, were less militant about civil rights than those who were members of predominantly white denominations, such as Episcopalians, members of the United Church of Christ, Presbyterians, and Catholics. The members of the various religious sects and cults were the least militant. The conclusion: "Until such time as religion loosens its hold over these people or comes to embody to a greater extent the belief that man as well as God can bring about secular change, and focuses more on the here and now, religious involvement may be seen as an important factor working against the radicalization of the Negro public."[88] Nevertheless, the church has been the focal point of organizing for protest, and a small minority of militant ministers have been powerful catalysts without which the movement might never have achieved the success it has.

With the ascendancy of black nationalist ideology beginning in the second half of the 1960s, black Christian religious leaders and people have attempted to make Christianity serve the cause of black liberation through the empowerment of blacks, especially those in predominantly white churches. Within traditional Protestant denominations and Catholic churches, all-black caucuses and other organizations have developed to demand a greater degree of decision-making authority in these churches. In addition, several black clergymen have advocated what is generally called a black theology of liberation.[89] They maintain that if Christianity is to survive in the black community it must align itself with the oppressed and concern itself more with the correction of present injustices than with other-worldly matters. Other religious leaders have built a theology based on the notion that Christ was black.[90] This position holds that the black church must be in the forefront of the movement for black liberation.

Black nationalist sentiment has made its impact on black religion. While the vast majority of black churches no doubt continues to remain aloof from the movement for black liberation, focusing instead on other-worldly matters, increasing numbers of black theologians and rank-and-file members have embraced the thrust of black nationalism.

• • •

Three of the primary social institutions in the black community are the family, politics, and religion. Each of these institutions generally parallels its counterpart in the larger society, but each has its distinct elements. The differences result from a long history of oppression. There is some evidence that urbanization and improvements in standard of living are minimizing the differences, especially in family patterns and religious practices. The likelihood is, however, that because of the racist nature of American society, and because of increasing black consciousness, the distinctive aspects of the institutions will persist.

Politics is perhaps the institution in which the greatest changes have taken place in recent years. Armed with the vote, black people are turning to politics as a means of forcing the society to address itself to the needs of their communities.

SELECTED BIBLIOGRAPHY

AIKEN, CHARLES. *The Negro Votes.* San Francisco: Chandler Publishing Co., 1962.

BAILEY, HENRY A., ed. *Negro Politics in America.* Columbus, Ohio: Charles E. Merrill Co., 1967.

BANFIELD, EDWARD, and JAMES Q. WILSON. *City Politics.* Cambridge, Mass.: Harvard University Press, 1963.

BERNARD, JESSIE. *Marriage and the Family among Negroes.* Englewood Cliffs, N.J.: Prentice-Hall, 1966.

BILLINGSLEY, ANDERW. *Black Families in White America.* Englewood Cliffs, N.J.: Prentice-Hall 1968.

BLOOD, ROBERT A., JR., and DONALD M. WOLFE. *Husbands and Wives.* Glencoe, Ill.: Free Press, 1960.

BROGAN, D. W. *Politics in America.* New York: Harper & Brothers, 1954.

CLEAGE, ALBERT B., JR. *Black Christian Nationalism.* New York: William Morrow & Co., 1972.

——. *The Black Messiah.* New York: Sheed & Ward, 1969.

CONE, JAMES H. *A Black Theology of Liberation.* Philadelphia: J. B. Lippincott Co., 1970.

DU BOIS, W. E. B. *Black Reconstruction.* New York: Harcourt, Brace & Co., 1935.

FRAZIER, E. FRANKLIN. *Black Bourgeoise.* Glencoe, Ill.: Free Press, 1957.

——. *The Negro Church in America.* New York: Schocken Books, 1964.

——. *The Negro Family in the United States.* Chicago: University of Chicago Press, 1966.

GREENBERG, EDWARD S., et al., eds. *Black Politics.* New York: Holt, Rinehart & Winston, 1971.

GRIER, WILLIAM H., and PRICE M. COBBS. *The Jesus Bag.* New York: McGraw-Hill, 1971.

HAMILTON, CHARLES V. *The Black Preacher in America.* New York: William Morrow & Co., 1972.

HILL, ROBERT. *The Strengths of Black Families.* New York: Emerson Hall Publishers, 1972.

HUNTER, FLOYD. *Community Power Structure.* Chapel Hill: University of North Carolina Press, 1953.

JOHNSTON, RUBY F. *The Development of Negro Religion.* New York: Philosophical Library, 1954.

KING, MARTIN LUTHER, JR. *Stride Toward Freedom.* New York: Harper & Brothers, 1958.

LADNER, JOYCE. *Tomorrow's Tomorrow: The Black Woman.* New York: Doubleday & Co., 1971.

LECKY, ROBERT S., and H. E. WRIGHT, eds. *Black Manifesto: Religion, Racism, and Reparations.* New York: Sheed & Ward, 1969.

LEVY, MARK R., and MICHAEL S. KRAMER. *The Ethnic Factor.* New York: Simon & Schuster, 1972.

LEWINSON, PAUL. *Race, Class, and Party.* New York: Oxford University Press, 1932.

MARX, GARY. *Protest and Prejudice.* New York: Harper & Row, 1969.

MATTHEWS, DONALD R., and JAMES W. PROTHRO. *Negroes in the New Southern Politics.* New York: Harcourt, Brace & World, 1966.

MAYS, BENJAMIN E., and JOSEPH W. NICHOLSON. *The Negro's Church.* New York: Institute of Social and Religious Research, 1933.

MYRDAL, GUNNAR. *An American Dilemma: The Negro Problem and Modern Democracy.* New York: Harper & Brothers, 1944.

The Negro Handbook. Chicago: Johnson Publishing Co., 1966.

PETTIGREW, THOMAS F. *A Profile of the Negro American.* Princeton, N.J.: D. Van Nostrand Co., 1964.

RAINWATER, LEE, and WILLIAM L. YANCEY, eds. *The Moynihan Report and the Politics of Controversy.* Cambridge, Mass.: MIT Press, 1967.

SILBERMAN, CHARLES S. *Crisis in Black and White.* New York: Random House, 1964.

STAPLES, ROBERT, ed. *The Black Family: Essays and Studies.* Belmont, Calif: Wadsworth Publishing Co., 1971.

STONE, CHUCK. *Black Political Power in America.* New York: Bobbs-Merrill Co., 1968.

U.S. Department of Labor, Office of Policy Planning and Research. *The Negro Family: The Case for National Action.* Washington, D.C.: Government Printing Office, 1964.

WALTON, HANES. *Black Politics.* Philidelphia: J. B. Lippincott Co., 1972.

WILLIE, CHARLES V., ed. *The Family Life of Black People.* Columbus, Ohio: Charles E. Merrill Co., 1970.

WILMORE, GAYRAUD S. *Black Religion and Black Radicalism.* New York: Doubleday & Co., 1972.

WILSON, JAMES Q. *Negro Politics: The Search for Leadership.* Glencoe, Ill.: Free Press, 1960.

Youth in the Ghetto. New York: Harlem Youth Opportunities Unlimited, 1964.

NOTES

[1]See E. Franklin Frazier, *The Negro Family in the United States* (Chicago: University of Chicago Press, 1966), especially chap. 10.

[2]See, e.g., ibid., chap. 5.

[3]Jessie Bernard, *Marriage and the Family among Negroes* (Englewood Cliffs, N.J.: Prentice-Hall, 1966), pp. 10–13.

[4]*The State of Black America 1985* (Washington, D.C.: National Urban League, 1985), p. 16.

[5]U.S. Bureau of the Census, *Statistical Abstract of the United States, 1985* (Washington, D.C.: Government Printing Office, 1985) p. 45.

[6]See Andrew Billingsley, *Black Families in White America* (Englewood Cliffs, N.J.: Prentice-Hall, 1968), pp. 16–21.

[7]Robert B. Hill, *The Strengths of Black Families* (New York: Emerson Hall, 1972), p. 42.

[8]*Statistical Abstract, 1985*, p. 735.

[9]U.S. Bureau of the Census: *1980 Census of Housing: General Housing Characteristics, United States Summary* (Washington, D.C: Government Printing Office, 1983), tables 6,7.

[10]Ibid., tables 83,84.

[11]See E. Franklin Frazier, *Black Bourgeoisie* (Glencoe, Ill.: Free Press, 1957), pp. 82–83.

[12]U.S. Department of Labor, *The Negro Family: The Case for National Action* (Washington, D.C.: Government Printing Office, 1965), p. 5.

[13]Many of the criticisms have been reprinted in Lee Rainwater and William Yancey, eds., *The Moynihan Report and the Politics of Controversy* (Cambridge, Mass.: MIT Press, 1967).

[14]"Remarks of the President at Howard University, June 4, 1965," in ibid., p. 130.

[15]*Statistical Abstract, 1985*, p. 57.

[16]See C. Eric Lincoln, "The Absent Father Haunts the Negro Family," *New York Times Magazine,* November 28, 1966, p. 60.

[17]*Statistical Abstract, 1972*, p. 51.

[18]*New York TImes,* April 8, 1970, p. 1.

[19]Adelaide Hill and Frederick Jaffe, "Negro Fertility and Family Size Preferences: Implications for Programming of Health and Social Services," in *The Negro American,* ed. Talcott Parsons and Kenneth Clark (Boston: Houghton Mifflin, 1966), pp. 210–13.

[20]See Joyce Ladner, *Tomorrow's Tomorrow: The Black Woman* (New York: Doubleday, 1971), pp. 220–25.

[21]Bernard, *Marriage and The Family,* pp. 50–55.

[22]U.S. Bureau of the Census, *Status of the Black Population, 1972,* p. 68.

[23]For a review of such studies, see Thomas F. Pettigrew, *A Profile of the Negro American* (Princeton, N.J.: Van Nostrand, 1964), pp. 15–24.

[24]W. Mischel, "Father-Absence and Delay of Gratification: Cross-Cultural Comparisons," *Journal of Abnormal and Social Psychology* 63 (1961), 116–24.

[25]Pettigrew, *Profile of the Negro American,* p. 19.

[26]Ibid., p. 20.

[27]Hill, *Strengths of Black Families,* p. 49.

[28]Judith Cummings, "Breakup of Black Family Imperils Gains of Decades, *New York Times,* November 20, 1983, pp. 1,56.

[29]Ibid., p. 56.

[30]"Information on Fertility Patterns: Focus on Black Adolescents," (New York: Alan Guttmacher Institute, n.d.)

[31]*The State of Black America 1985* (Washington, D.C.: National Urban League, 1985), pp. 6–9.

[32]*Teenage Pregnancy: The Problem That Hasn't Gone Away* (New York: Alan Guttmacher Institute, 1981), p. 4.

[33]"Teenage Pregnancy in Developed Countries: Determinants and Policy Implications," *Family Planning Perspectives* 17 (March/April 1985), p. 35.

[34]See Russell Middleton and Snell Putney, "Dominance in Decisions in the Family: Race and Class Differences," *American Journal of Sociology* 65 (May 1960), 605–9. However in a study of black and white families in the Detroit, Michigan, area and in southeastern Michigan it was reported that whereas the majority of white families were egalitarian (54 percent), the largest percentage of black families were dominated by the wife. The husband was found to be dominant in 19 percent of the black families; the wife was dominant in 44 percent; and 38 percent were egalitarian. See Robert A. Blood, Jr., and Donald M. Wolfe, *Husbands and Wives* (Glencoe, Ill.: Free Press, 1960), pp. 34–36.

[35]Allison Davis and Robert J. Havighurst, "Social Class and Color Differences in Child Rearing," *American Sociological Review* 11 (December 1946), 698–710.

[36]See, e.g., Martha S. White, "Social Class, Child Rearing Practices, and Child Behavior," *American Sociological Review* 22 (December 1957), 704–12.

[37]Zena S. Blau, "Exposure to Child-Rearing Experts: A Structural Interpretation," *American Journal of Sociology* 69 (May 1964), 596–608.

[38]See, e.g., Andrew Billingsley, *Black Families in White America;* Hill, *Strengths of Black Families;* Ladner, *Tomorrow's Tomorrow;* Robert Staples, ed., *The Black Family: Essays and Studies* (Belmont, Calif.: Wadsworth, 1971); Charles V. Willie, ed., *The Family Life of Black People* (Columbus, Ohio: Merrill, 1970).

[39]Hill, *Strengths of Black Families,* p. 4.

[40]See Arthur Cosby, "Black-White Differences in Aspirations among Deep South High School Students," *Journal of Negro Education* 40 (Winter 1971), 17–21; Edward Harris, "Personal and Parental Influences in College Attendance," *Journal of Negro Education* 39 (Fall 1970), 305–13; Bernard Rosen, "Race, Ethnicity, and the Achievement Syndrome," *American Sociological Review* 24 (February 1959), 47–60.

[41]Cited in Rayford W. Logan, *The Negro in the United States* (Princeton, N.J.: Van Nostrand, 1957), p. 51.

[42]These data are reported in *The Negro Handbook* (Chicago: Johnson, 1966), pp. 271–74.

[43]W. E. B. Du Bois, *Black Reconstruction* (New York: Harcourt, Brace, 1935), p. 371.

[44]See, e.g., Gunnar Myrdal, *An American Dilemma* (New York: Harper, 1944), pp. 479–86.

[45]See D. W. Brogan, *Politics in America* (New York: Harper, 1954). pp. 116ff. See also Oscar Glantz, "The Negro Voter in Northern Industrial Cities," *Western Political Quarterly* 13 (December 1960), 999–1010.

[46]For a review of these acts and ruling see Charles Aiken, *The Negro Votes* (San Francisco: Chandler Publishing Co., 1962).

[47]Ibid., pp. 21–25.

[48]See Paul Lewinson, *Race, Class, and Party* (New York: Oxford University Press, 1932); Myrdal, *American Dilemma*, pp. 485–86.

[49]Floyd Hunter, *Community Power Structure* (Chapel Hill: University of North Carolina Press, 1953), chap 5.

[50]Ibid., p. 184.

[51]See Edward Banfield and James Q. Wilson, *City Politcs* (Cambridge, Mass.: Harvard University Press, 1963), chap. 20.

[52]Frazier, *Black Bourgeoisie*, pp. 224–29.

[53]See James Q. Wilson, "The Negro in Politics," in *The Negro American*, ed. Parsons and Clark (Boston: Houghton Mifflin, 1966); for a study of the changing role of blacks in Southern political life, see Donald R. Matthews and James W. Prothro, *Negroes and the New Southern Politics* (New York: Harcourt, Brace, 1966).

[54]U.S. Bureau of the Census, *Statistical Abstract of the United States, 1985*, p. 253.

[55]See Russell Middleton, "The Civil Rights Issue and Presidential Voting among Southern Negroes and Whites," *Social Forces* 40 (March 1962), 209–15; Henry Lee Moon, "The Negro Vote in the Presidential Election of 1956," *Journal of Negro Education* 26 (Summer 1957), 219–30.

[56]James Q. Wilson, *Negro Politics: The Search for Leadership* (Glencoe, Ill.: Free Press, 1960), especially chap. 12; Matthews and Prothro, *Negroes and the New Southern Politics*, chap. 7.

[57]These data are reported in *Black Elected Officials: A National Roster 1984* (Washington, D.C.: Joint Center for Political Studies, 1984).

[58]*Congressional Quarterly Weekly Report*, April 13, 1985, pp. 675–81.

[59]The following data are from *Black Elected Officials*.

[60]*New York Times*, October 1, 1973, p. 1.

[61]"Statement to the President of the United States by the Congressional Black Caucus, March 25, 1971," *Review of Black Political Economy* (Winter/Spring 1971), 101–19.

[62]See Tobe Johnson, *Metropolitan Government: A Black Analytical Perspective* (Washington, D.C.: Joint Center for Political Studies, 1972); *Blacks and Metro-Politics* (Washington D.C.: Joint Center for Political Studies, 1972).

[63]For a discussion of the limitations of political action, see James Q. Wilson, "The Changing Political Position of the Negro," in *Assuring Freedom to the Free*, ed. Arnold Rose (Detroit, Mich.: Wayne State University Press, 1964), pp. 163–84.

[64]See Melville Herskovits, *The Myth of the Negro Past* (New York: Harper, 1941), especially chap. 7: "The Contemporary Scene: Africanisms in Religious Life."

[65]E. Franklin Frazier, *The Negro Church in America* (New York: Schocken Books 1964), p. 6.

[66]Ibid., p.8.

[67]Myrdal, *American Dilemma*, p. 860.

[68]Benjamin E. Mays and Joseph W. Nicholson, *The Negro's Church* (New York: Institute of Social and Religious Research, 1933), pp. 29–33.

[69]Frazier, *Negro Church in America*, pp.42–44.

[70]Myrdal, *American Dilemma*, p. 861.

[71]Frazier, *Negro Church in America*, pp. 55–57.

[72]These data and those which follow are derived from several sources, including Constant H. Jacquet, ed., *Yearbook of American and Canadian Churches 1985* (Nashville, Tenn.: Abingdon Press, 1985); Ned Polanski and John Williams, eds., *The Negro Almanac: A Reference Work on the Afro-American* (New York: Wiley, 1983); *Statistical Abstract, 1985*.

[73]Myrdal, *American Dilemma*, p. 864.

[74]St. Clair Drake and Horace Cayton, *Black Metropolis* (New York: Harcourt, Brace, 1945), pp. 412–16.

[75]*Youth in the Ghetto* (New York: Harlem Youth Opportunities Unlimited, 1964), p. 111.

[76]Myrdal, *American Dilemma*, pp. 866–67.

[77]Ruby F. Johnston, *The Development of Negro Religion* (New York: Philosophical Library, 1954), pp. 129–30.

[78]Frazier, *Negro Church in America,* pp. 76–81.

[79]See Joseph H. Fichter, "American Religion and the Negro," in *Negro American,* ed. Parsons and Clark, pp. 401–22.

[80]*Negro Handbook,* p. 307.

[81]E. Franklin Frazier, *The Negro in the United States* (New York: Macmillan, 1957), p. 351.

[82]Mays and Nicholson, *The Negro's Church,* pp. 238–41.

[83]Martin Luther King, Jr., *Stride Toward Freedom* (New York: Harper, 1958).

[84]See Kenneth Clark, "The Civil Rights Movement: Momentum and Organization," in *Negro Americans,* ed. Parsons and Clark, pp. 595–625.

[85]See Carleton L. Lee, "Religious Roots of the Negro Protest," in *Assuring Freedom to the Free,* ed. Rose, pp. 45–71.

[86]Fichter, "American Religion and the Negro," pp. 401–22.

[87]Gary T. Marx, *Protest and Prejudice* (New York: Harper & Row, 1969), pp. 94–105.

[88]Ibid., p. 105.

[89]See James H. Cone, *A Black Theology of Liberation* (Philadelphia: Lippincott, 1970).

[90]See Albert B. Cleage, Jr., *Black Christian Nationalism* (New York: Morrow, 1972).

CHAPTER SIX
SOCIAL DEVIANCE

"I can conceive of no Negro native to this country who has not, by the age of puberty, been irreparably scarred by the conditions of his life. . . . The wonder is not that so many are ruined but that so many survive."[1] This statement by James Baldwin capsulizes the role of environmental factors in producing in black Americans deviations from the professed norms of the larger society. Black people are forced to live under harsh conditions in the United States, yet high standards of civic responsibility are expected of them.

No discussion of social deviance among black Americans can ignore the role of racism in American life. Individuals, social agencies, and social institutions responsible for the enforcement of social norms in American society operate within a long-established framework which precludes equality of treatment for black citizens. In no case is this situation more pronounced than in the relationship between the police and the black community. Police officers, like citizens in general, operate with a set of assumptions about black people which predisposes them to giving blacks differential treatment.[2] In this regard, the police do not differ significantly from other public officials in the United States. Therefore such circumstances must enter into any discussion of the extent and causes of social deviance among black people in the United States.

This chapter focuses on three areas in which behavior is reported to exceed the "tolerance limit of the community."[3] Crime and delinquency, mental illness, and drug addiction have been selected because of the availability of research findings in these areas and because other areas (e.g., family problems) are discussed elsewhere.

CRIME AND DELINQUENCY

Statistics on crime and delinquency in the United States are notoriously inaccurate. In addition to differences among various administrative agencies in methods of compiling statistics on criminal and delinquent behavior, special problems arise in connection with black people.[4] The position occupied by black people in a racist society means that they are more likely than whites to be arrested, indicted, and convicted. Furthermore, black people are less likely than white persons to receive probation, parole, suspended sentence, pardon, or commutation of the death sentence.[5] In short, black people are discriminated against in the administration of justice, just as they are in virtually every aspect of American life. Also, only about one-third of the crimes committed each year are reported to the police. The relative proportion of crimes recorded for black people, therefore, must be questioned.

For a variety of reasons, official statistics on black criminality are exaggerated.[6] Many acts that are considered crimes among black persons are not considered as such when they are committed by white persons. In several political subdivisions laws relating to such practices as segregation and vagrancy are especially designed for black people. Black men have been arrested and convicted for such acts as "looking at a white woman" and refusing to comply with the racial etiquette of the South. Black people are frequently blamed and falsely convicted for crimes which have actually been committed by white persons.

Black people are especially vulnerable to misuse of power by the police. Police sometimes arrest blacks on the slightest suspicion and obtain "confessions" through the excessive use of force. Similarly, blacks are often arrested in police raids as a means of earning fees. Once arrested, blacks face a series of acts of discrimination in the courts, on the part of juries, judges, and prosecutors. Antiblack prejudice on the part of court officials frequently results in blacks' being convicted for crimes they have not committed. One of the most clear-cut cases of discriminatory behavior is the disproportionately high percentage of black people executed under capital punishment. Between 1930 and 1983, 53 percent of the 3,870 persons executed in the United States were black.[7]

Because they are poor and frequently unable to pay fines, convicted blacks are more likely than convicted white persons to be sentenced to prison. On their arrival at prison, blacks again encounter a series of acts of discrimination. Prison officials share the same antiblack prejudice that pervades the larger society. Black prisoners are frequently required to perform the most difficult work tasks. They are less likely to be pardoned because they cannot usually exert the political pressure necessary for such acts. Similarly, they are discriminated against in the use of parole as a method of release and rehabilitation.

Despite the many shortcomings in collecting crime statistics and in the administration of justice for black people, official reports usually form the basis for estimating the extent of criminal behavior in the United States. These statistics report that the crime rate for black people exceeds that for whites in all categories. The proportionate number of arrests is greater, as is the rate of commitments to state and federal prisons.

Crime

Official crime statistics in the United States have been reported yearly since 1930 by the Federal Bureau of Investigation (FBI) of the Department of Justice. These data are based on the number of arrests reported by police departments throughout the United States. In 1982 reports were received from law-enforcement agencies having jurisdiction over 93 percent of the population. Reports are made in accordance with a handbook supplied to local law-enforcement officials by the FBI. This handbook outlines the procedures for scoring and classifying crimes. Thus the annual report of the FBI is the most comprehensive index of arrests available.

According to the 1982 report, blacks, comprising 12 percent of the population, accounted for 27.8 percent of the arrests for criminal acts. (See table 6-1.) The proportion of arrests varied by offenses charged. More than three-fifths (61 percent) of all persons arrested for gambling were black, compared with only 9.3 percent of the persons arrested for violating liquor laws. In all categories of offenses, however, the rate of arrests for black people was higher than that for white persons. Assuming that the arrests reported by the FBI represent a reasonably reliable indicator of conventional crimes committed in the United States, arrests for specific offenses in which blacks significantly exceed their proportion in the total population may provide some clues to an explanation of differential rates of criminality among black and white persons.

Inspection of the table reveals little about the crimes for which black people are arrested other than the general observation that they are vastly overrepresented in the total arrests when compared with their numbers in the population. However, a few paterns emerge. (1) The rate of arrests for those crimes which are defined as "serious" (the first seven in the table) was greater than for "minor" crimes. For example, black people accounted for more than one-half of the arrests for murder and nonnegligent manslaughter and for robbery, and nearly one-half of all arrests for forcible rape. (2) The arrest rate for black people was lowest for major crimes directly related to socioeconomic status. These crimes, including forgery and counterfeiting, fraud, and embezzlement, generally involve the use and misappropriation of money and defrauding. They usually involve larger financial transactions than blacks are capable of engaging

TABLE 6-1   Total Arrests and Black Arrests, United States, 1982

Offense Charged	Total	Black	Percent Black
All Arrests	10,000,078	2,777,145	27.8
1. Murder and nonnegligent manslaughter	18,475	9,174	49.7
2. Forcible rape	28,179	13,991	49.7
3. Robbery	137,562	83,522	60.7
4. Aggravated assault	257,607	99,842	38.8
5. Burglary	433,744	137,494	31.7
6. Larceny-theft	1,137,329	379,373	33.4
7. Motor vehicle theft	108,279	33,989	31.4
8. Arson	16,810	4,159	24.7
9. Other assaults	448,166	155,125	34.6
10. Forgery and counterfeiting	79,772	28,479	35.7
11. Fraud	268,969	87,683	32.6
12. Embezzlement	7,288	1,173	23.9
13. Stolen property; buying, receiving, possessing	114,007	41,750	36.6
14. Vandalism	200,208	37,706	18.8
15. Weapons; carrying, possessing, etc.	163,461	60,865	37.2
16. Prostitution and commercialized vice	110,713	53,112	48.0
17. Sex offenses, except forcible rape & prostitution	66,083	13,700	20.7
18. Drug abuse violations	562,390	156,369	27.8
19. Gambling	36,539	22,287	61.0
20. Offenses against family & children	45,260	16,292	36.0
21. Driving under the influence	1,379,180	148,221	10.7
22. Liquor laws	402,690	37,395	9.3
23. Drunkenness	1,033,385	162,387	15.7
24. Disorderly conduct	760,687	303,164	39.9
25. Vagrancy	32,127	10,820	33.7
26. All other offenses, except traffic	1,949,405	636,461	32.6
27. Suspicion	8,885	1,740	19.6
28. Curfew and loitering law violations	78,564	23,995	30.5
29. Runaways	114,334	16,351	14.3

Source: Compiled from Federal Bureau of Investigation, *Crime in the United States, 1982: Uniform Crime Reports,* table 36, p. 184.

in and positions in the social structure which are usually denied black people. (3) The arrest rate for black people was especially high for the illegal possession of weapons (37.2 percent of total), prostitution and commercialized vice (48 percent of total), and gambling (61 percent of total). The latter two crimes are clearly related to the precarious economic position which black people occupy, whereas the possession of weapons is no doubt a function of the frustrations which result from this depressed state.

The arrest rate for black people may be compared with the rate of court commitments and with the characteristics of prisoners in federal prisons. In 1972, 27.5 percent of all persons arrested were black. In the same year blacks accounted for 27 percent of all court commitments to federal prisons but 33 percent of all prisoners confined in federal prisons.[8] There is, therefore, a sizable discrepancy between the rate of court commitments and the proportion of prisoners in federal prisons. This discrepancy represents, among other things, discrimination on the part of court personnel, the inability of black people to pay cash fines in lieu of prison sentences, the lack of access to bail and efficient legal counsel, and discrimination insofar as pardon and parole are concerned. Furthermore, the average sentence for blacks in federal prisons in 1972 was 45.4 months, compared to 34.8 months for whites. And white prisoners served an average of 17.7 months, compared to 22.9 months for blacks.[9]

On the state level, in 1970 nonwhites accounted for 43 percent of persons in prisons.[10] This figure probably represents an underenumeration because data are not included for seventeen states, including some with large black populations, such as Alabama, Louisiana, Michigan, New Jersey, and Virginia. California affords a fairly typical example. Blacks accounted for approximately 7 percent of the population, but nonwhites comprised 31 percent of all convicts in that state's prison.[11] In addition, 45 percent of the persons sentenced to terms of one year or longer are nonwhite. For the black urban male there is little chance that he will not encounter arrest sometime during his lifetime.

Because of the shortcomings enumerated above, it is impossible to say that black people commit a disproportionately high percentage of crimes in the United States.[12] Numerous reasons for their high arrest rate may be advanced. (1) In the United States black people occupy a separate and subordinate economic and social position, which leads to frustration. Their frustrations are usually displaced in acts of aggression against fellow blacks, thus leading to a high proportion of arrests for intraracial criminal acts. (2) As Mydral has demonstrated, the caste system under which black people live operates in such a way as to prevent them from identifying with the society and the law. The very legal system itself is manipulated to discriminate against black people.[13] (3) Black persons far more than white persons are forced to live in deteriorated sections of cities. These areas are characterized by widespread poverty, poor housing, restrictions on settlement, and limited outlets for recreation and employment. "Out of these and similar conditions arise elements conducive to greater criminality, as well as other forms of pathology, among the Negro population."[14] (4) The high arrest rate among black people is partially a function of their reaction to having their means to success blocked by discriminatory behavior. "Crime may thus be utilized as a means of escape, ego enhancement, expression of aggression, or upward mobility."[15] Black people have internalized the cultural goals of the larger society, but the socially acceptable means for achieving these goals are unavailable to them. (5) Black people are overrepresented in the lower class, and recorded crime tends to be concentrated in this class.[16] "White-collar crime," the middle- and upper-class specialty, is far less likely to be recorded as such.[17] Poor people, both black and white, live in a society in which they are surrounded by affluence, yet must live in poverty. The association between economics and recorded crime is a pronounced one.

Juvenile Delinquency

It is impossible to estimate the amount of juvenile crime committed in the United States for the same reasons that statistics on crime in general are unreliable indicators of criminal behavior.[18] Age, rather than offense, is the defining characteristic of juvenile delinquents, and the age at which an offender is defined as a juvenile varies from state to state. Usually, however, juveniles are defined as persons under the age of 18. As with adults, black youths are far more likely to be arrested for criminal acts than white youths. In 1982, for example, the FBI reported that blacks accounted for 26.3 percent of all arrests of persons under 18 years of age.[19] Other investigations corroborate these findings.[20] The same factors operating to inflate the black crime rate in general must be considered in any discussion of juvenile delinquency among blacks. Black youths encounter the same types of discrimination as do black adults. Studies report that black youths accused of criminal acts are more likely to be institutionalized than white youths and that they are likely to be committed younger, for less serious offenses, and with fewer court appearances.[21]

Even when allowances are made for discrimination against black youths and for inaccuracies in reporting, rates of juvenile delinquency among blacks are reported to be especially high compared to rates for white youths in large urban centers. For example, betewen 1951 and 1962 the rate for central Harlem was reported to be at least twice as high as the rate for New York City as a whole.[22] Data on delinquency from predominantly black sections of several other cities—St. Louis, Missouri; Boston, Massachusetts; Minneapolis, Minnesota; Cleveland, Ohio; and Syracuse,

New York—indicate that the rates in these sections vary anywhere from twice to four times the rates for the cities as a whole.[23] It is reported that in 1960 almost one-third (31 percent) of the juvenile delinquents in the Lexington, Kentucky, Standard Metropolitan Statistical Area were blacks, although nonwhites comprised only 15 percent of the population from ages 5 to 19.[24] Black (and other minority) youths have a disproportionately high arrest rate in the United States, but the correlation is between poverty and arrest rather than race and arrest.

In addition to factors contributing to the high arrest rate among black people in general (as enumerated above), black youths in the United States are distinguishable from youths in the dominant society in ways which are likely to contribute to nonconforming behavior. Even when compared with black adults, black youths are especially vulnerable to arrest. For example, in one city where two-thirds of the police interviewed openly admitted antiblack prejudice, a policeman was asked why he had apprehended a black youth. He replied that he "looked suspicious," which he explained by saying, "He was a Negro wearing dark glasses at midnight."[25] The physical appearance of black youths frequently corresponds to the policeman's perception of the confirmed delinquent.

The family in which the black youth lives partially contributes to nonconforming behavior as defined by the dominant middle-class society. The black family, with its lower-class status, is more likely than the white family to be characterized by problems.[26] The family is frequently incomplete, often lacking the father. The incidence of arrest for juvenile delinquency among children from fatherless homes is greater than among children who come from homes where both parents are present. In such families the mother is frequently required to work outside the home, and the child lacks adequate parental supervision or guidance. Interpersonal relations between parents and children in poor families are frequently characterized by indifference, hostility, fear, and absence of sympathy and kindness. These elements are reported to be associated with delinquency in youth.[27]

Within the black community the youths frequently see assertive behavior as a means of obtaining and maintaining status.[28] Having been rejected, as well as subjected to constant threats, by the larger society and by middle-class blacks, these youths resort to assertive behavior. "Deviant conduct, therefore, might be approached as a nonconforming means of survival in a segregated, presumably hostile society."[29] Techniques are thereby developed for dealing with the emotional frustrations black youths encounter.

Finally, acts of deviance on the part of black youths are much more likely to come to the attention of official agencies than are those of white youths.[30] Deviant acts on the part of white youths are more likely to be handled by private social agencies, whereas for black youths they are handled by legal authorities.

Furthermore, a longitudinal study of juvenile delinquency tracked the criminal history of every person born in 1958 who lived in Philadelphia from 1968 to 1975. It is the largest study of juvenile delinquency ever attempted in the United States. Among other findings, the study reported that males were more than two and a half times more likely to become delinquent than females, and there was no difference between black and white teenagers.[31]

It cannot be overstated that arrest data do not necessarily coincide with the number of crimes committed. Indeed, the FBI reports that the proportion of crimes cleared by arrest in 1982 varied anywhere from 14 percent for auto theft to 74 percent for murder.[32] As illustrated by the so-called Watergate scandal which resulted from the 1972 presidential-election campaign, crime in the United States is widespread, even among the highest elected and appointed officials in government. While the seriousness of crimes by government officials is minimized by some politicians, they have involved many millions of dollars and affected the lives of millions of people the world over, among them thousands of innocent people in Indochina who died during the Vietnam War. The government of the United States is noted for its lawlessness.

While conventional criminality among black people in the United States has become a national issue ("law and order" is the code name), little notice is given to the criminal acts of the police and other law-enforcement personnel against black people. Each year thousands of black people, especially youths, are killed by the police, often without provocation. Such incidents are hardly considered newsworthy, but when a policeman is killed by a black person, with or without provocation, it becomes an important issue. A study of police practices in Chicago in 1970 and 1971 revealed that the Chicago police killed more civilians than the police in any other major city. It concluded: "The burden of this high death rate fell on blacks far out of proportion to their numbers. A black in Chicago was over six times as likely as a white to be killed by the police."[33] In this regard Chicago is not significantly different from other American cities.

Finally, black nationalist ideology has had its impact on convicts in prisons throughout the country. Large segments of black prisoners see themselves as political prisoners, either because economic circumstances are responsible for their incarceration or because they are charged with conventional criminality as a means of imprisoning them for their political views.[34] Life is made especially difficult for prison inmates who express some degree of political awareness. The massacre of thirty-two inmates (largely black) at the Attica Correctional Facility in New York in 1971 on the orders of the governor of the state is but one of the hundreds of such incidents yearly in the United States. These murders were not considered criminal acts either on the part of the governor who ordered them or the state troopers who carried out his orders.

MENTAL ILLNESS

Statistics on the incidence of mental illness among black people are both insufficient and contradictory. Since black people are separated from the larger society by a caste barrier which relegates them to a precarious existence, the assumption is frequently made that they must suffer a higher incidence of mental illness than do white Americans. This theory holds that for black people the U.S. social environment is one of oppression and that this situation adversely affects their mental health. Numerous social pressures to which blacks, more than white Americans, are exposed leave their impact on their personalities. Such circumstances, it is assumed, contribute to differentially high rates of mental illness among black people.

The deinstitutionalization of mental patients from public hospitals in the 1960s served to severely limit the data because most black mental patients had been confined to public hospitals. White mental patients, on the other hand, had often been confined in private institutions or received treatment on an outpatient basis. Added to this complication is the practice, in recent years, of supplying data on mental illness without designating the race of patients.

Mental illness is usually divided into two types, psychoses and psychoneuroses. Psychoses are more easily diagnosed and are therefore more often studied. However, studies show conflicting findings. For a period of three decades one researcher studied the incidence of mental illness among black persons, compared with white persons, in New York State. The statistics for New York State are reasonably complete for patients hospitalized for psychoses because they are collected by a central agency from both public and private hospitals. Malzberg reports that in 1930 and 1931, the rate of first admissions of blacks to mental hospitals or mental wards in other hospitals was 150.6 per 100,000 population, compared with 87.7 whites per 100,000 population, or a ratio of 1.7 to 1.[35] By 1939 both black and white rates had increased, but the black rate of increase is reported to have been greater—48 percent, compared with a 14 percent increase among whites.[36] Malzberg reports that between 1948 and 1951 blacks continued to have significantly higher rates of hospitalization for psychoses than whites.[37] Moreover, in 1960 and 1961 blacks constituted only 8.4 percent of the population of New York State but accounted for 13.8 percent of the admissions to mental hospitals.[38] Although the differential between blacks and whites had diminished, blacks were still over-represented in first admissions to mental hospitals in New York State.

The data from New York State showed a persistent excess of psychoses among blacks. Findings from other states have frequently differed, however.[39] It was reported that in Pennsylvania from 1943 to 1947 the incidence of mental illness was higher for blacks than for whites. In South Carolina the numbers of blacks in state mental hospitals in 1948 were proportionate to their numbers in the population. A comparable finding was reported for Mississippi from 1945 for 1947. Data from Louisiana reported that the incidence of mental illness among whites was greater than among blacks in 1941. A study in Illinois reported no greater incidence of psychoses among blacks than among whites in 1948.[40] A study of the Cincinnati, Ohio, General Hospital revealed that the proportion of black admissions to the psychiatric wards was not significantly higher than the ratio of blacks in the population of that city.[41]

An impressively comprehensive study in Baltimore, Maryland, reported that blacks did not have higher rates of psychoses than whites.[42] Data reported in this study were based on sample surveys and on public and private institutional rates. In state hospitals nonwhite rates were higher, but in private hospitals and Veterans Administration hospitals rates were higher among whites. And among the noninstitutional population the white rate of psychosis was more than ten times as great as the black rate. The overall rate from all sources in Baltimore was 9.46 per 1000 whites, compared with 7.04 per 1000 blacks. Finally, a widely publicized study reported that in Virginia the rates of black mentally ill patients had always been higher than those for whites and that there had been a significant increase in the black rate.[43]

The findings from these diverse studies have been so contradictory as to make generalizations hazardous. Nevertheless, the assumption that black people suffer disproportionately high rates of the most serious forms of mental illness persists.[44] Furthermore, two later studies reported an inverse correlation between social class and the incidence of psychoses.[45] Since blacks are overrepresented among the poor, it might be expected that psychoses would be more prevalent among them, but it is generally reported that white Americans, more than blacks, are likely to suffer from psychoneuroses, the milder form of mental illness. Pasamanick reported that in Baltimore the rate of psychoneuroses among whites was more than twice as great as among blacks. The rate among whites was reported to be 62 per 1000 population, compared with 28 per 1000 among blacks.[46] Williams and Carmichael reported that the incidence of psychoneuroses among black people in state hospitals was much lower than among whites. In New York State it was reported that the rate of psychoneuroses among whites was three times as great as among blacks from 1949 to 1951.[47] Both Hollingshead and Redlich, and Srole et al., reported a direct correlation between social class and the prevalence of psychoneuroses. Again, since black people are underrepresented among the middle class, it might be expected that the incidence of psychoneuroses among them would be lower than among white Americans. Although the data on psychoneuroses are less complete, they are also less contradictory than data on psychoses.

Psychoses are usually considered to be of two types, organic and functional. Studies reporting the differential incidence of mental illness among blacks and whites report that blacks are more likely to suffer from such organic psychoses as general paresis and alcoholic psychoses and from such functional psychoses as dementia praecox (schizophrenia); whites are more likely to suffer from manic depressive (functional) psychoses.[48] Pettigrew, after a review of studies of mental illness among blacks, concluded: "Particular psychoses contribute disproportionately to the greater Negro rates. Schizophrenia, the bizarre condition of social withdrawal and personality disorganization, is especially frequent among Negro first admissions."[49] Therefore it is reported that the incidence of mental illness among black people is greater for both organic and functional psychoses.

Pasamanick reported that Baltimore nonwhites had higher rates of mental deficiency than whites. He reported that between 1952 and 1955 the rate was 21.3 per 1000 black population, compared with 13.2 per 1000 white population. He attributed this difference to environmental (rather than hereditary) factors, such as lack of motivation and less stimulation among poor people.

Conflicting data on the differential incidence of mental illness among blacks and whites usually result from incompleteness and from difficulties in diagnosing mental illness. As one writer has concluded, ". . . inadequate appreciation of the sociological dimensions in the differential racial environments may lead the researcher or clinician to overlook variations in the development of the personality with consequent difficulties in assessing etiological factors, accurate diagnosis, or therapeutic proceedings."[50] Nevertheless, differentially high rates, when reported, are usually explained in terms of social factors. For example, the Malzberg studies explain the differential in New York State as a function of migration, which results in a more precarious standard of living. Furthermore, statistics are more often reported for public than for private institutions. Because black people are overrepresented among the poor, they are forced to seek treatment in public institutions, whereas white Americans more often seek care in private institutions or through noninstitutional arrangements. Black people are often denied treatment in private hospitals and clinics. Williams and Carmichael reported in 1949 that "no private institution in the United States at the present time will accept the

Negro as a mental patient, and the number of whites treated in these institutions is difficult to evaluate . . ."[51]

Data from southern states, which generally show that black people are proportionately represented in mental hospitals, no doubt reflect a tendency to hospitalize only the most severe cases of mental illness among black people. This tendency may result in underenumeration. On the other hand, the overrepresentation of black people in some studies may reflect faulty diagnoses. Clinical studies on mental illness among black people, which frequently report extreme paranoia, may actually describe an accurate perception of the hostile environment in which they are forced to live. As Kardiner and Ovesey have written, "Such anxieties mean one thing in the white and another in the Negro. In the white they mean paranoid tendencies; but not in the Negro. For the latter, to see hostility in the environment in a normal perception."[52]

By far the most comprehensive report on mental disorders among America's black population in recent years is the report of the subpanel on mental health of blacks prepared for the President's Commission on Mental Health in 1978.[53] This report emphasizes the role of race in mental illness. "The Subpanel recognizes that it is largely the environment created by institutional racism, rather than intrapsychic deficiencies in Black Americans as a group, that is responsible for the overrepresentation of Blacks among the mentally disabled."[54] Black mental professionals have questioned the applicability of traditional models of mental health to the black community. It is their position that individual functioning must be viewed within the context of social, political, economic, and other institutional forces with which the individual must cope.

The subpanel report questions the many conflicting findings of other studies of mental illness among blacks and notes that several such studies have shown correlations between social class and mental illness. And some studies compare low-income blacks with middle-class whites. Given the inadequacies and contradictions of many studies, the subpanel reports that "in 1970, the rates of institutionalized persons per 100,000 population were 1412.7 for blacks, but only 1004.3 for whites."[55] Between 1950 and 1970 the rate of institutionalization for black people increased but decreased for whites. The rates for nonwhite men increased by 56 percent, compared to a 21 percent decrease for white men; for nonwhite women it increased by 14 percent while the rate for white women decreased by 39 percent.[56]

Black males show the highest rates of mental disorders; furthermore, those in the 18–34 age group show the highest rate, compared to other age and racial groups. In addition, data show that blacks are admitted, committed, or sentenced for custodial care in mental institutions sooner than whites, their admissions to mental institutions are less likely to be voluntary, and they are less likely to be committed by a spouse or offspring.

Table 6-2 presents data on inpatient admissions to state and county mental hospitals in 1975. From this table it can be seen that black admissions in each age category far exceeded that for whites. The same pattern holds for admissions to outpatient clinics in the same year. In some cases (e.g., those 65 years of age and older) black admissions to outpatient clinics were more than the white rate. These data represent what the subpanel considers to be an important shortcoming. The mental health professionals are largely white, and blacks have been abused by such practitioners on numerous occasions.

While the studies show that the highest incidence of mental disorders occur to black males, there are some instances in which stresses have served to compound the problems among black females. In some cases they face stressful problems because of race and sex and ultimately because of old age. For example, 1975 data show that significantly more black women were admitted to state and county hospitals for most of the severe mental disorders than white women. Except for depressive disorders, where black women were admitted at about one-half the rate of white women, the figures show that of every 100,000 persons, black women have higher rates of schizophrenia (118.2 admissions versus 42.8 for white women), alcohol disorders (50.1 for black women, 12.4 for white women), organic brain disorders (blacks 17.3, whites 7.8), and personality disorders (9.8 for blacks and 6.6 for whites.).[57]

Additional research concludes that political-social factors (e.g., poor

TABLE 6-2   Age-Specific Rates per 100,000 Population of Inpatient Admissions to State and County Mental Hospitals by Race, Sex, and Age, 1975

Age on Admission	White			Black		
	Both Sexes	*Male*	*Female*	*Both Sexes*	*Male*	*Female*
Total admission	296,151	190,788	105,363	83,367	53,646	29,721
	Rates per 100,000 Population					
All Ages	161.1	214.2	111.2	344.2	469.5	232.2
Under 18 years	31.6	39.3	23.6	77.8	103.1	52.2
18–24 years	234.0	343.9	129.4	539.6	892.1	241.8
25–44 years	270.2	349.3	194.2	688.3	1032.7	406.3
45–64 years	213.4	276.0	155.7	414.1	414.2	413.9
65 years plus	85.3	130.9	54.0	171.9	210.8	143.7
Median age	35.2	34.3	37.3	32.1	30.0	38.0

Source: *President's Commission on Mental Health 1978*, p. 832.

housing, lack of educational opportunity, poverty, frustration, powerlessness) are the primary causes of mental disorders among blacks.[58] This position corresponds to that of the subpanel of the president's Commission on Mental Health. Finally, a report prepared for the National Urban League also supports these findings.[59]

The harshness of the environment in which black people are forced to live may contribute to the reports of their overrepresentation of Americans suffering from functional psychoses. Studies indicate that the culture in which one lives plays an important role in the incidence of psychoses and that the incidence varies from culture to culture.[60] The effect of American culture on black people has been summarized by Kardiner and Ovesey: Cultural factors "force the Negro to live within the confines of a caste system which not only interferes seriously with all varieties of social mobility through class lines, but simultaneously, tends to stifle effective protest by the threat of hostile retaliation by the majority of whites. Such oppression cannot but leave a permanent impact on the Negro's personality."[61]

Because of these cultural factors two black psychiatrists have urged black people to develop adaptive devices in order to survive in the United States. "For his own survival, then, he [the black man] must develop a *cultural paranoia* in which every white man is a potential enemy unless proved otherwise and every social system is set against him unless he personally finds out differently."[62] This body of traits is called the "black norm."

That living in a state of oppression in the United States has contributed to a disproportionately high incidence of mental illness among black people is usually assumed, but empirical data, where they exist, are so contradictory as to preclude firm generalizations.

DRUG ADDICTION (SUBSTANCE ABUSE)

Data on the extent of drug addiction in the United States are extremely crude because the use of narcotics for nonmedical purposes is generally prohibited by federal, state, and municipal laws. Nonmedical users and dispensers of narcotics must exercise secrecy in these activities, and addicts usually become known only when they are arrested or when they seek treatment. Therefore, published statistics probably represent a small fraction of the narcotics addicts in the United States.

Large segments of the population of the United States have come to rely on drugs to counter the alienation which is so widespread in many areas of life. The National Commission on Marihuana and Drug Abuse, after extensive research, reported that "chemically induced mood alteration is taken for granted and is generally acceptable in contemporary America." The commission reported that in 1971 retail sales of alcohol (wine, beer, and

hard liquor) amounted to $24.2 billion; that in 1970 the retail sales of pre-
scribed barbiturates, stimulants, and tranquilizers amounted to $972 milion;
and that over-the-counter sales of mood-altering agents (excluding stimulants) amounted to 32.7 million.[63]

Through the years drug addiction has come to be associated with
those drugs which have been declared illegal except for medical purposes,
and it is these drugs that are of concern here. Several types of addicting
drugs are commonly used in the United States. They may be classified in
two broad types, stimulants and depressants. The stimulants include cocaine, benzedrine, and mescaline. The depressants, which induce sleep
and lessen nervous tension, include morphine and all its derivatives (e.g.,
heroin, dilaudid, and codeine), synthetic analgesics (e.g., methadone and
demerol), and the hypnotics and sedatives (e.g., bromides and barbiturates). Although habitual marijuana use is considered a form of drug
addiction by lawmakers and narcotics-control personnel, it is not considered by medical practitioners to be so because it does not usually entail
physiological dependence.

Statistics show that among drug addicts heroin (a depressant) is used
by a vast majority.[64] An early study of 1036 patients in a federal hospital
for narcotic addicts reported that morphine was preferred by the patients
and that it was the first used and the last used by a majority. This drug
was followed in expressed preference and usage by heroin.[65] The typical
addict is likely to take cocaine, heroin, morphine, or a similar drug intra-
venously. In recent years such practices as glue sniffing, gasoline addiction, and the use of hallucinogenic drugs (LSD, psilocybin, and mescaline)
have reportedly increased, especially among younger Americans.

The Federal Bureau of Narcotics was created in 1930 to implement
laws governing the use and sale of narcotics and to supervise the production and importation of these drugs. One of its primary functions is
the apprehension of violators of an elaborate network of narcotics-control laws. According to the Federal Bureau of Narcotics, which compiles
statistics on drug addiction from state police reports, there were approximately 60,000 addicts in the United States in 1965. This figure was
obviously a gross underenumeration, as one study estimated that there
were 90,000 addicts in New York City alone.[66] Estimates of the number
of narcotic addicts in the United States vary widely. A 1970 Ford Foun-
dation-sponsored study of drug abuse estimated that there were between
150,000 and 250,000 active heroin addicts in the United States. The
following year this study team revised its estimate to between 250,000
and 300,000.[67] This study limited its definition of drug abuse to heroin,
marijuana, stimulant and depressant drugs, and hallucinogens. Such
drugs as alcohol and nicotine were excluded. This study reported that
addicts were heavily concentrated in slum sections of large cities, with
half living in New York City. Blacks, Puerto Ricans, and Mexican-Ameri-

cans comprised somewhere between 60 and 70 percent of the country's heroin addicts.

The National Commission on Marihuana and Drug Abuse, unlike the Ford Foundation researchers, includes both alcohol and tobacco as drugs, for they are used for mood alteration, and compulsive use often leads to psychological and physical dependence. It was estimated by the commission that there were some 560,000 active addicts in the country, and that between one-half and three-fifths of the nation's opiate-dependent persons reside in New York City.[68] The commission reported that experience with sedatives, tranquilizers, and stimulants, both legally and illegally obtained, was higher among whites than among other racial groups. Heroin addiction was reported to be disproportionately high among young males in urban areas, especially members of minority groups. The incidence of dependence on depressant drugs in general was found to be higher among minority-group males than the general male population.[69] The report emphasized that drug use was not a cause but a concomitant of other social problems such a alienation, anomie, and economic deprivation. A study of drug addiction in New York City found the reported rate to be seven times as high in central Harlem as in the city as a whole.[70]

Although data on drug addiction are inadequate, all available evidence indicates that black people are disproportionately represented among reported narcotic addicts. (It must be remembered, however, that reported addicts probably represent a small proportion of those addicted to the use of narcotics.) Most known narcotic addicts use depressant drugs, such as heroin and morphine, which serve as a means of escape from the precarious existence which black people in the United States lead. Clausen describes their effects: "Their depressant actions include relief of pain, muscular relaxation, drowsiness or lethargy, and (before extreme tolerance has been developed) euphoria, a sense of well-being and contentment."[71] Similarly, other economically deprived groups, such as Puerto Ricans and Mexican-Americans, are overrepresented among reported narcotic addicts. In 1965, Puerto Ricans accounted for 13.1 percent of all narcotic addicts reported by the Federal Bureau of Narcotics; Mexican-Americans accounted for 5.6 percent.[72]

Drug addiction in the United States is an urban phenomenon. More than one-half (51.6 percent) of the addicts reported by the Federal Bureau of Narcotics live in New York, primarily in New York City. One-fourth live in California and Illinois, mainly in Los Angeles and Chicago. The remaining one-fourth live in other large cities, such as Detroit, Philadelphia, Washington, D.C., Baltimore, and Newark. Each of these cities contains large proportions of deprived blacks. Drug addiction is most prevalent in urban areas because of the lack of institutional (family, religious) controls, the accessibility of supply, greater anonymity (decreasing the likelihood of detection), and the presence of social norms favorable to such behavior.

Drug addiction is most acute among young males. Approximately 83 percent of all reported addicts were male, and almost half (46.5 percent) of them were between the ages of 21 and 30. Fifty percent were over 30 years of age, and nearly 38 percent were between 31 and 40. Of addicts under 21 years of age, black youths were vastly overrepresented, but the proportion was significantly lower than among older black addicts. Blacks constituted only one-fourth of the addicts under 21 years of age, and Puerto Ricans constituted another one-fifth. These figures indicate that within the category with the highest rates of unemployment—young adult black and Puerto Rican males—the rate of drug addiction is highest. Furthermore, the high rate of drug addiction among adolescents no doubt reflects the increasing use of drugs among middle-class white youth.

Drug addiction is most prevalent in those sections of metropolitan centers that are more often inhabited by members of ethnic minorities. Certain social characteristics prevail throughout these areas.[73] These areas have high rates of crime, prostitution, and out-of-wedlock births. Family problems are widespread, and the areas are densely populated. Living quarters tend to be deteriorated, and families frequently live in cramped quarters, often with several people sharing a single bedroom. Mothers frequently work outside the home, and fathers experience difficulties providing support for the family. Children rely heavily on peer groups for support and that often results in gangs and other youth groups within which social pressures force experimentation with narcotics.

According to one researcher, a distinctive subculture of drug addicts exists.[74] Within this subculture the young drug addict displays a highly developed sense of taste in clothes, speaks with a distinctive vocabulary, thrives on the exploitation of women, and, in general, maintains a superior attitude accompanied by a disdain for work and the conventional daily routine. He is frequently able to live without working, and his main purpose in life is to experience the "kick," an unconventional experience which serves to distinguish him from those he defines as "squares." The ultimate "kick" is the use of heroin because of the extreme proscription on its use in conventional middle-class society.

Recent studies of substance abuse, like earlier ones, provide conflicting data on the problem as it affects blacks and whites. In 1982 the National Institute on Drug Abuse reported that in that year alcohol abuse was considerably higher among white youths, young adults, and adults, than the same categories among blacks. For marijuana use, however, the institute reported no racial differences except among adults, and in this group slightly higher rates were found among blacks.[75] A sample survey of young men who had registered for Selective Service in the years 1962–72, found that lifetime use of drugs among them varied by race and the type of drug.[76] These data, presented in table 6-3, were also collected by the National Institute on Drug Abuse.

TABLE 6-3   Lifetime Use of the Drug Classes By Race, 1976 (Percentages)

Used	Total (2510)	White (2103)	Black (303)	Spanish (48)	Other (56)
Tobacco	88	88	87	83	88
Alcohol	97	97	94	94	98
Marihuana	55	54	65	54	48
Psychedelics	22	22	25	21	18
Stimulants	27	28	25	23	27
Sedatives	20	20	24	13	20
Heroin	6	5	14	6	5
Opiates	31	31	34	15	29
Cocaine	14	13	24	10	11

Source: National Institute on Drug Abuse, Research Monograph Series 5: *Young Men and Drugs: A Nationwide Study*, p. 15.

As can be seen from the table, the major differences were reported for marijuana, heroin, and cocaine, with blacks being the greater users. These data are also questionable because it is unlikely that young black men use either marijuana or cocaine to a greater extent than their white counterparts. Indeed, cocaine is reported in the media to be the drug of choice for young white people, especially those in the middle class. Furthermore, it is so expensive that relatively few blacks can afford to purchase the drug on a regular basis.

Some findings from other studies: Nonopiates (e.g., amphetamines and barbiturates) are more prevalent in the white community than in the black community. The major drug of choice in both black and white communities is alcohol, but blacks drink at an earlier age than whites. Blacks are likely to be either abstainers or heavy drinkers as opposed to moderate users. The reverse is true for whites. Blacks more often than whites are to be found in drug-treatment programs. Most studies show that at least half of the persons enrolled in methadone-maintenance programs in the 1970s were black. Finally, substance abuse is said to be involved in 50 percent of all violent deaths, and deaths from chronic liver disease and cirrhosis are twice as frequent among blacks as among whites.[77]

The evidence (such as it is) indicates that black people are overrepresented among drug users and abusers in the United States. Despite the shortcomings of the data, they are persuasive. The daily experiences of black people, in many regards, are traumatic. The use of narcotizing drugs represents one means of escaping a harsh environment.

•   •   •

Data on crime and delinquency, mental illness, and drug addiction among black Americans are inadequate and, in some cases, contradictory.

However, it is frequently reported that black people contribute disproportionately high rates to each of these social problems in the United States. Because of discrimination in the administration of justice, the reported differentially high crime and delinquency rates among black people must be questioned. It is virtually impossible for black Americans to secure impartial treatment at any step in the judicial process. It is possible that black people commit proportionately more conventional crimes than white Americans, but economic and social factors are responsible. The racist nature of American society frequently forces them to resort to nonconforming behavior as a means of surviving the daily hazards to which they are subjected.

The inadequacy of statistics on mental illness renders the making of firm generalizations impossible. Furthermore, subcultural differences between black Americans and mental-health personnel call the validity of diagnoses into question. As a form of social deviance the extent of drug addiction as reported in official sources is questionable. The likelihood is, however, that the precarious existence which black people lead gives rise to disproportionately high rates of drug addiction.

When black people deviate disproportionately from the norms of society, such behavior must be explained as resulting from the social environment. These phenomena (crime and delinquency, mental illness, and drug addiction) are referred to as "social problems" because they are products of the society in which they are found. For black citizens American society is one which has, through the years, made it difficult for them to conform to standards of behavior the society sets for all citizens.

SELECTED BIBLIOGRAPHY

BAUGHMAN, E. EARL. *Black Americans: A Psychological Analysis.* New York: Academic Press, 1971.

CICOUREL, AARON V. *The Social Organization of Juvenile Justice.* New York: John Wiley & Sons, 1968.

CLARK, KENNETH. *Dark Ghetto.* New York: Harper & Row, Publishers, 1965.

CLINARD, MARSHALL B. *Sociology of Deviant Behavior.* New York: Holt, Rinehart & Winston, 1963.

COHEN, ALBERT K. *Delinquent Boys.* Glencoe, Ill.: Free Press, 1955.

COMER, JAMES P. *Beyond Black and White.* New York: Quadrangle Books, 1972.

CRESSEY, DONALD. "Crime." In *Contemporary Social Problems.* Edited by Robert K. Merton and Robert A. Nisbet. New York: Harcourt, Brace & World, 1966.

CROSSACK, MARTIN M. *Mental Health and Segregation.* New York: Springer Publishing Co., 1965.

DAVIS, ANGELA Y. *If They Come in the Morning.* New York: New American Library, 1971.

Dealing With Drug Abuse: A Report to the Ford Foundation. New York: Praeger Publishers, 1972.

Federal Bureau of Investigation. *Crime in the United States, 1982: Uniform Crime Reports.* Washington, D.C.: Government Printing Office, 1983.

Federal Bureau of Prisons. *National Prisoner Statistics—State Prisoners: Admissions and Releases, 1970.* Washington, D.C.: Bureau of Prisons, 1971.

———. *Statistical Report, Fiscal Years 1971 and 1972.* Washington, D.C.: Bureau of Prisons, 1973.

GLEUCK, SHELDON, and ELEANOR GLEUK. *Unraveling Juvenile Delinquency.* Cambridge, Mass.: Harvard University Press, 1950.

GRIER, WILLIAM, and PRICE COBBS. *Black Rage.* New York: Bantam Books, 1968.

HOLLINGSHEAD, AUGUST B., and FREDERICK C. REDLICH, *Social Class and Mental Illness.* New York: John Wiley & Sons, 1958.

JACKSON, GEORGE. *Soledad Brother.* New York: Bantam Books, 1970.

JAHODA, MARIE. *Race Relations and Mental Health.* New York: Columbia University Press, 1960.

JONES, REGINALD, ed. *Black Psychology.* New York: Harper & Row, Publishers, 1972.

KARDINER, ABRAM, and LIONEL OVESEY. *The Mark of Oppression.* New York: World Publishing Co., 1962.

KNIGHT, ETHERIDGE, ed. *Black Voices from Prison.* New York: Pathfinder Press, 1970.

MALZBERG, Benjamin. *The Mental Health of the Negro.* Albany, N.Y.: Research Foundation for Mental Hygiene, 1962.

————. *Statistical Data For the Study of Mental Disease among Negroes in New York State.* Albany, N.Y.: State Department of Mental Hygiene, 1955.

MITFORD, JESSICA. *Kind and Usual Punishment: The Prison Business.* New York: Alfred A. Knopf, 1973.

MYERS, J. K., and B. H. ROBERTS. *Social Class, Family Dynamics, and Mental Illness.* New York: John Wiley & Sons, 1959.

National Commission on Marihuana and Drug Abuse, *Drug Use in America: Problem in Perspective.* Washington, D.C.: Government Printing Office, 1973.

National Institute on Drug Abuse. Research Monograph Series 5. *Young Men and Drugs: A Nationwide Survey.* Washington, D.C.: National Institute on Drug Abuse, 1976.

PARKER, SEYMOUR, and ROBERT KLINER. *Mental Illness in the Urban Negro Community.* New York: Free Press, 1966.

PELL, EVE, ed. *Maximum Security: Letters From Prison.* New York: E. P. Dutton Co., 1972.

PETTIGREW, THOMAS F. *A Profile of the Negro American.* Princeton, N.J.: D. Van Nostrand Co., 1964.

The Police and Their Use of Fatal Force in Chicago. Evanston, Ill.: Chicago Law Enforcement Study Group, 1972.

POUSSAINT, ALVIN F. *Why Blacks Kill Blacks.* New York: Emerson Hall Publishers, 1972.

President's Commission on Law Enforcement and Administration of Justice, *The Challenge of Crime in a Free Society.* Washington, D.C.: Government Printing Office, 1967.

President's Commission on Mental Health 1978. Washington, D.C.: Government Printing Office, 1978.

SCHULZ, DAVID A. *Coming Up Black,* Englewood Cliffs, N.J.: Prentice-Hall, 1969.

SROLE, LEO, et al. *Mental Health in the Metropolis: The Midtown Manhattan Study.* New York: McGraw-Hill Book Co., 1962.

SUTHERLAND, E. H. *White Collar Crime.* New York: Dryden Press, 1949.

THOMAS, ALEXANDER, and SAMUEL SILLEN. *Racism and Psychiatry.* New York: Brunner Mazel Publishers, 1972.

THOMAS, CHARLES W., ed. *Boys No More: A Black Psychiatrist's View of Community.* Beverly Hills, Calif.: Glencoe Press, 1971.

U.S. Bureau of the Census. *Statistical Abstract of the United States, 1985.* Washington, D.C.: Government Printing Office, 1985.

WILCOX, ROGER C. ed. *The Psychological Consequences of Being a Black American.* New York: John Wiley & Sons, 1971.

WILLIE, CHARLES, V., et al., eds. *Racism and Mental Health.* Pittsburgh, Pa.: University of Pittsburgh Press, 1973.

Youth in the Ghetto. New York: Harlem Youth Opportunities Unlimited, 1964.

NOTES

[1] James Baldwin, *Notes of a Native Son* (Boston: Beacon Press, 1957), p. 71.

[2] See, for example, Aaron V. Cicourel, *The Social Organization of Juvenile Justice* (New York: Wiley, 1968); Jerome H. Skolnick, *Justice Without Trial: Law Enforcement in Democratic Society* (New York: Wiley, 1966).

[3]See Marshall B. Clinard, *Sociology of Deviant Behavior* (New York: Holt, 1963), pp. 22–31.

[4]See, for example, Ronald H. Beattie, "Problems of Criminal Statistics in the United States," *Journal of Criminal Law, Criminology and Police Science* 46 (July–August 1955), 178–86.

[5]See Donald Cressy, "Crime," in *Contemporary Social Problems*, ed. Robert K. Merton and Robert A. Nisbet (New York: Harcourt, Brace, 1966), pp. 151–53; Guy B. Johnson, "The Negro and Crime," *Annals of the American Academy of Political and Social Science* 271 (September 1941), 93–104; Gunnar Myrdal, *An American Dilemma* (New York: Harper, 1944), pp. 966–79.

[6]This discussion relies heavily on Johnson, "The Negro and Crime," pp. 95–103.

[7]U.S. Bureau of the Census, *Statistical Abstract of the United States, 1985* (Washington, D.C.: Government Printing Office, 1985), p. 186.

[8]Federal Bureau of Prisons, *Statistical Report, Fiscal Years 1971 and 1972* (Washington, D.C.: Bureau of Prisons, 1973), p. 38.

[9]Ibid., p. 168.

[10]Federal Bureau of Prisons, *National Prisoner Statistics—State Prisoners: Admissions and Releases, 1970* (Washington, D.C.: Bureau of Prisons, 1971), p. 1.

[11]Ibid., p. 10.

[12]See, for example, J. T. Blue, "The Relationship of Juvenile Delinquency, Race, and Economic Status," *Journal of Negro Education* 17 (Fall 1948), 469–77; Earl R. Moses, "Differentials in Crime Rates Between Negroes and Whites Based on Comparisons of Four Socio-Economically Equated Areas," *American Sociological Review* 12 (August 1947), 411–20.

[13]Myrdal, *American Dilemma*, pp. 975–76.

[14]Moses, "Differentials in Crime Rates," p. 420; See also Albert K. Cohen, *Delinquent Boys* (Glencoe, Ill.: Free Press, 1955); and W. B. Miller, "Lower Class Culture as a Generating Milieu of Gang Delinquency," *Journal of Social Issues* 14 (1958), 5–19.

[15]Thomas F. Pettigrew, *A Profile of the Negro American* (Princeton, N.J.: Van Nostrand, 1964), p. 156.

[16]Albert J. Reiss, Jr., and Albert L. Rhodes, "The Distribution of Juvenile Delinquency in the Social Structure," *American Sociological Review* 26 (October 1961), 720–32; Calvin F. Schmid, "Urban Crime Areas: Part I," *American Sociological Review* 25 (August 1960), 527–42; Calvin F. Schmid, "Urban Crime Areas: Part II," *American Sociological Review* 25 (October 1960), 655–78.

[17]E. H. Sutherland, *White Collar Crime* (New York: Dryden Press, 1949).

[18]See Albert K. Cohen and James F. Short, "Juvenile Delinquency," in *Contemporary Social Problems*, ed. Merton and Nisbet, pp. 90–91.

[19]Federal Bureau of Investigation, *Crime in the United States, 1982: Uniform Crime Reports* (Washington, D.C.: Government Printing Office, 1983), p. 185.

[20]Joseph H. Douglass, "The Extent and Characteristics of Juvenile Delinquency among Negroes in the United States," *Journal of Negro Education* 28 (Summer 1959), 214–29.

[21]Sidney Axelrod, "Negro and White Male Institutionalized Delinquents," *American Journal of Sociology* 57 (May 1952), 569–74; Mary H. Diggs, "Some Problems and Needs of Negro Children as Revealed by Comparative Delinquency and Crime Statistics," *Journal of Negro Education* 19 (1950), 290–97; Irving Piliavin and Scott Briar, "Police Encounters with Juveniles," *American Journal of Sociology* 60 (September 1964), 206–14.

[22]*Youth in the Ghetto* (New York: Harlem Youth Opportunities Unlimited, 1964), p. 138.

[23]Kenneth Clark, *Dark Ghetto* (New York: Harper & Row, 1965), pp. 86–87.

[24]James K. Ball, Alan Ross, and Alice Simpson, "Incidence and Estimated Prevalence of Recorded Delinquency in a Metropolitan Area," *American Sociological Review* 29 (February 1964), 90–93.

[25]Piliavin and Briar, "Police Encounters with Juveniles," p. 212.

[26]Ruth S. Cavan, "Negro Family Disorganization and Juvenile Delinquency," *Journal of Negro Education* 28 (Summer 1959), 240–51.

[27]See Sheldon Glueck and Eleanor Glueck, *Unraveling Juvenile Delinquency* (Cambridge, Mass.: Harvard, 1950).

[28]Kenneth Clark, "Color, Class, Personality and Juvenile Delinquency," *Journal of Negro Education* 28 (Summer 1959), 240–51.

[29]Mozell Hill, "The Metropolis and Juvenile Delinquency among Negroes," *Journal of Negro Education* 28 (Summer 1959), 278.

[30]Douglass, "Juvenile Delinquency among Negroes," p. 215.

[31]Reported in the *New York Times*, December 8, 1985, p. 61.

[32]Federal Bureau of Investigation, *Crime in the United States*, p. 156.

[33]*The Police and Their Use of Fatal Force in Chicago* (Evanston, Ill.: Chicago Law Enforcement Study Group, 1972), p. 74.

[34]See, for example, Angela Y. Davis, *If They Come in the Morning* (New York: New American Library, 1971); George Jackson, *Soledad Brother* (New York: Bantam, 1970); Etheridge Knight, ed., *Black Voices From Prison* (New York: Pathfinder, 1970); Jessica Mitford, *Kind and Usual Punishment: The Prison Business* (New York: Knopf, 1973); Eve Pell, ed., *Maximum Security: Letters From Prison* (New York: Dutton, 1972).

[35]Benjamin Malzberg, *Statistical Data for the Study of Mental Disease among Negroes in New York State, 1939–1941* (Albany, N.Y.: State Department of Mental Hygiene, 1955), p. 1.

[36]Ibid., p. 9.

[37]Benjamin Malzberg, *The Mental Health of the Negro* (Albany, N.Y.: Research Foundation for Mental Hygiene, 1962).

[38]Benjamin Malzberg, *New Data on Mental Disease among Negroes in New York State, 1960–1961* (Albany, N.Y.: Research Foundation for Mental Hygiene, 1965).

[39]Data for Pennsylvania, South Carolina, and Louisiana are reported in Ernest Y. Williams and Claude P. Carmichael, "The Incidence of Mental Disease in the Negro," *Journal of Negro Education* 18 (Summer 1949), 276–82.

[40]Helen V. McLean, "The Emotional Health of Negroes," *Journal of Negro Education*, 18 (Summer 1949), 283–90.

[41]A. B. Sclare, "Cultural Determinants in the Neurotic Negro," *British Journal of Medical Psychology* 26 (1953), 279–88.

[42]Benjamin Pasamanick, "Some Misconceptions Concerning Differences in Racial Prevalence of Mental Disease," *American Journal of Orthopsychiatry* 33 (January 1963), 72–86; Benjamin Pasamanick, "A Survey of Mental Disease in the Urban Population," *American Journal of Psychiatry* 119 (October 1962), 229–305.

[43]David C. Wilson and Edna M. Lantz, "Culture Change and Negro State Hospital Admissions," *American Journal of Psychiatry*, 114 (July 1957), 25-32.

[44]Cf. Thomas F. Pettigrew, *A Profile of the Negro American*, p. 75.

[45]See August B. Hollingshead and Frederick C. Redlich, *Social Class and Mental Illness* (New York: Wiley, 1958); Leo Srole et al., *Mental Health in the Metropolis: The Midtown Manhattan Study* (New York: McGraw-Hill, 1962).

[46]Pasamanick, "Racial Prevalence of Mental Disease," p. 83.

[47]Malzberg, *New Data on Mental Disease*, pp. 58–59.

[48]Malzberg, *Study of Mental Disease*, pp. 4–6; Malzberg, *New Data on Mental Disease*, pp. 51–59; Benjamin Malzberg, "Mental Disease Among Native and Foreign Born Negroes in New York State," *Journal of Negro Education* 25 (Spring 1956), 175–181; Wilson and Lantz, "Culture Change," p. 32.

[49]Pettigrew, *Profile of the Negro American*, p. 75.

[50]R. A. Schermerhorn, "Psychiatric Disorders among Negroes: A Sociological Note," *American Journal of Psychiatry* 112 (May 1956), 882.

[51]Williams and Carmichael, "Mental Disease in the Negro," pp. 281–82.

[52]Abram Kardiner and Lionel Ovesey, *The Mark of Oppression* (New York: World, 1962), p. 343.

[53]*President's Commission on Mental Health 1978* (Washington, D.C.: Government Printing Office, 1978).

[54]Ibid., p. 823.

[55]Ibid., p. 830.

[56]Ibid., p. 831.

[57]Ibid., p. 858.

[58]Carolyn R. Payton, "Substance Abuse and Mental Health: Special Prevention Strategies Needed for Ethnics of Color," *Public Health Reports* 96 (January–February 1981), 20–25.

[59]Woodrow Jones, Jr., "Preventing Mental Disorders in the Black Community," *Urban League Review* 9 (Winter 1985–86), 32–38.

[60]See Joseph W. Eaton and Robert J. Weil, *Culture and Mental Disorders* (New York: Free Press, 1955).

[61]Kardiner and Ovesey, *Mark of Oppression,* p. 11.

[62]William H. Grier and Price M. Cobbs, *Black Rage* (New York: Bantam, 1968), p. 149.

[63]National Commission on Marihuana and Drug Abuse, *Drug Use in America: Problem in Perspective* (Washington, D.C.: Government Printing Office, 1973), pp. 42–44.

[64]Federal Bureau of Narcotics, *Annual Report on Narcotic Addiction in the United States* (Washington, D.C.: Treasury Department, 1966), table I.

[65]Michael J. Pescor, "A Statistical Analysis of the Clinical Records of Hospitalized Drug Addicts," *Public Health Reports,* supplement 143 (1938), appendix, p. 24.

[66]*Report of Study of Drug Addiction among Teenagers* (New York: Mayor's Committee on Drug Addiction, 1951).

[67]*Dealing with Drug Abuse: A Report to the Ford Foundation* (New York: Praeger Publishers, 1972), p. 4.

[68]National Commission on Marihuana and Drug Abuse, *Drug Use in America,* p. 173.

[69]Ibid., pp. 52, 111, 144.

[70]*Youth in the Ghetto* (New York: Harlem Youth Opportunities Unlimited, 1964), pp. 144–45.

[71]John A. Clausen, "Drug Addiction," in *Contemporary Social Problems,* ed. Merton and Nisbet, p. 197.

[72]Federal Bureau of Narcotics, *Annual Report.*

[73]See Clausen, "Drug Addiction," pp. 210–12; Isidor Chein, "Narcotics Use among Juveniles," in *Narcotic Addiction,* ed. John A. O'Donnell and John C. Bail (New York: Harper & Row, 1966), pp. 123–41.

[74]See Harold Finestone, "Cats, Kicks, and Color," *Social Problems* 18 (July 1957), 3–13.

[75]*Statistical Abstract, 1985,* p. 118.

[76]National Institute on Drug Abuse, Research Monograph Series 5: *Young Men and Drugs: A Nationwide Survey* (Washington, D.C.: National Institute on Drug Abuse, 1976).

[77]These findings are reported in Patrick R. Clifford and Antonio Rene, "Substance Abuse among Blacks: An Epidemiological Perspective," *Urban League Review* 9 (Winter 1985–86), 52–58.

CHAPTER SEVEN
ASSIMILATION INTO AMERICAN SOCIETY

The extent to which black Americans are assimilated into the larger society is the subject of considerable debate. They were among the earliest arrivals to North America, but they were quickly stripped of their native African cultures. Their tribal organization, religion, family life, and language were systematically destroyed. It thus became necessary for them to adopt the patterns of life of the white Europeans with whom they were forced to live. The adoption of Western culture became a difficult task, for they were permitted to assimilate into the society only to the extent that their services could be utilized by their white rulers. In general, they were forced to live a dual existence: their lives had to be structured in terms of the demands made on them by the larger society and in terms of the necessity to survive in a generally hostile environment. When formal slavery ended more than a century ago, it was replaced by a caste system, which prevented substantial alteration of the dual environment within which black people lived. A rigid system of segregation and discrimination replaced the institution of slavery, and this system continues to preclude assimilation into the larger society.

Being in the society but not a part of it has fostered a conflict among black Americans: some strive to identify with white middle-class values and others reject all aspects of white culture. The former attitude sometimes leads to negative identification (self-hatred), while the latter frequently manifests itself in black nationalism. The majority of blacks would no doubt welcome the chance to become assimilated into the larger society. To the extent that there are forces among blacks resisting such an eventuality, these forces are a result of widespread rejection by white Americans.

There have been few systematic attempts to examine the extent to which black people are assimilated into the larger society, partly because the assimilation process has only recently been systematically analyzed. Milton Gordon sees the process of assimilation as one involving several steps of subprocesses.[1] Each step represents a "type" or "stage" in the assimilation process. He identifies seven variables by which one may gauge the degree to which members of a particular group are assimilated into the host society which surrounds them. The stages and the subprocesses follow.[2]

TYPE OR STAGE OF ASSIMILATION	SUBPROCESS OR CONDITION
Cultural or behavioral assimilation	Change of cultural patterns to those of host society
Structural assimilation	Large-scale entrance into cliques, clubs, and institutions of host society, on primary-group level
Marital assimilation	Large-scale intermarriage
Identificational assimilation	Development of a sense of peoplehood based exclusively on host society
Attitude receptional assimilation	Absence of prejudice
Behavior receptional assimilation	Absense of discrimination
Civic assimilation	Absence of value or power conflict

It is possible to apply these variables systematically to the status of black people in the United States at the present time in an attempt to determine the extent to which these people have assimilated into American society.

CULTURAL ASSIMILATION

To what extent have black Americans adopted the cultural patterns of the larger society in which they find themselves? The systematic stripping of the slaves of their African cultures was detailed in chapter 1.[3] Debate persists, however, on the extent and nature of the survival of African cultures among black people in the United States. In the more than three and one-half centuries that black people have inhabited what is now the United States, they have adopted the culture of the larger society to the extent that it is difficult to detect any significant vestiges of their original cultures. In North America small numbers of slaves were scattered over a large area on numerous plantations and farms. Even when a sizable number of slaves were held by the same owner, they were likely to have been from a variety of cultures in Africa. Under such circumstances the retention of aspects of their original cultures was difficult. In addition, they were forbidden to speak their native languages, and their family patterns were systematically destroyed. Although it is still possible to detect survivals in religious life,[4] Christianity made significant inroads among the slaves, and their religious practices developed along the lines of those of white Christians. Indeed, ". . . the religion of the slaves was, in essence, strikingly similar to that of the poor, illiterate white men of the antebellum South."[5] In other aspects of culture as well, few survivals of African civilizations remain.

There have been frequent attempts by individual blacks and organizations to reemphasize aspects of traditional African cultures, but among the majority of blacks these attempts have been unsuccessful. Historically the most successful of these movements was the Universal Negro Improvement Association, led by Marcus Garvey.[6] The most recent is the Muslim Mission (popularly known as the Black Muslims), led originally by Elijah Muhammad and now by his son, Marith Deen Muhammad.[7] In urban areas throughout the United States Black Nationalist groups continue to search for aspects of their past that were destroyed by the institution of slavery.

According to Gordon, the extent to which black people have adopted the cultural patterns of the host society varies by class. He sees the middle- and upper-class blacks as being totally acculturated, while "lower-class Negro life . . . is still at a considerable distance from the American cultural norm."[8] A vast majority of black Americans are poor (lower class), and in some respects their cultural patterns deviate from those of the larger society. To a large extent, however, these differences are a function of class rather than race. Gordon's analysis posits "middle-class white Protestant Americans as constituting the 'core society.' " Clearly many poor blacks deviate from the norms of this group, as do poor, white Protestant Americans. In the sense that poor blacks adhere to lower-class American culture patterns, they may be said to be acculturated. Poor blacks in the rural South are not significantly different from their poor, white counterparts in food habits or religious practices, for example. They eat the less expensive foods and tend to be more emotional in their religious practices, but the same phenomena are true of poor, rural, white southerners. Blacks in non-southern urban areas may differ in this regard from poor whites in the same areas, but the differences are a function of their southern, not their African, heritage.

Middle- and upper-class blacks are hardly distinguishable from white Americans of comparable social-class level in many cultural patterns. There is even some evidence that they frequently overconform to middle-class standards of behavior in religious observances, in dress, in sexual behavior, and in child-rearing practices.[9] But this does not mean that black culture is a myth; Blauner has convincingly demonstrated that it is not.[10]

In recent years there have been several studies of various aspects of black life in the United States which attempt to demonstrate that a distinctive culture exists among American blacks. These studies have focused on language, patterns of family life, styles of dress, patterns of social organization, music, and other elements of culture.[11] Some maintain that the distinctive culture patterns of the black community are primarily a result of African survivals, while others see them as resulting mainly from a life of oppression in the United States.

Inasmuch as blacks were initially denied the right to participate in the culture of the larger society, while at the same time they were not permitted to practice their original cultures, they had to create a way of life (culture) in a hostile environment. In many regards these cultural patterns differ from those of the dominant society. To maintain that significant segments of the black community have largely assimilated the culture of the larger society is not to deny that cultural (or subcultural) differences persist. While serious scholarly research on black culture is relatively recent in its origin, black people have maintained through the years that in many respects their way of life differs from that of white Americans. It is perhaps necessary to await more definitive research in the area before concrete conclusions can be reached. However, it seems fair to say that in many respects the acculturation process is virtually complete for large segments of the black community.

STRUCTURAL ASSIMILATION

Black Americans usually maintain their own separate institutions within the black community. (See chapter 3.) Historically this situation has not resulted from voluntary isolation; rather, a caste system of segregation and discrimination against them has precluded their large-scale entrance into cliques, social clubs, and other social organizations and activities along with white Americans on a primary-group level. However, with increasing racial pride among black people today, voluntary racial separation is not uncommon. In the "rank order of discriminations" against blacks by white southerners, as enumerated by Gunnar Myrdal, activites specifically concerned with personal relations, such as dancing, bathing, eating, and drinking together with blacks, followed closely after intermarriage and interracial sexual relations as forbidden behavior.[12] Such practices are more characteristic of the South than elsewhere, but in general they characterize the relations between black and white persons throughout the United States. The caste system, which separates blacks and whites, dictates that members of these two social categories should not associate in any relationships which imply social equality. This ban generally extends to marriage, dancing, eating together, and social visiting.

The traditional pattern of relations between black and white American has been slightly altered in recent years, but in general the pattern of almost total isolation of the black community from the white community persists. As black people continue to settle in the central cities of the largest urban areas, the isolation is becoming more pronounced. Studies of black-white relations in the South show the pervasiveness of rigid segregation along racial lines in the major social groups and institutions.[13] The tradition in the South is deeply rooted in the mores, and social change is slow. Indeed, it is unlikely that any significant change will occur in the near future.

Outside the South the isolation of the black community is only slightly less pronounced than in the South. Most white Americans live their lives with only the slightest awareness of the lives of their black fellow citizens except during periods of racial unrest. A vast majority of the blacks who live outside the South live in urban areas, but those who live in small towns live isolated lives compared to their urban counterparts. Two studies illustrate the dearth of interracial association beween blacks and whites in small northern cities. In Elmira, New York, it is reported that the black community is so isolated that its inhabitants think of themselves not as citizens of Elmira but as citizens of the black community. Such references as "all over town" or "the prettiest girl in town" do not refer to Elmira but to the specific section in which the blacks are concentrated.[14] Given such conditions as these, it is clear that blacks have not entered into social groups and activities with their white coresidents. Social contacts between the two groups are minimal.

In a small Connecticut town it was reported: "While Negro-white neighborhood relations are friendly, they are characterized for the most part by lack of contact between the two races."[15] The blacks maintained their own church, and in public social activites sponsored by other churches, discrimination against blacks was evident. There were few adult interracial social contacts. Only two of the many formal organizations, the Chamber of Commerce and the town band, had black members. On the adolescent level a similar pattern was discerned. Social contact between black and white persons was, in this case, limited to athletic and recreational activities. The school system was found to be the only institution in which black and white citizens participated with some degree of equality.

In large cities outside the South there is little social contact between blacks and whites. Social life of blacks tends to be centered around their own social, civic, and religious organizations.[16] Recently, however, middle- and upper-class blacks have often participated freely with whites in social groups. Nevertheless, the vast majority of blacks continue to have only superficial social contact with white persons. The maintenance of rigid residential segregation is a strong deterrant against the structural assimilation of blacks into the life of the larger society.

Structural assimilation may be subdivided into primary and secondary assimilation.[17] Those social institutions which are rooted in the black community (e.g., schools) are primary, and those either partially (e.g., schools) or totally (e.g., economic activities) located in the white community are secondary to the black community. When this dichotomy is made, it is clear that assimilation has progressed at a much more rapid pace in secondary institutions than in those which are primary. Inasmuch as primary institutions tend to be in the private sector of American life and those which are secondary tend to be public, the interest of black people has been more in secondary assimilation than in primary assimilation.

MARITAL ASSIMILATION

The United States represents a society which has attempted to curb the process of racial amalgamation through legislation forbidding the marriage of blacks and nonblacks. Historically most states have enacted laws forbidding the marriage of black and white persons. Although these laws were disregarded in some states, they were rigidly enforced in others, thereby limiting the number of black-white interracial marriages. The penalties for violating these antimiscegenation laws varied by state, ranging up to $2000 in fines and terms of imprisonment up to ten years.[18]

These antimiscegenation laws were gradually repealed in most nonsouthern states, but at the time the Supreme Court declared them unconstitutional in 1967, sixteen states still had such laws recorded. Even in those states where the laws had been repealed, social mores strongly forbidding intimate interpersonal association across racial lines limited the number of black-white intermarriages. The result has been that such marriages have occurred infrequently in the United States.

Data on the incidence of black-white intermarriages are somewhat limited, but sufficient evidence exists to give a reasonable picture of the extent to which the phenomenon occurs. One writer reports that, in 1956, 1137 black-white intermarriages were contracted, of which 90 percent involved black men and white women. This number represents 0.07 of 1 percent of the total of 1,569,000 marriages contracted in the United States during that year.[19] Another writer reports that in 1939, black-white interracial marriages accounted for only eight out of every 10,000 marriages in the country.[20]

The most comprehensive data on interracial marriage is provided by the United States Bureau of the Census.[21] According to the bureau, there were 65,000 black-white married couples in 1970, 167,000 in 1980, and 164,000 in 1983, representing an increase of nearly 300 percent in the decade of the 1970s. Of the black-white married couples, black men tended to marry white women about twice as often as black women married white men. Between 1980 and 1983 the total number had declined by about 3000. The Bureau of the Census reports data on interracial marriages involving blacks with spouses who are other than white (e.g., Asian). In 1970 there were 245,000 such marriages, in 1980 there were 484,000, and in 1983 there were 555,000. Of these interracial married couples in 1983, 24,000 involved a black husband, and 9000 involved a black wife.

Data from states and municipalities confirm the relative infrequency of black-white intermarriage. In Connecticut, for the seven-year period from 1953 to 1959, there were a total of 285 marriages between black and white persons out of a total of 125,746 marriages, or 2.3 per 1000 marriages.[22] The highest rate of interracial marriages was recorded for Los Angeles during the period from 1924 to 1933, when 1.2 per 100 marriages were reported. California then enacted a law forbidding interracial marriages. When this law was nullified by a state court in 1948, there was no significant increase in the number of interracial marriages involving black and white persons. During a thirty-month period (November 1948 to April 1951) the rate of interracial marriages was 56 per 10,000. Of this number approximately 20.5 percent involved black men, and 7.4 percent involved black women.[23]

From 1916 to 1937 the percentage of black-white marriages among all marriages involving blacks varied from 1.7 percent to 4.8 percent. In Boston for the period from 1914 to 1938 black-white marriages constituted approximately 5.2 percent of all marriages involving blacks.[24] In Chicago between 1925 and 1938 the percentage of black men married to white women was 2.1, while the figure for white men married to black women was 0.6 of 1 percent.[25] Data from Washington, D.C., show that between 1940 and 1948, of the 97,599 marriage licenses issued, only 26 involved black-white marriages.[26] From the foregoing data it is clear that black-white intermarriage in the United States is an uncommon phenomenon.

IDENTIFICATIONAL ASSIMILATION

The position of black people in the United States is unique. They form one of the largest and oldest minorities in the country. Racially distinct from the majority, they are highly visible as a minority group. They were enslaved for more than two and one-half centuries, and they continue to be rather widely regarded as racially inferior. Consequently, they are responded to as blacks rather than as Americans. The circumstances under which they live virtually preclude their development of a sense of peoplehood based exclusively on the host society. They are forced to think of themselves as a separate ethnic group rather than simply as Americans.

Despite the many difficulties black people have encountered, their allegiance to the United States is clear. Their interest appears to be in being accorded full citizenship. For example, in a nationwide survey conducted in 1963 an overwhelming majority of blacks (81 percent) indicated that they thought the United States was worth fighting for in a war.[27] Similarly, when asked in 1966 to rank black leaders, a nationwide sample of blacks ranked integrationist leaders such as Martin Luther King, Jr. and Roy Wilkins higher than the more militant anti-integrationist leaders such as Stokely Carmichael and Elijah Muhammad.[28] Surveys conducted for the National Advisory Commission on Civil Disorders in fifteen cities which had experienced black rebellions in the summer of 1967 reported a growing disenchantment on the part of blacks. In Detroit, of those who participated in the rebellion, 34.9 percent said the country was not worth fighting for in case of a major world war, while 15.5 percent of those who did not participate answered similarly. In Newark 52.8 percent of those who reported participating in the rebellion said they did not think the country was worth fighting for in case of a world war, while 27.8 percent of those who did not participate gave the same response.[29] In general, then, it appears than the main concern for a vast majority of America's blacks is that they be accorded the same rights of citizenship as other Americans.

When legal slavery ended in the United States, black people were not permitted to enter into the mainstream of society, as were their counterparts in Brazil and the Caribbean. Rather, a situation developed in which all blacks, no matter what the extent of their achievement might have been, were regarded simply as blacks; a black could never expect to be accorded treatment comparable to that of a white American, regardless of the latter's lack of achievement. A black is not just another public official, he or she is a *black* public official: the black justice of the Supreme Court, the black mayor of Washington, D.C., the black senator from Massachusetts, and so on. When the official's position is known, he is accorded a certain amount of deference regardless of his race. However, if his position is not known, he is responded to by most Americans as "just another black," and he would be treated accordingly in most situations. White Americans do not see black people as individuals, distinguishable from one another; rather, they see them as an indistinguishable mass. Under such circumstances they are responded to indiscriminately. The black farm laborer and the Nobel Prize winner are both simply blacks, with all that the word implies. One black respondent, in commenting on job relations with white fellow workers, said: "I don't care how a white person treats you. They have a feelin' in 'em that you're colored—I know my place, no matter where I am."[30] This respondent, in a northern city, accurately defined the general attitude of white Americans toward blacks.

Forced into such a position of a self-conscious minority, the tendency of members of that group to think of themselves collectively is inevitable. When a fellow black achieves a certain distinction, it becomes a source of pride for other blacks. Conversely, when a fellow black is charged with some act which meets with social disapproval, it becomes a source of embarrassment for other blacks.[31] In other words, to black Americans, as well as to white Americans, one is either black or white, and one responds in terms of these two categories. To a black *us* means blacks and *them* means white persons.[22]

Finally, Louis Harris and Associates conducted a national survey of black and white attitudes on several issues during the last week of December 1984 and the first week of January 1985. Interviewers asked respondents whether they agreed with the statement, "Even though we call America a melting pot of religious and racial minorities, there is still a lot of prejudice against minority groups." Fully 94 percent of blacks responded affirmatively, compared with 84 percent of whites.[33] Such views on the part of black people may be said to represent a lack of identificational assimilation among them.

Because black people have occupied an oppressed and segregated status in the United States for centuries, the likelihood of their developing a sense of "peoplehood" with white Americans seems remote. Indeed, in recent years, although they have made some gains in the realm of integration, there appears to be a growing tendency for black people to develop a strong sense of identification with other blacks, an increasing pride on their part in being black. Such ingroup identification militates against the development of a sense of identification with the host society.

ATTITUDE-RECEPTIONAL ASSIMILATION

Studies of prejudice among white Americans generally indicate that antiblack prejudice is widespread in the United States. Intensity of attitudes vary, depending on the region of the country, social-class level, age, religion, and other variables, but in general antiblack prejudice is the social norm among white Americans. There is some indication of change in attitudes insofar as the more impersonal dimensions of prejudice are concerned, especially in recent years,[34] but in certain realms attitudes remain firmly antiblack.

The earliest studies of prejudice indicate that white Americans maintained strongly negative attitudes toward intimate association with nonwhite persons, especially black persons. In the 1920s an overwhelming majority of white Americans indicated that they would reject blacks as relatives through marriage (98.6 percent), as personal friends in social clubs (90.9 percent), and as neighbors (88.2 percent).[35] In the 1960s the pattern still held: 84 percent of white persons reported that they would object to a close friend or relative marrying a black, and 51 percent said they would object to black neighbors.[36]

The extent of antiblack prejudice in the United States has been reported in several other studies. In one nationwide study of prejudice only 5 percent of white persons interviewed received the lowest possible score on a four-point scale of prejudice; 48 percent received the highest possible score.[37] In a study of white veterans in Chicago, only 8 percent expressed tolerant attitudes toward blacks.[38] A 1966 nationwide survey of white attitudes toward blacks provides data on the extent of anti-black prejudice in the United States.[39] At least one-half of all respondents subscribed to stereotypes about blacks, such as, blacks are different (52 percent), and blacks have looser morals (50 percent). Furthermore, significant proportions of white persons indicate that they would object to close association with blacks in a variety of situations—for example: having a black child to supper (42 percent), trying on clothes blacks have tried on (31 percent), using the same restrooms as blacks (22 percent), and sitting next to a black in a movie (21 percent).

The Cornell Studies in Intergroup Relations reported a significant degree of antiblack prejudice in communities throughout the United States in the 1950s.[40] In these studies prejudice was indicated by the acceptance of antiblack stereotypes, such as, "Generally speaking, Negroes are lazy and ignorant," and the manifestations of social-distance feelings, such as finding it distasteful (1) to eat at the same table with a black, (2) to dance with a black, (3) to go to a party and find that most of the people there are black, and (4) to have a black person marry someone in their family. Prejudiced responses on these items varied anywhere from virtually all respondents disapproving of the marriage of a relative to a black to more than one-third (34 percent) of all respondents on the West Coast endorsing the antiblack stereotype.

Opposition to integration in public schools and housing provides some indication of change in attitudes of white persons toward black person. In 1942 only one-third (30 percent) of white Americans expressed the opinion that black and white children should go to the same school; by 1963 the percentage had more than doubled (63 percent). Slightly more than one-third (35 percent) of all white Americans approved of residential integration in 1942, and by 1963, 61 percent expressed approval.[41]

Some studies show that white attitudes toward desegregation have become more favorable in recent years in spite of the racial strife caused by the black rebellions. The University of Chicago's National Opinion Research Center conducted surveys of racial attitudes at intervals between 1942 and 1970. These surveys included two questions, one on white attitudes toward segregation in public transportation, and one on attitudes toward segregation in public education.[42] In 1942, 44 percent of white Americans endorsed integrated public transportation; in 1970 the figure had doubled to 88 percent. On the more sensitive issue of school integration, white Americans during the same period changed their attitudes from 30 percent favorable in 1942 to 75 percent in 1970. On the question of interracial marriage, however, about one-half of whites expressed the opinion in 1970 that laws should prohibit the marriage of blacks and whites. A Gallup survey in 1971 found that only 29 percent of adult white Americans expressed approval of marriages between blacks and whites.[43]

The Survey Research Center of the University of Michigan conducted surveys on the attitudes of whites toward blacks between 1964 and 1970.[44] In 1964, 38 percent of whites expressed the view that the government should enforce school-integration laws, and by 1970 there was a slight change to 41 percent. Regarding government-enforced desegregation of public accommodations, such as hotels and restaurants, positive attitudes increased from 41 percent in 1968 to 56 percent in 1970. On the question of open housing, in 1964 53 percent supported the position that blacks should be permitted to live wherever they could afford; the percentage had increased to 67 in 1970.

Antiblack prejudice, while on the decline, remains deeply rooted in society.[45] The daily newspaper accounts of resistance both to racial integration in public schools and racial integration in housing throughout the United States attest to the extent to which prejudice is institutionalized in the society. A 1985 Harris survey found that one-fourth (25 percent) of all whites agreed with the statement, "Blacks have less ambition than most other people."[46] Such a finding indicates the depth of antiblack prejudice existing in the United States. The likelihood that the situation for blacks in the United States will ever reach the point that they do not encounter prejudiced attitudes is remote.

Furthermore, a reduction in prejudice does not necessarily mean a change in the status of black people, for prejudice is not the sole ingredient in racism. More crucial for blacks in this regard are the institutionalized practices which maintain white dominance. That is, the racism in the institutions of the society precludes social justice for blacks. So long as these practices endure, the mere reduction of negative attitudes will not significantly alter the status of black people.

BEHAVIOR-RECEPTIONAL ASSIMILATION

The prejudiced attitudes of white Americans are frequently translated into discriminatory behavior. Hence black Americans experience difficulty in securing employment, housing, and education; they are treated differentially in the administration of justice. In the South they experience discrimination in voting and in places of public accommodation. Indeed, discrimination against black people in the United States is institutionalized.[47] Like prejudiced attitudes, discriminatory practices vary depending on the region of the country. Outside the South black people experience little difficulty in voting or gaining access to places of public accommodation, but in housing, employment, and education discrimination against black people is commonplace in all regions. Discriminatory practices relegate black people to an inferior status in the United States and affect each aspect of their lives. When they are forced into inferior schools, they receive inferior education, which relegates them to inferior employment, which in turn relegates them to inferior housing. The cycle is complete. Furthermore, their low status makes them "inferior," and their "inferiority" justifies acts of discrimination against them. The product of past discrimination is cited to justify continued discrimination.

Acts of discrimination are a manifestation of the legacy of slavery. Although these acts have been practiced since emancipation, they were intensified and extended in scope between 1890 and 1925. For example, Mississippi passed a statewide law requiring separate taxis for black and white persons as late as 1922.[48] Few attempts were made by the federal government to deal with antiblack discrimination until the 1950s, although executive orders had ostensibly dealt with discrimination as early as World War II. The most sweeping federal attempt to deal with these practices was the Civil Rights Act of 1964.

Perhaps the area in which discrimination against black people is most widespread is housing. Throughout much of the present century the mere entry of a black family into a neighborhood inhabited by white Americans, when such was possible, has stimulated mob violence. Discrimination in housing is so widespread that virtually all black families that attempt to leave neighborhoods inhabited by blacks are likely to experience acts of discrimination relating to housing.[49] Discrimination in housing is not limited to low-income blacks. Many well-known, upper-class blacks—baseball players, opera singers, popular entertainers, judges, and educators—have experienced difficulty in finding housing outside the black neighborhoods of large cities. For example, "The scientist Percy Julian, upon purchasing a fine home in Oak Park in 1951, encountered threats to his person, harassment of his children, and serious attempts to bomb and burn him out. But he stood his ground (hiring a private watchman for two years to guard the place) and finally won acceptance as a respected citizen of that upper-class Chicago suburb."[50] The pattern of widespread discrimination against black people in housing is nationwide. In every American city it is possible to tell the race of a citizen by his or her address. There is no large American city in which blacks and whites share the same neighborhoods to any great extent.[51]

Repeated attempts to prohibit discrimination in housing have met with little success. On November 20, 1962, the president of the United

States issued an executive order barring discrimination by reason of race, color, religion, or national origin in the "sale or rental of residential property and related facilities owned by the federal government or aided or assisted by it."[52] Prior to that time several states and municipalities had enacted legislation barring racial discrimination, and the Supreme Court had ruled in 1948 that federal and state courts could not enforce restrictive covenants in housing. Most housing in the United States is privately owned and financed, and few municipal and state laws and, prior to the Fair Housing Act of 1968, no federal laws, covered such housing. Furthermore, where laws forbid discrimination in housing, enforcement is virtually nonexistent.

Feelings among white Americans about sharing housing and neighborhoods with black people are strongly negative, as was evidenced by the racist mobs gathered in Chicago in 1966 and in Milwaukee in 1967 when civil rights activists demonstrated against discrimination in housing. In Milwaukee the demonstrations were led by a Roman Catholic priest, and during one of them a mob of angry white persons carried a simulated coffin which read, "God is White" and "Father Groppi Rest in Hell." Others carried a placard reading, "You no we're alright, uptight, Out of Sight, We no we're Right, Cause We're WHITE."[53] Because discrimination in housing is so deeply rooted, it is unlikely that black people will achieve equal opportunity in housing in the near future. In 1964 the citizens of California voted overwhelmingly (4.5 million to 2.4 million) in favor of an amendment providing that "Neither the state nor any subdivision or agency thereof shall deny, limit, or abridge, directly or indirectly, the right of any person, who is willing or desires to sell, lease, or rent any part or all of his real property, to decline to sell, lease, or rent any part or all of his real property, to such a person or persons as he, in his absolute discretion, chooses."[54] A South African novelist, on a visit to the United States, summed up the situation in these words: ". . . school segregation is dying, but in housing the Negro's dilemma is grim. In most places they can either live quietly in the slums or dangerously elsewhere."[55]

In the United States the ability of the individual to earn a living is largely his or her responsibility. Federal, state, and municipal governments have, however, from time to time, enacted legislation to assure that black people would enjoy equal employment opportunities with other Americans. The first of these attempts was an executive order banning discrimination in war industries, government training programs, and government industries. It was issued by the president in 1941, after blacks threatened a massive march on Washington to protest discrimination in the national defense program. Since that time many federal, state, and municipal laws—most recently the Civil Rights Act of 1964—ostensibly forbade racial discrimination in employment. Nevertheless, discrimination against blacks continues. Because of acts of discrimination, it is frequently difficult for black males to fulfill their potentials as husbands and fathers. They are literally the last to be hired and the first to be fired.

Discrimination exists not only in securing employment but also in the type of employment to which black Americans are relegated. (See chapter 4.) Because of discrimination against them in employment, the median income of black families in 1985 was only slightly more than one-half the white median family income. In the same occupational category and with comparable experience, black people can expect to earn anywhere from one-half to nine-tenths of what their white counterparts earn.[56] Some of the differential in income may be attributed to lack of training on the part of blacks, but the major factor accounting for these differentials is discrimination in employment.[57]

Discrimination in securing employment continues on a wide scale. It is most clearly reflected in differential rates of unemployment for black and white workers, and it is one of the most cruel forms of discrimination. At no time between 1954 and 1985 was the unemployment rate for black workers less than twice the rate of white unemployment.[58] Some black unemployment must be attributed to structural changes in the economy, and black workers are likely to be less well trained than white workers, but high rates of black unemployment exist for black workers *at all levels of skill.* That is, black professional workers are just as likely to have significantly higher rates of unemployment than white professionals as are black unskilled workers compared to white unskilled workers. Furthermore, blacks are likely to be unemployed for longer periods than their unemployed white counterparts.

All types of economic discrimination against black citizens are rooted in the tradition of economic exploitation, dating back to the slave era. Since it is no longer possible for white Americans to own blacks as property, it is through discriminatory practices that the exploitation of black workers is maintained. Since such practices have become institutionalized throughout the years, the prospects for black workers are not promising.

Overt discrimination in education is prevalent throughout the United States. The major factor affecting the quality of education for blacks outside the South is *de facto* segregation of public schools, which results in the overwhelming majority of black pupils attending schools which are either totally black or predominantly black. *De facto* segregation in public schools, of course, results from residential discrimination in most cases. As late as 1980 more than 65 percent of all blacks in public schools in the United States attended schools that were more than 50 percent black in enrollment.[59] The pupils of these all-black or predominantly black schools are denied equality of educational opportunity. In virtually every school district, South and non-South, where the schools are racially segregated, facilities for black pupils are inferior—there are more pupils per teacher, the buildings are older, and the schools are less well equipped.[60]

In the South in recent years public school desegregation has proceeded at a faster rate than outside that region. As of 1980, 17.7 percent of all black pupils attended schools that were 99 to 100 percent minority. In the South the percentage was 14, in the Northeast it was 27.1, in the Midwest 28, and in the West 10 percent.[61] Even as the federal government pressed southern school boards to comply with the Supreme Court decision of 1954, and the Civil Rights Act of 1964, the northern pattern of de facto segregation continues, because of the exodus of white families to the suburbs. And it seems likely that the practice of differential facilities in schools attended primarily by blacks will continue.

Discrimination in the administration of justice, at all levels, is as characteristically American as any other aspect of the culture. (See chapter 6.) Probably the most prevalent form of discrimination in the administration of justice is police misconduct, which often takes the form of excessive use of force, sometimes culminating in the death of blacks. Such police misconduct has been the stimulus for riots and uprisings in American cities. Within the context of American society the conviction of police officers for acts of brutality is rare. It is somehow felt that violence committed by law-enforcement officials is invariable justified.

In the South law-enforcement officials are known to have cooperated with other racists in committing acts of violence against black people and their sympathizers.[62] In Neshoba County, Mississippi, the county sheriff, his deputy, and a policeman were among the twenty-one persons charged by the Federal Bureau of Investigation with the murder of three civil rights workers in June 1964. The U.S. Commission on Civil Rights listed various forms of police misconduct in Birmingham, Alabama; Cairo, Illinois; Baton Rouge, Louisiana; Jackson, Mississippi; and Memphis, Tennessee—all cities it which blacks had held civil rights demonstrations in 1963. Police officials acted to curb the rights of citizens to speak freely, assemble peaceably, and petition the government for redress of grievances.[63]

Police misconduct is not limited to the South. As more and more black people settle in the centers of large cities, relations with police officials are being increasingly strained. Black sections of cities are patrolled by an increasingly hostile police force. Their attitudes and behavior are closer to that of occupying forces than public servants who are responsible to the citizens in these communities.[64] Acts of police misconduct toward black people were responsible for several of the outbreaks of violence which became characteristic urban summer phenomena.

Discrimination in the administration of justice is not limited to police misconduct. It is characteristic of law enforcement in general. Such a situation has led many blacks to manifest little respect for the legal system of the United States. One civil rights leader issued a statement which contained the following:

> I am charged with inciting black people to commit an offense by way of protest against the law, a law which neither I nor any of my people have any say in preparing. . . .
> I consider myself neither morally nor legally bound to obey laws made by a body in which I have no representation. That the will of people is the basis of the authority of government is a principle universally acknowledged as sacred throughout the civilized world and constitutes a basic foundation of this country. It should be equally understandable that we, as black people, would adopt the attitude that we are neither morally nor legally bound to obey laws made without our consent and which seek to oppress us.[65]

Outside the South, where approximately one-half the black people in the United States live, there is little, if any, discrimination against blacks in voting. Within the South, however, such discrimination is widespread. (See chapter 5.) After several unsuccessful attempts to curb discrimination against blacks attempting to vote, Congress passed the Civil Rights Act of 1964, the first title of which concerned black voting rights. Again in 1965 Congress passed a voting rights law specifically designed to ensure the franchise to blacks. The enforcement of these laws has not yet assured blacks in the Deep South that they can exercise their voting rights, but increasingly large numbers have voted in recent elections. Nevertheless, various extralegal measures perpetuate discriminatory practices in voting.

CIVIC ASSIMILATION

There appears to be a growing conflict between black and white persons concerning some fundamental "value and power" interests in the United States. Although such conflicts are not new, only in recent years have they manifested themselves openly. Inasmuch as blacks share the same religion and other basic culture elements with the majority of white Americans, there are fewer conflicts than is the case with some other minority groups. Nevertheless, blacks constitute one of the groups which has shared less than equally in the basic rewards of society, both in goods and services. They have faced discrimination in every aspect of American life, and today they are overrepresented among the country's poor. The result of such a set of circumstances has led to serious questions about the professed cultural values of society.

The major civic conflicts between black and white Americans appear to be in two areas: (1) the disproportionate distribution of power in society, and (2) the lack of responsibility on the part of government toward citizens. The former was clearly evident in the Black Power movement and the latter in such organizations as Mothers for Adequate Welfare, the National Welfare Rights Organization, the Poor People's Campaign, and the New York Citywide Coordinating Committee of Welfare Recipients, a coalition of welfare-action groups in New York City.

The Black Power movement first gained prominence in the spring of 1966. It was a direct result of the almost total lack of control by black people of the institutions and agencies which are responsible to them. As Stokely Carmichael, the man most responsible for the interest in Black Power, viewed the concept, it referred to political, economic, and judicial control, by black people, in areas where they were in a majority. In areas where they were in a minority, it referred to a sharing of control. "It means the creation of power bases from which black people can work to change statewide and nationwide patterns of oppression through pressure from strength—instead of weakness."[66] In other words, Black Power means that blacks, like other minorities, should organize themselves into power blocs, a fundamental aspect of the pluralist pressure group process in American society.

Black Americans have always been, and continue to be, overrepresented among the nation's poor. They frequently find it impossible to secure employment during periods of general economic prosperity. When such a situation results, they are forced to partake in a dehumanizing system of social welfare whose meager allowances are provided grudgingly. They have organized to demand welfare payments adequate for a minimal standard of living. For example, in New York City thousands of welfare recipients filed claims for welfare funds which they maintained the city owed them for such necessities as winter coats and beds.[67] Such a development in the United States represented the first time that a group of Americans demanded a satisfactory standard of living *as a right.*

The Freedom Budget prepared by the A. Philip Randolph Institute had as its aim the achievement of freedom from want by 1975. The basic objectives included restoring full employment, assuring adequate income for those employed, guaranteeing maximum adequate level of income for those who could not or should not be employed, providing a decent home for all Americans, and providing medical care and educational opportunity for all.[68] It was assumed by the authors of this report that the federal government should take primary responsibility for achieving these objectives.

In May 1968 the Southern Christian Leadership Conference (SCLC) organized the Poor People's Campaign. The idea for campaign originated with the late Martin Luther King, Jr., founder and past president of this organization. It was led by Ralph David Abernathy, his succesor as president of SCLC. The objective of the Poor People's Campaign was to demonstrate the plight of America's poor and to demand government reforms necessary to eradicate poverty and racism in the United States. Several demands were made to government officials at all levels. These include the expansion of federal manpower programs to provide one million new jobs a year, the establishment of a guaranteed minimum income, the construction of millions of new low-rent housing units, the liberalizing of the surplus foods program, the repeal of punitive welfare legislation, and other benefits in education, health care, and human rights.

To dramatize its demands, the Poor People's Campaign erected a shantytown on the mall at the Lincoln Memorial in Washington D.C., to house the thousands of poor people—American Indians, blacks, Mexican Americans, Puerto Ricans, white people—who had made the trip to Washington from all parts of the country, traveling by bus, foot, mule, train, and private automobile. Others were housed in local churches and schools.

The Poor People's Campaign was organized on the assumptions that poverty, illiteracy, disease, and destitution are unnecessary in the United States at the present time and that it is the responsibility of the government to establish a satisfactory standard of living for all of its citizens.

In general, there appears to be a growing awareness among black people in the United States that responsibilities between citizens and government are reciprocal. That is, the government has the right to make certain demands on citizens, and citizens have similar right to make certain demands on their government. Throughout most of American history the former idea has been accepted, but the latter has not.

Although it must be said that, at the present time, there are few areas of value or power conflict between black and white Americans, there are some crucial conflicts, and in all likelihood these conflicts will intensify as demands are made by black people for greater sharing in society. As the conflicts intensify, their resolution is likely to become more difficult.

●   ●   ●

From the preceding analysis one must conclude that among black people, assimilation has not been accomplished in most aspects of American life. Blacks are to some extent acculturated, for they share the culture of the larger society. However, there is minimal structural, marital, and identificational assimilation. They continue to experience widespread prejudice and discrimination; therefore, in terms of attitude-receptional and behavior-receptional assimilation, they lag behind many other minorities. On the civic assimilation variable, the process is uneven. Few conflicts exist at present, but where there is conflict, it is fundamental, and the likelihood is that these conflicts will increase.

The prospects for the complete assimilation of black people into American life are extremely grim. Perhaps the single most important impediment to this process is the extent to which racism has become institutionalized in American life. White Americans refuse to accept black people as equals. Black Americans, on the other hand, have endeavored through the years to achieve assimilation into the large society through peaceful legal means. They have been constantly rebuffed. This is in large measure a function of racial privilege. White Americans resist the assimilation of blacks because this would jeopardize the privileges that they enjoy at the expense of black people. Consequently a small but growing number of black people are now questioning the desirability of total assimilation. Thus it seems fair to say that the likelihood of complete assimilation is indeed remote.

SELECTED BIBLIOGRAPHY

BETTELHEIM, BRUNO, and MORRIS JANOWITZ, *Social Change and Prejudice.* New York: Free Press, 1964.

BLAUNER, ROBERT. *Racial Oppression in America.* New York: Harper & Row, Publishers, 1972.

BRINK, WILLIAM, and LOUIS HARRIS, *Black and White.* New York: Simon & Schuster, 1967.

———. *The Negro Revolution in America.* New York: Simon & Schuster, 1964.

CAMPBELL, ANGUS. *White Attitudes toward Black People.* Ann Arbor, Mich.: Institute for Social Research, 1971.

CLARK, KENNETH B. *Dark Ghetto.* New York: Harper & Row, Publishers, 1965.

CONOT, ROBERT. *Rivers of Blood, Years of Darkness.* New York: Bantam Books, 1967.

COX, OLIVER C. *Caste, Class and Race.* Garden City, N.Y.: Doubleday & Co., 1948.

DAVIS, ALLISON, BURLEIGH GARDNER, and MARY GARDNER. *Deep South.* Chicago: University of Chicago Press, 1937.

DILLARD, J. L. *Black English: Its History and Usage in the United States.* New York: Random House, 1972.

DOLLARD, JOHN. *Caste and Class in a Southern Town.* New Haven, Conn.: Yale University Press, 1937.

DRAKE, ST. CLAIR, and HORACE CAYTON. *Black Metropolis.* New York: Harcourt, Brace & Co., 1945.

FRAZIER, E. FRANKLIN. *Black Bourgeoisie.* Glencoe, Ill.: Free Press, 1957.

———. *The Negro in the United States.* New York: Macmillan Co., 1957.

A Freedom Budget For All Americans. New York: A. Philip Randolph Institute, 1966.

GOLDSTEIN, RHODA L., ed. *Black Life and Culture in the United States.* New York: Thomas Y. Crowell & Co., 1971.

GORDON, ALBERT I. *Intermarriage: Interfaith, Interracial, Interethnic.* Boston: Beacon Press, 1964.

GORDON, MILTON M. *Assimilation in American Life.* New York: Oxford University Press, 1964.

GREENBERG, JACK, *Race Relations and American Law.* New York: Columbia University Press, 1959.

HANNERZ, ULF. *Soulside: Inquiries Into Ghetto Culture and Community.* New York: Columbia University Press, 1969.

HERSKOVITS, MELVILLE J. *The Myth of the Negro Past.* New York: Harper & Brothers, 1941.

KNOWLES, LOUIS L., and KENNETH PREWITT. *Institutional Racism in America.* Englewood Cliffs, N.J.: Prentice-Hall, 1969.

LAURENTI, LUIGI. *Property Values and Race: Studies in Seven Cities.* Berkeley: University of California Press, 1960.

LEWIS, HYLAN. *Blackways of Kent.* Chapel Hill: University of North Carolina Press, 1955.

LIEBOW, ELLIOT. *Tally's Corner: A Study of Negro Streetcorner Men.* Boston: Little, Brown and Co., 1967.

McENTIRE, DAVIS. *Residence and Race.* Berkeley: University of California Press, 1960.

MARX, GARY. *Protest and Prejudice.* New York: Harper & Row, Publishers, 1969.

MENDELSON, WALLACE. *Discrimination.* Englewood Cliffs, N.J.: Prentice-Hall, 1962.

MYRDAL, GUNNAR. *An American Dilemma: The Negro Problem and Modern Democracy.* New York: Harper & Brothers, 1944.

NORTHWOOD, L.K., and ERNEST BARTH. *Urban Desegregation.* Seattle: Unversity of Washington Press, 1965.

POWDERMAKER, HORTENSE. *After Freedom.* New York: Viking Press, 1939.

Report of the National Advisory Commission on Civil Disorders. New York: Bantam Books, 1968.

SILVER, JAMES W. *Mississippi: The Closed Society.* New York: Harcourt, Brace & World, 1964.

SUTHERLAND, ELIZABETH, ed. *Letters From Mississippi.* New York: McGraw-Hill Book Co., 1965.

TAEUBER, KARL, and ALMA Taeuber. *Negroes in Cities.* Chicago: Aldine Publishing Co., 1965.

U.S. Department of Health, Education, and Welfare, Office of Education. *Equality of Educational Opportunity.* Washington, D.C.: Government Printing Office, 1966.

WHITTEN, NORMAN E., and JOHN F. SZWED. eds. *Afro-American Anthropology: Contemporary Perspectives.* New York: Free Press, 1970.

WILLIAMS, ROBIN M., JR. *Strangers Next Door: Ethnic Relations in American Communities.* Englewood Cliffs, N.J.: Prentice-Hall, 1964.

WOOODWARD, C. VANN. *The Strange Career of Jim Crow.* New York: Oxford University Press, 1957.

NOTES

[1]Milton M. Gordon, *Assimilation in American Life* (New York: Oxford University Press, 1964), chap. 3.

[2]Ibid., p. 71.

[3]See also E. Franklin Frazier, *The Negro in the United States* (New York: Macmillan, 1957), chap. 1.

[4]See Melville J. Herskovits, *The Myth of the Negro Past* (New York: Harper, 1941); Frazier, *Negro in the United States,* pp. 14–19.

[5]Kenneth M. Stampp, *The Peculiar Institution* (New York: Knopf, 1956), p. 377.

[6]See Edmund D. Cronon, *Black Moses* (Madison: University of Wisconsin Press, 1964).

[7]See E. U. Essien-Udom, *Black Nationalism* (Chicago: University of Chicago Press, 1962); C. Eric Lincoln, *The Black Muslims in America* (Boston: Beacon Press, 1961).

[8]Gordon, *Assimilation in American Life,* p. 76.

[9]See, for example, E. Franklin Frazier, *Black Bourgeoisie* (Glencoe, Ill.: Free Press, 1957).

[10]Robert Blauner, "Black Culture: Myth or Reality?" in *Afro-American Anthropology: Contemporary Perspectives,* ed. Norman E. Whitten, Jr., and John F. Szwed (New York: Free Press, 1970), pp. 347–66.

[11]See J. L. Dillard, *Black English: Its History and Usage in the United States* (New York: Random House, 1972); Rhoda L. Goldstein, ed., *Black Life and Culture in the United States* (New York: Crowell, 1971); Ulf Hannerz, *Soulside: Inquiries Into Ghetto Culture and Community* (New York: Columbia University Press, 1969); Whitten and Szwed, *Afro-American Anthropology.*

[12]Gunnar Myrdal, *An American Dilemma* (New York: Harper, 1944), p. 60.

[13]See, for example, Allison Davis, Burleigh Gardner, and Mary Gardner, *Deep South* (Chicago: University of Chicago Press, 1940); John Dollard, *Caste and Class in a Southern Town* (New Haven, Conn.: Yale University Press, 1937); Hylan Lewis, *Blackways of Kent* (Chapel Hill: University of North Carolina Press, 1955); Hortense Powdermaker, *After Freedom* (New York: Viking, 1939).

[14]Robert B. Johnson, "Negro Reactions to Minority Group Status," in *American Minorities,* ed. Milton L. Barron (New York: Knopf, 1957), pp. 192–212; Robin M. Williams, Jr., *Strangers Next Door* (Englewood Cliffs, N.J.: Prentice-Hall, 1964), pp. 235–43.

[15]Frank F. Lee, "Race Relations Pattern in a Small Town," *American Sociological Review* 19 (1954), 138–43.

[16]St. Claire Drake and Horace Cayton, *Black Metropolis* (New York: Harcourt, Brace, 1945); Kenneth B. Clark, *Dark Ghetto* (New York: Harper & Row, 1965). Research conducted

in a suburban community thirteen miles from Detroit, Michigan, indicates that this pattern holds there. See Stanley Weiss, "The Contextual Effect: A Mosaic of Social Class Phenomena as Reflected through Subcultural Life within a Bi-Racial Metropolitan Community," Seminar on the Metropolitan Community (University of Michigan, 1966).

[17]See E. Franklin Frazier, "The Negro Middle Class and Desegregation," *Social Problems* 4 (April 1957), 291–301; Donald L. Noel, "Minority Responses to Intergroup Situations," (department of sociology, Ohio State University).

[18]See Brewton Berry, *Race and Ethnic Relations* (Boston: Houghton Mifflin, 1958), p. 250.

[19]Louis Lomax, "Interracial Marriage—An American Dilemma," *Pageant*, November 1957, p. 6.

[20]Albert I. Gordon, *Intermarriage: Interfaith, Interracial, Interethnic* (Boston: Beacon Press, 1964), p. 2.

[21]*Statistical Abstract 1985*, p. 38.

[22]Gordon, *Intermarriage*, p. 267.

[23]John H. Burma, "Research Note on the Measurement of Interracial Marriage," *American Journal of Sociology* 57 (1952), 587–89.

[24]Gordon, *Intermarriage*, p. 265.

[25]Ibid., p. 267.

[26]Helen Schaffer, "Mixed Marriage," *Editorial Research Reports*, vol. 1, May 1961.

[27]William Brink and Louis Harris, *The Negro Revolution in America* (New York: Simon & Schuster, 1964), p. 61.

[28]William Brink and Louis Harris, *Black and White* (New York: Simon & Schuster, 1967), p. 54.

[29]*Report of the National Advisory Commission on Civil Disorders* (New York: Bantam, 1968), p. 135.

[30]Williams, *Strangers Next Door*, p. 246.

[31]See Seymour Parker and Robert Kleiner, "Status Position, Mobility, and Ethnic Identification of the Negro," *Journal of Social Issues* 20 (April 1964), 85–102.

[32]Johnson, pp. 192–212.

[33]Harris Survey, 1985.

[34]See Paul B. Sheatsley, "White Attitudes toward the Negro," in *The Negro American*, ed. Talcott Parsons and Kenneth B. Clark (Boston: Houghton Mifflin, 1966), pp. 303–24.

[35]Emory S. Bogardus, *Immigration and Race Attitudes* (Boston: Heath, 1928), p. 25.

[36]Brink and Harris, *Negro Revolution in America*, p. 148.

[37]Donald L. Noel and Alphonso Pinkney, "Correlates of Prejudice: Some Racial Differences and Similarities," *American Journal of Sociology* 69 (1964), 610; see also Alphonso Pinkney, "The Anatomy of Prejudice" (Ph.D. thesis, Cornell University, 1961), chap. 3.

[38]Bruno Bettelheim and Morris Janowitz, *Social Change and Prejudice* (New York: Free Press, 1964), p. 130.

[39]Brink and Harris, *Black and White*, p. 136.

[40]Williams, *Strangers Next Door*, chap. 4.

[41]Sheatsley, "White Attitudes toward the Negro," pp. 305–8.

[42]Andrew M. Greeley and Paul B. Sheatsley, "Attitudes toward Racial Integration," *Scientific American*, (December 1971), pp. 13–19.

[43]*New York Times*, November 19, 1971, p. 57.

[44]Angus Campbell, *White Attitudes toward Black People* (Ann Arbor, Mich.: Institute for Social Research, 1971), chap. 7.

[45]In addition to the studies cited above, other studies include the following: Reva W. Allman, "A Study of the Social Attitudes of College Students," *Journal of Social Psychology* 53 (1961), 33–51; Herbert Hyman and Paul B. Sheatsley, "Attitudes toward Desegregation," *Scientific American* (July 1964), pp. 16–23; Russell Middleton, "Ethnic Prejudice and Susceptibility to Persuasion," *American Sociological Review* 25 (1960), 679–86; Harold A. Nelson, "Expressed and Unexpressed Prejudices Against Ethnic Groups in a College Community," *Journal of Negro Education* 31 (1962), 125–31; Thomas F. Pettigrew, "Regional Differences in Anti-Negro Prejudice," *Journal of Abnormal and Social Psychology* 59 (1959), 28–36; Alphonso Pinkney, "Prejudice toward Mexican and Negro Americans: A Comparison," *Phylon* 24 (1963), 353–59.

[46]Harris Survey, p. 3.

[47]See Wallace Mendelson, *Discrimination* (Englewood Cliffs, N.J.: Prentice-Hall, 1962).

[48]See C. Vann Woodward, *The Strange Career of Jim Crow* (New York: Oxford University Press, 1957), p. 103.

[49]Eunice Grier and George Grier, "Equality and Beyond: Housing Segregation in the Great Society," in *The Negro American,* ed. Parsons and Clark, pp. 525–54; Davis McEntire, *Residence and Race* (Berkeley: University of California Press, 1960); L. K. Northwood and Ernest A. T. Barth, *Urban Desegregation* (Seattle: University of Washington Press, 1965).

[50]Richard Bardolph, *The Negro Vanguard* (New York: Vintage Books, 1961), pp. 286–88. Copyright holder: Holt, Rinehart & Winston, Inc.

[51]Karl E. Taeuber and Alma F. Taeuber, *Negroes in Cities* (Chicago: Aldine, 1965).

[52]U.S. Commission on Civil Rights, *Civil Rights '63: 1963 Report of the United States Commission on Civil Rights* (Washington, D.C.: Government Printing Office, 1963), p. 99.

[53]*New York Times,* September 17, 1967, p. 4E.

[54]Cited in Charles Abrams, "The Housing Problem and the Negro," in *The Negro American,* ed. Parsons and Clark, p. 519. This act was subsequently voided by the U.S. Supreme Court.

[55]Alan Paton, "The Negro in America Today," *Collier's,* October 29, 1954, p. 70.

[56]U.S. Bureau of the Census, *The Social and Economic Status of the Black Population in the United States, 1972* (Washington, D.C.: Government Printing Office, 1973), pp. 17–26.

[57]See Ralph Turner, "Foci of Discrimination in the Employment of Non-Whites," *American Journal of Sociology* 58 (November 1952), 247–56; Rashi Fein, "An Economic and Social Profile of the Negro American," in *Negro American,* ed. Parsons and Clark, p. 120.

[58]*Statistical Abstract 1985,* p. 447.

[59]*Statistical Abstract 1985,* p. 139.

[60]U.S. Department of Health, Education, and Welfare, Office of Education, *Equality of Educational Opportunity* (Washington, D.C.: Government Printing Office, 1966), p. 3.

[61]*Statistical Abstract 1985,* p. 139.

[62]Mendelson, *Discrimination,* chap. 5; James W. Silver, *Mississippi: The Closed Society* (New York: Harcourt, Brace & World, 1964); Elizabeth Sutherland, *Letters from Mississippi* (New York: McGraw-Hill, 1965); Howard Zinn, *SNCC: The New Abolitionists* (Boston: Beacon Press, 1964).

[63]U.S. Commission on Civil Rights, *Civil Rights '63,* pp. 107–25.

[64]See Robert Conot, *Rivers of Blood, Years of Darkness* (New York: Bantam, 1967); Tom Hayden, *Rebellion in Newark* (New York: Random House, 1967); Mendelson, *Discrimination,* chap. 5.

[65]This statement, issued by H. Rap Brown, chairman of the Student Nonviolent Coordinating Committee, is quoted in Staughton Lynd, "A Radical Speaks in Defense of S.N.C.C.," *New York Times Magazine,* September 10, 1967, p. 148.

[66]Stokely Carmichael, "What We Want," *New York Review of Books,* September 22, 1966, p. 5.

[67]*New York Times,* October 3, 1963, p. 1.

[68]*A Freedom Budget for All Americans* (New York: A. Philip Randolph Institute, 1966), pp. 2–3.

CHAPTER EIGHT
THE BLACK REVOLT
AND ITS CONSEQUENCES

The post-World War II era has been a period of rapid change in the United States and in the world. Although changes affecting the status of black Americans have been neither rapid nor widespread, they have occurred and they have generated greater expectations. The resistance of white Americans to change has made blacks apprehensive about the willingness of society to accord them treatment equal to what its white citizens receive. The caution with which public officials have moved to make amends for what are rather widely regarded as past injustices has created greater black militancy. The depth of antiblack sentiment in society has frequently been indicated by the negative response of white Americans to increased black militancy. Because white Americans insist upon determining the pace with which changes in race relations occur, a crisis has resulted. Blacks have learned from experience that positive changes affecting their status are more likely to result from political pressures than from altruism. In the mid-1950s it appeared that increased civil rights for blacks might become one of the major tasks to which American society might address itself for the first time in a century.

BEGINNINGS OF THE REVOLT: BLACK PERSISTENCE
AND WHITE RESISTANCE

The Supreme Court decision of May 1954 was welcomed by black Americans and their white supporters, who felt that somehow this act might signal the beginning of a new era in the relations between black and white

Americans. The decision outlawing segregation in public education had been expected, and black Americans felt that it would afford white Americans, especially those in the South, the opportunity to share in the worldwide movement for greater human rights. White southerners responded to the desegregation ruling not with feelings of relief, but with the establishment, during the summer, of White Citizens' Councils, which had as their primary function massive resistance to the ruling of the Supreme Court. Since the Supreme Court did not indicate how its ruling was to be implemented, school districts which had either required or permitted segregation reopened in September on a segregated basis (except those in Washington, D.C., and Baltimore, Maryland, where attempts were made to comply with the ruling of the Court). Throughout the South plans were made to do whatever became necessary to maintain the long-standing practice of racial segregation in schools. Statements by public officials in that region (governors, senators, representatives) supported the notion of massive resistance.

When the Supreme Court finally issued its implementation decree—that desegregation in public education should proceed "with all deliberate speed"—in May 1955, the forces opposing integration in public education had already organized themselves throughout the South.[1] Southerners were determined to maintain separate schools for black and white pupils, regardless of the ruling of the Supreme Court. The extent of their opposition came as a surprise to blacks and their white supporters. It appeared that their hopes for a new era in race relations would not materialize. If a ruling of the highest court in the country could be met with such contempt by those responsible for maintaining the constitutional rights of citizens, how could black people ever expect to be accorded rights equal to those of white Americans?

Signs of growing unrest were evident among black Americans. African colonies were demanding and receiving independence from European colonial powers, and it appeared that all of Africa would achieve political freedom before black people in the United States would be able to assert the fundamental rights of service in places of public accommodation or attendance at schools supported by taxes imposed on them. Later in the summer of 1955, Emmett Till, a 14-year-old black boy from Chicago, visiting in Money, Mississippi, was kidnapped and lynched. He was accused of having whistled at a white woman, and, characteristically, those responsible for his murder were never apprehended. Feelings of disillusionment were widespread in black communities.

On December 1, 1955, a black seamstress, Rosa Parks, boarded a public bus in Montgomery, Alabama. She took a seat in the section set aside for blacks. Shortly thereafter she was ordered to vacate her seat so a white man could occupy it. She refused and was arrested. When word of the arrest spread through the black community, the Montgomery Bus

Boycott was organized.[2] The bus boycott lasted for more than a year, ending in December 1956, when the Supreme Court upheld a lower-court ruling outlawing racial segregation on buses in Montgomery.

This massive demonstration of solidarity among blacks in opposition to long-standing practices of segregation and discrimination can be considered the first major act of resistance by blacks in modern times and signaled the birth of what might be called the black revolt.[3] The story of the Montgomery Bus Boycott spread throughout black communities in the United States and served as an impetus for similar acts in other cities. Tallahassee, Florida, and Birmingham, Alabama, followed with bus boycotts. Nonviolent resistance to what was considered an "evil" system composed of "unjust" laws became the official means of dealing with the caste system of the South. The philosophy of nonviolence, according to its principal spokesman, contains the following elements: (1) active resistance to "evil," (2) attempts to win one's opponent through understanding, (3) directing one's attack against forces of "evil" rather than against persons performing such acts, (4) willingness to accept suffering, without retaliation, (5) refusal to hate one's opponent, and (6) the conviction that the universe is on the side of justice.[4]

As the nonviolent resistance movement spread, massive opposition to social change in the realm of race relations was intensified by white southerners. One hundred southern members of Congress signed the Southern Manifesto, opposing the Supreme Court decision of 1954. They vowed "to use all lawful means to bring about a reversal of this decision which is contrary to the Constitution." Accordingly, laws implementing massive resistance to desegregation were enacted in Alabama, Georgia, Louisiana, Mississippi, South Carolina, and Virginia. While the Southern Manifesto did not explicitly call for the use of violence as a means of preventing black pupils from attending schools with white pupils, its impact generated violence.

A federal court ordered officials at the University of Alabama to admit a black student in February 1956. Her appearance on campus was met by mob violence from white students and others who were determined to maintain an all-white student enrollment.[5] She was removed from campus when the rioting flared and was forced to sue for readmission. The university officials responded with permanent expulsion on the grounds that she had made unfair statements about the University of Alabama.

On the elementary- and secondary-school levels violence became the accepted means of preventing desegregation. In September 1956 a mob prevented black pupils from enrolling at the public high school in Mansfield, Texas. Mobs demonstrated against school integration in Clinton, Tennessee, and in Sturgis and Clay, Kentucky. In the latter cases it became necessary to deploy the National Guard to protect the black pupils.

In the following years, when black parents attempted to enroll their children in schools with previously all-white enrollments, they were met with acts of violence, frequently directed at them by white women. One of the more highly publicized of these events occurred at Central High School in Little Rock, Arkansas, in 1957.[6] The courts had approved a desegregation plan, submitted by the Little Rock School Board, calling for the gradual desegregation of public schools beginning with the admission of nine black students to Central High School. The evening before they were scheduled to enroll, the governor announced that he would dispatch the National Guard to the school because of the possibility of violence. When the first black pupil appeared two days later, she was met by thousands of jeering white citizens, who barred her from entering the building and by 270 National Guardsmen. Weeks later the National Guardsmen were withdrawn; nine black pupils entered the school, but local citizens forced them to withdraw. Mob violence in Little Rock continued to keep the black pupils from entering the school until the president ordered 1000 paratroopers to Little Rock and federalized 10,000 members of the Arkansas National Guard to ensure their enrollment. This action represented the first time since Reconstruction that federal troops had been sent into the South to protect the rights of black people. Finally, on September 25, the nine black students entered Central High School. Federal troops remained at Central High School throughout the school year. At the beginning of the following school year the governor of Arkansas ordered all high schools in the city closed for the school year 1958–59. This was ostensibly done to prevent "impending violence and disorder." When the schools finally reopened in 1959, black pupils enrolled in both Central High School and another high school, which had previously maintained a policy of admitting only white pupils.

Little Rock was not alone in its policy of massive resistance to integration through the closing of public schools. When desegregation was ordered for the Virginia cities of Norfolk, Charlottesville, and Front Royal, the governor responded by closing the schools involved. In Prince Edward County, Virginia, resistance to desegregation was so strong that the county's public schools were closed from 1959 to 1964.

In the years immediately following 1954, little desegregation of public schools was accomplished. Every September, at the beginning of the school year, one could expect the news wires to carry stories of violence directed toward black pupils. These pupils were frequently required to walk through racist mobs to get to class, and, once in the classroom, they experienced a variety of insults and physical abuse from younger racists.[7]

On the college level desegregation was not achieved without violence. At both the University of Mississippi and the University of Alabama the admittance of blacks triggered violence from white students. In fact, the admission of one black student to the University of Mississippi in 1962 triggered violence which ended in two deaths and one hundred injuries. It was finally necessary to station 12,000 federal troops on the campus to assure the attendance of this student in classes. Federalized National Guardsmen were required to escort two black students to classes at the University of Alabama in 1963.

THE CIVIL RIGHTS MOVEMENT

By 1960 desegregation of public education was proceeding at a slow pace, and in the Deep South massive resistance remained an effective answer to the Supreme Court's ruling and to the demands of blacks. Feelings of despair over the school-segregation issue were widespread in the black community. The federal government assumed no responsibility for assuring enforcement of blacks' declared constitutional rights. The responsibility for desegregating schools rested with blacks themselves, and when they sought admission for their children to desegregated schools, it was frequently a long, costly, and complicated court procedure. Segregation and discrimination were still the social norms throughout the South, and all-white southern juries continued to refuse to convict white persons responsible for lynching black people.

In February 1960 four black college students in North Carolina sought service at a lunch counter in a five-and-dime store. When they were denied service, they remained seated. The manager ordered the lunch counter closed, but they remained seated, reading their textbooks. The news of their actions quickly spread throughout the country, and within a few days the "sit-in" movement had spread to fifteen cities in five southern states. Whenever a group of black people appeared at a lunch counter, a mob of southern whites appeared to heckle and jeer them. But the actions of the students inspired many others, black and white, to support them. Because of the determined resistance to desegregation of southern white persons and because of the strong determination of blacks for social change in race relations, thousands of white Americans joined forces with the blacks to give birth to the civil rights movement. Black college students organized the Student Nonviolent Coordinating Committee (SNCC) to coordinate activities aimed at desegregating places of public accommodation in the South. Peaceful demonstrations, led by college students, occurred in every major city where racial segregation was practiced openly. Thousands of blacks and their white supporters were jailed for violating local segregation laws. The lunch counter demonstrations were accompanied by nationwide economic boycotts of the stores which maintained practices of segregation. Within a period of one and a half years it is reported that at least 70,000 black and white persons participated in the sit-in movement. More than 3600 were arrested, and some 141 students and 58 faculty members were expelled by college authorities for their activities. Altogether, one or more establishments in each of 108 southern and border cities had been desegregated because of the sit-ins.[8]

The combined effects of these demonstrations and boycotts forced several of the larger chain stores to abandon practices of segregation in service and discrimination in employment. The example then spread to other areas: "wade-ins" were held at segregated public beaches, and "kneel-ins" were attempted in segregated churches. Always these demonstrators were peaceful, in keeping with the philosophy of nonviolent direct action. However, in virtually all cases there was violence from white persons determined to maintain white supremacy at all costs.

The Interstate Commerce Commission had ruled in 1955 that racial segregation of passengers in buses, waiting rooms, and travel coaches involved in interstate travel violated these passengers' constitutional rights. Nevertheless, individual bus drivers and local law-enforcement personnel continued to require blacks to sit separated from white passengers. In February 1961 the director of the Congress of Racial Equality (CORE) announced that members of the organization would test the effectiveness of this ruling by staging a series of "freedom rides" throughout the South. Other civil rights organizations joined this effort, and in May a group of black and white activists started their journey from Washington, D.C., to New Orleans, Louisiana. When the bus reached Anniston, Alabama, it was bombed and burned by a mob of local white persons, and the group of freedom riders was beaten. In Montgomery, Alabama, the presence of the freedom riders met with such hostility that it was necessary to dispatch four hundred U.S. marshals to keep order.

The freedom riders were jailed, beaten, or both in Alabama, Louisiana, and Mississippi. There were more than a dozen freedom rides in the South, and these rides combined the efforts of the four major civil rights organizations. In addition to CORE and SNCC, the National Association for the Advancement of Colored People (NAACP) and the Southern Christian Leadership Conference (SCLC) participated. The freedom rides involved more than one thousand persons, and the legal expenses they incurred exceeded $300,000.[9] As a result of these activities, the Interstate Commerce Commission issued an order outlawing segregation on all buses and in all terminal facilities.

The civil rights movement appealed to increasingly large numbers of white Americans. Demonstrations protesting all forms of segregation and discrimination were conducted throughout the United States, especially in the South. There were attacks on legally imposed segregation in the South and de facto segregation elsewhere and on discriminatory practices throughout the country. There were demonstrations at public libraries, swimming pools, public parks, and seats of municipal government throughout the Deep South and Border South. Discrimination against black people in voting became a special target for civil rights activists, based on the assumption that once armed with the franchise, blacks would be in a position to elect public officials sympathetic to their demands. The Civil Rights Act of 1960 provided for the appointment of federal voting referees to receive applications to qualify voters if it could be proved that a person had been denied the right to vote because of race. Throughout the South voter-registration schools were set up in churches. The response of many white southerners was characteristic of their resistance to change in existing practices. Black churches were bombed and burned. Churches had traditionally been exempt from the tyranny which southern blacks encountered daily, and now it appeared that they were not safe even in their houses of worship. Appeals to federal officials were in vain, and the reign of terror continued unabated. Arrests for these activities were rare, for local policemen often supported such activities. Black people and their white supporters remained nonviolent despite daily provocations and beatings.[10]

On occasion one city was selected to be a major target of civil rights demonstrations. SNCC selected Greenwood, Mississippi, as the site of its emancipation centennial campaign, in response to an attempt to assassinate one of its field workers. They organized a massive voter-registration campaign and were met by heavily armed policemen with police dogs. When they attempted to escort local Mississippi blacks to register to vote, they were attacked by the police and their dogs.[11] The late Martin Luther King, Jr., selected Birmingham, Alabama, as SCLC's major site of antisegregation demonstrations during the centennial year. Birmingham was one of the most rigidly segregated larger cities in the South, and it was felt that if segregation barriers there could be penetrated, it would make for less difficulty elsewhere. The demonstrators were met in Birmingham by a force of police and firefighters led by a well-known segregationist. Police and firefighters were ordered to use a variety of techniques to curb the demonstrations, including fire hoses, cattle prods, and police dogs. For several days the demonstrators met greater brutality from law-enforcement personnel than they had ever encountered previously, and the police and firefighters were supported in their acts by an injunction from a local judge prohibiting protest marches. When the demonstrators defied this injunction, hundreds of them were jailed. The constitutional right of citizens to petition peacefully for redress of grievances was violated, and the Department of Justice issued a statement that it was watching the situation but that it was powerless to act. It was decided by the leaders of the demonstrations that schoolchildren should participate along with adults. They, too, were met by police clubs, dogs, and fire hoses. The pictures of the repressive measures used by the police and firefighters alerted the nation and the world to the extremes which segregationists would resort to in order to maintain white supremacy.

A turning point was reached in Birmingham when following a meeting of the Ku Klux Klan, the home of the brother of the late Martin Luther King, Jr., and the motel which had served as King's headquarters and residence were bombed. Thousands of black demonstrators abandoned the philosophy of nonviolence and took to the streets with bottles and stones. They burned houses and stores and stoned police and passing cars. Before the uprising ended, they had burned a nine-block area of the city. When the demonstrators had requested federal protection from police dogs, fire hoses, and police clubs, the president had announced that no federal agency could act. However, when the blacks stoned white policemen and other citizens, federal troops were dispatched to Alabama within hours. Apparently the latter constituted acts of violence, while the former did not.

Demonstrations in many other southern and border cities followed those in Birmingham. Danville, Virginia, and Cambridge, Maryland, were among the most prominent. During the summer of 1963 some thirty-five homes and churches were bombed or burned, at least 10 people were killed, and more than 20,000 demonstrators were arrested. Thousands of others were shocked by cattle prods, set upon with high-pressure fire hoses, bitten by police dogs, and beaten by police. The summer demonstrations culminated in August, when 250,000 blacks and their white supporters participated in the March on Washington, the largest civil rights demonstration in history. As a direct outgrowth of these demonstrations Congress enacted the Civil Rights Act of 1964. The major provisions of this act are as follows: (1) sixth-grade education was established as a presumption of literacy for voting purposes; (2) segregation and discrimination in places of public accommodation were outlawed; (3) public facilities (parks, playgrounds, libraries, and so on) were desegregated; (4) the attorney general was authorized to file school-desegregation suits; (5) discrimination was outlawed in all federally assisted activities; (6) discrimination by employers or unions with one hundred or more employees or members was outlawed; (7) the attorney general was authorized to intervene in private suits in which persons alleged denial of equal protection of the laws under the Fourteenth Amendment.

The leaders of several civil rights organizations, after achieving the victory which this act signaled, decided to concentrate their activities on voter registration and education. They had been urged by the Department of Justice to concentrate on these activities instead of street demonstrations. Consequently, in 1964 the Mississippi Summer Project was organized. Thousands of black and white activists journeyed to Mississippi to engage in activities aimed at improving the status of that state's nearly one million blacks. They concentrated on voter education and registration and on "freedom schools."[12] The activists were subjected to a serious initial setback when three of their volunteers were abducted and murdered by a mob of local racists.[13] Throughout the summer they were subjected to a variety of harassments and abuse. The casualty list was high: by October 21 at least 3 persons had been killed, 80 were beaten, 3 were wounded by gunfire in 35 shootings, more than 35 churches were burned, 35 homes and other buildings were bombed, and more than 1000 persons had been arrested. In addition, several unsolved murders of local blacks were recorded.[14]

The Civil Rights Act of 1964 contained a provision ensuring blacks the right to vote in all elections. However, when they attempted to register, a variety of techniques, especially intimidation, kept them from exercising this right. Consequently, the major effort for 1965 was the campaign to ensure the right to vote. Resistance to black voting rights was strong. Several civil rights organizations decided to focus their attention on Alabama, which had been one of the most intransigent in this regard. Attempts to register blacks failed, and a march from Selma to Montgomery was planned to dramatize the plight of that state's black citizens. Thousands of black activists and their white suporters gathered in Selma for the march. Several attempts to march were thwarted by the police, under orders from a local sheriff. Acts of excessive use of force by police were widespread, and these acts motivated additional thousands of citizens, including many clergymen, from all over the United States to join the activists in Selma. The march finally materialized but not without violence. Two white activists and one black were killed and scores of others were injured.

The Selma-to-Montgomery march stimulated the Voting Rights Act of 1965, which made it possible for southern blacks to register and vote with little difficulty. It was also the last mass demonstration of the civil rights movement. During the years of peak activity the civil rights movement enlisted the support of thousands of Americans, both black and white. Its nonviolent, direct-action approach was responsible for many of the changes affecting the status of southern blacks. But its goals and methods were hardly applicable to the problems facing the many blacks in urban slums throughout the country. Thousands of blacks and their white supporters had combined for what was felt to be the most significant movement for social change in the United States.[15] The issues were clear, and although there were differences on means toward achieving the goals, a coalition of many groups had united to work for a common end: the eradication of segregation and discrimination in American life. To a significant degree they were successful in achieving greater civil rights for blacks, but black Americans remained basically an oppressed underclass of citizens.

DESPAIR IN THE SLUMS

By 1965 approximately half of all the blacks in the United States lived outside what is generally regarded as the South (see chapter 2), primarily in the slums of urban areas. For the most part, the lives of those in nonsouthern urban areas have not been affected by the gains of the civil rights movement. A majority (three-fifths) of those remaining in the South are also crowded into the slums of urban areas, and although their lives have in some ways been affected by the civil rights movement, they too suffer from the gap between promise and performance. A vast majority of blacks, then, live under conditions of hopelessness and despair. Little hope for change in their depressed status was apparent in 1965. At a time when the economy of the country was experiencing continued expansion, the median family income of black people was only slightly more than one-half (54 percent) of the median white family income. Eleven years after the Supreme Court outlawed segregation in public education, schools in the United States as a whole were more segregated than ever before. The unemployment rate for black people remained chronically high. Vast sums which had been allocated for public low-income housing had been diverted into middle-income housing which slum dwellers could not afford. At least thirty-six murders of civil rights workers in the South had been recorded, only three of which led to convictions, with no sentence of more than ten years' imprisonment.

Many of the millions of recent black migrants from the South are from farms. Mechanization of agriculture and racist terror forced them to leave the cotton fields. They packed their bags and boarded buses headed for New York City, Chicago, Detroit, Los Angeles, and other large cities. Many thought that these moves were into less hostile territory. Upon their arrival they were forced into slums in the centers of these cities. They arrived poorly educated and lacking in skills. They were in many ways similar to the great waves of European immigrants who entered the United States during the last decades of the nineteenth century and the first decades of the twentieth century. However, no provision was made to ease the transition for these migrants, as had been done for white European refugees. As one observer commented:

> Had Northern cities received hundreds of thousands of immigrants from Europe in the past few decades, no doubt all sorts of emergency provisions would have been made to help settle the newcomers, make them welcome, provide food, clothing, an shelter for them, and enable them to find work. Southern Negroes obtained no such courtesy, and what recognition they did get was calculated to remind them that white Americans may fight among themselves but in the clutch know how to stand together as a race.[16]

These migrants quickly learned that outside as well as within the South their place in the society had been clearly designated for them.

Federal measures ostensibly aimed at improving the standard of living for urban blacks have either been inadequate or have not been enacted by Congress. Many of the appropriations under the Economic Opportunity Act of 1964 never reached the persons they were designed to assist. In some cases as much as half the money in antipoverty programs was utilized for administrative purposes. The congressional elections of 1966 saw conservatives elected in many states, and the administration virtually abandoned many of its civil rights proposals in response to what was interpreted as an upsurge of antiblack feeling among the electorate. Several cities had experienced violent black demonstrations in 1964 and 1965, and conservatives seeking public office based much of their campaign on curbing "crime in the streets" (i.e., black uprisings.). In such a climate either proposed legislation was defeated (e.g., the rat-control bill) or the requested appropriation was significantly reduced (e.g., the model-cities bill). In the end, politics took precedence over the welfare of poor people, a significant proportion of whom are black.

The powerlessness of black Americans is clear. The communities in which they live are not significantly different from colonial territories in the underdeveloped world. They have no control over the institutions in their communities which are technically responsible to them. Virtually all black communities are among the major depressed areas in the country. The chief support for the communities comes from outside sources; the economy is dominated by people who do not and would not live in the communities. The inadequately maintained houses are often owned by affluent (and often politically powerful) suburban residents. The schools are staffed and controlled by outsiders. Law and order are maintained by suspicious and frightened police, who frequently resort to the excessive use of force on the slightest provocation. When these residents are able to secure employment, they provide a cheap labor supply for the white community. Yet they are forced to pay prices far in excess of those paid by affluent suburban citizens for inferior products available in stores in slum neighborhoods. In many ways, then, the black community in the 1960s represented what might be called a form of internal colonialism. As one social scientist has written: "The dark ghetto's invisible walls have been erected by the white society, by those who have power, both to confine those who have *no* power and to perpetuate their powerlessness. The dark ghettos are social, political, and—above all—economic colonies. Their inhabitants are subject peoples, victims of the greed, cruelty, insensitivity, guilt, and fear of their masters."[17] Most white citizens are unaware of the conditions in these communities until the residents, as a result of their feelings of hopelessness and despair, rebel against conditions through what have come to be traditional summer uprisings.

One of the most articulate and perceptive leaders to address himself to the millions of poor blacks in the slums was Malcolm X. He was a product of slum life and had experienced virtually all aspects of destitution so common to poor black people in the United States.[18] Because of his abilities, he achieved an international reputation as a spokesman for the aspirations of poor black people. Malcolm X was feared and admired by both black and white Americans, and frequently the same individual shared both sentiments. He was often misunderstood, although his speeches were clear. He urged black people to consolidate their efforts and to link their struggle with that of their African brothers as a means of achieving political, economic, and social equality. He did not feel that integration into the larger society was either likely or necessary in the near future. Therefore he advocated a policy of group solidarity. As a means of achieving this solidarity, he constantly advocated positive identification (i.e., pride in blackness). Malcolm X urged white Americans who sympathized with the aspirations of black people to organize themselves and work within the white community in an effort to rid it of its racist practices. He did not advocate the initiation of violence, but he was a strong proponent of armed self-defense as a means of meeting violent attacks by racists. Few leaders have been so misunderstood as Malcolm X. As a social critic, his exegesis of American society was severe but meticulous. In many ways he was the inaugurator of the Black Power movement.

BLACK POWER

For all practical purposes the civil rights movement ended in 1965. The following year civil rights organizations appeared to be searching for some cause around which to rally as a means of continuing their protest activities. Although implementation was lagging, they had won important victories: the Civil Rights Act of 1964, the Voting Rights Act of 1965, and perhaps most important of all, the recognition by Americans that the low status of black people posed a serious social problem in a world where oppressed people were fighting for freedom and self-determination. The question, Where do we go from here? was asked by the leaders of the major civil rights organizations. In June 1966 James Meredith was shot as he started his freedom march through Mississippi. Immediately thereafter the leaders of several civil rights organizations gathered in Memphis, Tennessee, and made plans to turn the aborted march into a major civil rights campaign. During this march Stokely Carmichael, the chairman of SNCC, introduced a new and controversial slogan into the nomenclature of the movement to achieve greater civil rights for blacks. The concept of Black Power was first used in this context when the marchers reached Greenwood, Mississippi.[19] Field workers from SNCC had worked in this community, and, at a mass rally, when Carmichael proclaimed, "What we need is black power," he was cheered by the crowd of poor Mississipians.

The introduction of the concept of Black Power was debated by the leaders of CORE, SCLC, and SNCC. Martin Luther King and his associates from SCLC disapproved of its use, but the leaders of CORE and SNCC supported its use. A compromise was reached—that the concept was not to be used as the official slogan of the march—but it gained worldwide usage and generated a heated debate among the major black organizations.

Somehow the combination of the words *black* and *power* seemed to offend and frighten white Americans, especially some "liberal" white persons who had contributed time and money to the civil rights movement. To them the concept implied black supremacy (or reverse racism) and black violence. Consequently, they resigned from membership and withheld financial support from the more militant organization. Similarly, the more moderate civil rights organizations, such as the NAACP and the National Urban League, expressed their disapproval of Black Power. The organizations which had led the civil rights movement and which had cooperated in the major campaigns and demonstrations in the South were divided along ideological lines.

Those leaders advocating Black Power had attempted to define the concept, but such attempts were usually lost in the growing debate in the mass media of communications. To Stokely Carmichael of SNCC the concept spoke to the needs of black people at the time. It was a call to black Americans to liberate themselves from oppression by assuming control over their lives economically, politically, and socially. He said:

> Black Power means black people coming together to form a political force and either electing representatives or forcing their representatives to speak to their needs. It's an economic and physical bloc that can exercise its strength in the black community instead of letting the job go to the Democratic or Republican parties or a white-controlled black man set up as a puppet to represent black people. *We* pick the brother and make sure he fulfills *our* needs. Black Power doesn't mean antiwhite, violence, separatism, or any other racist things the press says it means. It's saying, "Look, buddy, we're not laying a vote on you unless you lay so many schools, hospitals, playgrounds, and jobs on us."[20]

Later he and Charles Hamilton elaborated on the concept of Black Power:

> It is a call for black people in this country to unite, to recognize their heritage, to build a sense of community. It is a call for black people to begin to define their own goals, to lead their own organizations, and to support those organizations. It is a call to reject the racist institutions and values of this society.
>
> The concept of Black Power rests on a fundamental premise: *Before a group can enter the open society, it must first close ranks.* By this we mean that group solidarity is necessary before a group can operate effectively from a bargaining position of strength in a pluralistic society.[21]

Floyd McKissick of CORE saw the following as elements of Black Power: increased political and economic power for blacks, improved self-image, the development of young, militant black leadership, the development of black consumer power, and strong resistance to police brutality in black communities.[22]

Although Martin Luther King, Jr., opposed the use of the concept of Black Power for a variety of reasons, he acknowledged that it had what he called a "positive meaning."[23] He saw it as a "cry of disappointment" and of despair with the present state of black-white relations. He also interpreted it as ". . . a call to black people to amass the political and economic strength to achieve their legitimate goals." Finally, he saw Black Power as "a psychological call to manhood." Despite its many positive features, King felt that the concept had too many negative values for it to serve as the basic strategy with which to meet the problems faced by black people at that time.[24] He believed that it embodied a philosophy of hopelessness about achieving basic changes in the structure of American society. In addition, as an integrationist, King saw the Black Power movement as one based on separation of the races in the United States. He rejected the notion that any group within the larger society could achieve equality through separation. Finally, as a foremost exponent of nonviolence, he felt that the concept was often a call for retaliatory violence, which, he maintained, could only serve to impede progress in race relations.

The more moderate leaders of civil rights organizations opposed the concept of Black Power from its inception. The leaders of the NAACP and the Urban League joined five other prominent black spokesmen and responded to the militant organization by placing an advertisement entitled "Crisis and Commitment" in numerous newspapers.[25] In response to the advocates of Black Power they enumerated what they considered to be the "principles upon which the civil rights movement rests." They included four points: (1) a commitment to the principle of racial justice through the democratic process, (2) the repudiation of violence, (3) a commitment to the principle of integration, and (4) a commitment to the principle that the task of bringing about integration is the common responsibility of all Americans, both black and white.

Some of the leading critics of Black Power have rejected the concept in favor of coalition politics. They felt that the concept was harmful to the movement for greater civil rights for America's blacks because "it diverts the movement from a meaningful debate over strategy and tactics, it isolates the Negro community, and it encourages the growth of anti-Negro forces." As an alternative to Black Power, they advocated a "liberal-labor-civil rights coalition which would work to make the Democratic Party truly responsive to the aspirations of the poor, and which would develop support for programs (specifically those outlined in A. Philip Randolph's $100 billion Freedom Budget) aimed at the reconstruction of American society in the interests of greater social justice."[26]

Supporters of Black Power rejected the notion of forming coalitions with predominantly white liberal, labor, and religious organizations. They insisted that those who advocated such coalitions were proceeding on the basis of three fallacious assumptions: (1) that the interests of black Americans were identical with the interests of these groups, (2) that a viable coalition could be established between groups with power and powerless blacks, and (3) that it was possible to sustain political coalitions on a "moral, friendly, sentimental basis; by appeals to conscience."[27]

The debate over Black Power continued. The more militant organizations, CORE and SNCC, were its chief proponents; the more moderate organizations, the NAACP and the Urban League, were strongly opposed; and SCLC adopted a middle position. In keeping with their position that Black Power means black consciousness and solidarity, the militant organizations urged their white supporters to form parallel organizations and to work with the white community to rid it of the racism endemic to American life. A coalition between black and white Americans was seen as unworkable. The major impediment to equality for black people was seen as the resistance of the white community. Consequently, CORE and SNCC urged their white supporters to work within their own communities.

Less than one year after the concept as first introduced, it had gained widespread prominence. In July 1967 the first National Conference on Black Power was held in Newark, New Jersey. This conference was attended by more than one thousand black delegates from forty two cities in thirty six states. They represented a broad cross section of black leaders, ranging from the militant black nationalists to employees of government agencies. One of the most significant aspects of the conference was that it brought together for the first time a wide assembly of black people who met in workshop sessions to define the concept of Black Power and who agreed to implement its components. When the conference ended, a series of resolutions had been passed, covering the following issues, among others: (1) the establishment of black financial institutions such as credit unions and nonprofit cooperatives, (2) the establishment of black universities, (3) selective purchasing and boycotting of white merchants in black communities, (4) the demand for a guaranteed annual income for all people, (5) a boycott by black athletes of international Olympic competition and professional boxing, in response to the stripping of the world heavyweight boxing title from Muhammad Ali, (6) boycotts of black churches which were not committed to the "black revolution," (7) boycotts of black publications accepting advertisements for hair straighteners and bleaching creams.

Meanwhile, Black Power gained wider acceptance among more radical white Americans. In November 1966 students at Oberlin College, in Oberlin, Ohio, held in intercollegiate conference entitled Black Power in the Urban Ghetto, in an effort to "eliminate the emotionalism which clouds the debate on Black Power and to try to point out the basic issues involved." At its annual meeting in August 1967, the National Student

Association, the largest organization of college students in the United States, resolved to support the implementation of the concept of Black Power "through any means necessary." In September the delegates attending the National Conference for New Politics in Chicago voted by a margin of more than two to one to support all resolutions of the Newark Black Power Conference and to support "black control of the political, economic, and social institutions in black communities."

Interest in the concept of Black Power was perhaps too recent in its origin to gain wide acceptance on its relevance to the problems faced by blacks. It had emotional implications which white Americans feared, but stripped of its emotional connotations, it meant the amassing by black people of the economic, political, and social power necessary to deal effectively with the problems they face as a powerless people relegated to a life of poverty in an affluent society. Furthermore, it was a call to black people to reject the social values (especially racism) which are responsible for their low status in the United States and to replace them with an ideology which embraces dignity and pride in blackness. Black solidarity was seen as a precondition to the achievement of these ends. Integration, it was felt, is much more likely to be achieved from a position of strength than from one of weakness.

The concept of ethnic power is not alien to American society. Historically, many ethnic groups have improved their status through the process of organizing themselves into power blocs. Indeed, historically, ethnic solidarity has been a fundamental aspect of American minority relations. One writer defended Black Power as follows:

> ...to the extent that "Black Power" expresses a determination to build a Negro Community which would be something more than euphemisms for the ghetto, it is a valid and necessary cry; to the extent that it expresses a despair of the one-by-one absorption of "deserving" Negroes into the general society and puts its faith instead in collective action aimed at dealing with collective fate, it is an intelligent response to the reality of American life.[28]

He saw the attempts to establish group loyalty among blacks, which was a fundamental aspect of Black Power, as an essential means of dealing with a basically hostile society. Although other minority groups have effectively organized themselves along religious and ethnic lines into political and economic power blocs as a means of improving their status, once this goal has been achieved, they have effectively combined forces and joined what blacks call the white power structure, which serves to perpetuate the low status of blacks. They may be of Irish, Italian, Jewish, or Polish extraction, but in encounters with blacks, racial homogeneity solidifies them. In short, black surbordination was achieved and has been maintained by the unabashed use of "white power."

Another writer, who saw Black Power as "the acquisition of power by Negroes for their own use, both offensively and defensively," defended the concept, especially its emphasis on black nationalism and black consciousness, as follows:

> It is important to establish a positive black identity in a great many sectors of the black communities, both North and South, rural and urban, lower and middle class. Indeed, it is both important and legitimate to teach black people (or any other ethnic minority) about their history, placing special emphasis upon the positive contributions of other black people. This black consciousness has the potential to create unity and solidarity among black people and to give them hope and self-confidence.[29]

She reported that Black Power achieved success among Mississippi blacks because attempts at racial integration in that state had failed.

The use of black political power to achieve black rights was not new. In 1941 black leaders effectively forced the president to issue an executive order banning discrimination in employment in industry doing business with the federal government. Such organizations as the Negro American Labor Council of the American Federation of Labor-Congress of Industrial Organizations and the all-black organizations within urban police departments exist to protect the interests of their members. The idea underlying the concept of Black Power, then, was not new. It gained new strength in the last half of the 1960s. In 1967 a nationwide organization of elected black public officials was formed to develop methods of utilizing their combined power to improve the status of black citizens. A nationwide group of black ministers met in November 1967 in an effort to make Black Power a force in American Protestant church policies. They were organizing to serve as a pressure group within the National Council of Churches in an effort to increase the number of blacks in policy-making positions and to "bring the resources of white churches into urban ghettos in such a way as to enhance Negro leadership."[30]

The civil rights movement was basically reformist, aimed at changing some aspects of the structure of American society insofar as black people were denied some of the rights guaranteed citizens in the Constitution. It was directed toward establishing the principle of legal equality as public policy and toward the responsibility of the federal government in protecting the constitutional rights of citizens. To a degree these goals have been achieved, or at least they have been accepted as a matter of principle. The Black Power movement, on the other hand, went beyond social reform. If the demands for political, economic, and social control by black people over the institutions which are responsible to them, along with the other changes necessary for the liberation of American blacks were achieved, American society will have undergone revolutionary changes. The civil rights movement did not address itself to the complex, deeply rooted problems facing black people in the slums of the United States. The Black Power movement did. In this sense, the Black Power movement might be said to have been the logical extension of the civil rights movement. Where the civil rights movement ended, the Black Power movement commenced; the demise of the civil rights movement gave birth to the black liberation movement.

THE CONSEQUENCES

The passage of the Civil Rights Act of 1964 and the Voting Rights Act of 1965, both of which resulted from massive civil rights campaigns conducted by black and white Americans in such places as Birmingham and Selma, Alabama, brought about a measure of change in the lives of southern blacks. The daily indignities which had characterized their lives for centuries had been somewhat ameliorated. To a degree they could share public facilities—libraries, restaurants, parks, and hotels—with white Americans. To a lesser degree they could exercise their constitutional right to vote. Many white Americans rejoiced that significant progress had been achieved in these realms, and to them the civil rights "revolution" was accomplished. They had demonstrated, marched, and suffered with their black brothers and sisters, and they had won. With this sense of accomplishment, they abandoned the civil rights movement. As long as black people were marching and singing "We Shall Overcome," they were eager to lend support. But they were unaware that the eradication of overt practices of racial segregation in public places and discrimination at the polls signaled only the first step toward equality for black people. Rather, they saw it as an end. Black people, on the other hand, were aware that the lives of few blacks outside the South had been affected by these changes. The southern black was beginning to achieve the token degree of equality which his counterpart outside the South had already achieved.

Collectively black people represent a vast underclass of citizens in the United States, and little attempt has been made to deal with their many long-standing problems—poverty, discrimination in employment, inadequate housing, and the like. Because of the expense involved, proposed remedies for these problems have not been taken seriously by many who have worked in the civil rights movement. Little expense had been incurred in accomplishing the modest gains of the civil rights movement, but to alter significantly the status of black people in the United States in a fundamental sense would be expensive, both in money and in psychological readjustment. It would no doubt cost billions of dollars, and white Americans would be forced to abandon one of America's longest-standing cultural myths—that of racial inferiority of the black person. Taken collectively, the price is too high for a vast majority of America's privileged class. Therefore the civil rights movement reached a deadlock: black Americans demanded equality, while most white Americans continued to cling to the ideology of white supremacy. This resistance to change resulted from the refusal of white Americans to relinquish their position of dominance that afforded them a variety of privileges denied to blacks.

The status of black people in the United States in 1986 indicates how much remains to be accomplished before black Americans will have achieved equality. Earnings and employment rates for blacks lag far behind those of white Americans. The average black earns approximately one-half of what the average white American earns, and the rate of unemployment among blacks is two and a half times as high as among white Americans. Furthermore, when unemployed, they are likely to remain in that state twice as long as white workers. A vast majority (three-fourths) of blacks hold menial jobs. They continue to do the low-paying, unskilled jobs essential for contemporary society. At least one-half of all black people live in substandard (slum) housing, for which they are forced to pay more than their white counterparts who enoy better-quality housing. These conditions contribute to low standards of health. For example, the infant mortality rate is twice as high for blacks as for white Americans. In education, most blacks continue to attend segregated public schools with inferior facilities. Consequently their achievement level lags behind that of white pupils.

Significant changes have been recorded in the lives of black Americans during the past two decades, but they have affected mostly only the small middle class. Today many blacks are employed in positions which heretofore had been reserved for white persons. However, the lives of the black masses in the urban slums remain unaffected. The appointment of a black to the Supreme Court or as chief administrative officer of Washington, D.C., hardly affects those persons living substandard lives in the many cities throughout the country. Such appointments symbolize a remote opportunity which mocks the plight of the members of the underclass and reinforces their despair. It is among the black people living in urban slums that despair is most pronounced. They became acutely aware that officials of the federal government were willing to commit annually ten times as much of the nation's resources to a war in Asia as they were to programs ostensibly designed to eradicate poverty at home. Similarly, they are aware that, proportionately, twice as many blacks as whites were killed in action in Vietnam. These factors, coupled with the lack of change in race relations, have contributed to the feelings of hopelessness which pervade black slums throughout the United States. Peaceful petition for redress of grievances has resulted in token change in the overt practices

of segregation and discrimination. It has not secured effective action regarding the more fundamental problems which a vast majority of black
people face.

One result of this lack of change in race relations was the massive
uprisings in black communities which for several years came to be a regular summer feature in the United States. Each summer hundreds of black
people struck at the structure of society through these uprisings. In the
summers of 1963–67 these phenomena occurred in hundreds of cities
throughout the country, often taking on the character of urban guerrilla
warfare, with the oppressed slum dwellers opposing the helmeted federal troops and local law-enforcement personnel. Federal, state, and local
officials were generally insensitive to the real meaning of these uprisings,
charging that they had been led by small bands of "extremists" directed
from Havana or Peking. But for a significant proportion of black people,
leaders as well as rank and file, the disturbances had a more positive than
negative impact. For example, approximately one-third (34 percent) of a
sample of blacks indicated that they felt that "riots" had helped their
cause. Among a sample of leaders more than two-fifths (41 percent) gave
a similar response. One-fifth of both categories of individuals (20 percent
of rank and file and 19 percent of leaders) indicated their belief that the
"riots" had hurt the cause of civil rights.[31]

The first of the major uprisings occurred in Watts, the black section
of Los Angeles, in August 1965.[32] In 1966 it was Cleveland, Ohio, and in
1967, Newark, New Jersey,[33] and Detroit, Michigan.[34] In 1967 alone these
uprisings occurred in some fifty-six cities in thirty-one states, resulting in
at least 84 deaths, 3828 injuries, 9550 arrests, and hundreds of millions of
dollars in property damage.[35]

The uprising in Watts lasted for five days. Thirty-four persons were
killed, more than 1000 were injured, some 4000 arrests were made, and
the estimated property damage was $40 million. More than 200 buildings
were destroyed by fire, and another 400 were damaged. Of those persons
killed, coroner's inquests indicated that 16 of the deaths of blacks had
been caused by the Los Angeles Police Department and 7 had been
caused by the National Guardsmen.[36] After the uprising many public
officials appeared to be more concerned about the property losses than
about the loss of human lives.

The Watts uprising signaled the end of the monopoly previously
held by the advocates of nonviolence as a method of protest among
blacks. At the peak of the uprising 10,000 black people took to the streets,
and for more than five days fought against a force of 15,500 police and
National Guardsmen. The police seized more than 850 weapons from the
demonstrators, and the uprising was finally suppressed.

Another major uprising occurred in Newark in July 1967 in which
26 persons were killed, more than 1100 injured, and more than 1600

jailed. Property damage was estimated at $15 million. The black community was occupied for several days by a force of 3000 National Guardsmen, 1400 local police, and 500 state troopers. A majority of the deaths resulted from gunfire from Newark police who have been described as racists. It is reported that one hundred black-owned stores were destroyed by the police.[37]

Immediately after the Newark uprising, Detroit experienced the bloodiest racial uprising in modern America. Forty-three people were killed, more than 2000 were injured, and more than 5000 were arrestd. Property damage exceeded $500 million. The black residents of Detroit engaged in a form of urban guerrilla warfare with heavily armed police and soldiers. Altogether 7000 National Guardsmen and 4700 paratroopers supplemented the 2500 members of the city and state police forces. With the use of tanks and machine guns the uprising was finally brought to an end after seven days of fighting. As with preceding urban uprisings, there were evidences of police brutality motivated by racism. It is reported that three young black men were executed by white policemen who found them with three white women in a motel room several blocks from the scene of the fighting.[38] Other blacks present insisted that the three men were unarmed and that the police were motivated by antiblack prejudice.

Each of these uprisings—Watts, Newark, and Detroit—was immediately triggered by what the black people involved considered unfair police action. Black people are often apprehended for minor infractions of the law for which white persons are rarely punished in similar circumstances. The police are seen as the society's enforcers of unfair standards of justice and as occupying forces, and many slum residents reject this legal authority. During uprisings police frequently shoot black people of all ages for such infractions of the law as looting stores. The assumption that property rights are more sacred than human life prevails. Black people, on the other hand, interpret the looting as a means of sharing in the material rewards of a society which has, through a variety of techniques, denied them their rightful share. Although seemingly trivial incidents involving law enforcement kindle slum uprisings, these are not the underlying cause of such phenomena. In urban slums black people are forced to live in poverty and deprivation. They utilize the uprisings as a means of bringing their economic plight (unemployment and low earnings) maintained by white racism to the attention of public officials, who have generally been insensitive to their status.[39] It is through the destruction caused by these uprisings that public officials in a highly materialistic society are made aware of the hopelessness and despair of these citizens.

The conditions under which black people live have improved somewhat in the last two decades, but these changes have heightened their feelings of relative deprivation in relation to the status of white Americans. This feeling of relative deprivation has led to the crisis in race relations, which nearly twenty years ago brought American society to the point where, as the National Advisory Commission on Civil Disorders concluded: "Our nation is moving toward two societies, one black, one white—separate and unequal."[40] The commission, which investigated the black uprisings of 1967, reported that these disorders were caused by the attitudes of white Americans toward black Americans: "White racism is essentially responsible for the explosive mixture which has been accumulating in our cities since the end of World War II."[41] Elsewhere the commission reported: "What white Americans have never fully understood—but what the Negro can never forget—is that white society is deeply implicated in the ghetto. White institutions created it, white institutions maintain it, and white society condones it."[42] Sociological studies of causes of present black militance generally attribute this phenomenon to the feeling of relative deprivation black people feel when compared to white Americans.[43]

White Americans frequently compare the socioeconomic status of black Americans with that of other people living outside the United States. Such comparisons are invalid because it is the relative status of black and white Americans which has precipitated the present crisis. Black people in the United States may enjoy a higher standard of living than do citizens of the so-called underdeveloped nations, but the gap between black and white Americans continues to be vast.

It is frequently maintained that the uprisings that swept American cities impeded the cause of black equality. Such phenomena may have increased antiblack prejudice, but at the same time their long-term effect may have improved the status of blacks insofar as decreased discrimination was concerned. In short, a reduction in discrimination is more important to the cause of black equality than an increase in prejudice. The so-called "riots" of 1967 resulted in the far-reaching report by the National Advisory Commission on Civil Disorders. If the recommendations of this report had been put into effect, the result would have been widespread change in the status of black people in the United States.

In the meantime, recent developments among black people are likely to alter the character of American race relations. One such development is the increasing political awareness of black college students. Since 1962 black students at the major colleges and universities throughout the United States have organized themselves into all-black clubs and are challenging established practices.[44] They question the content of courses and the hiring practices of these institutions, and reject integration into the white, middle-class social life of these schools. They read the works of black writers, most of whom rarely appear on reading lists for regular courses. They conduct discussions on topics such as black identity and publish newspapers and magazines. In short, they introduce the concept of Black Power on the college campus.

Students were among the earliest participants in the civil rights movement in the South, but black students at predominantly white colleges and universities outside the South were often more involved in fraternities, sororities, and other social activities than in questions of equality for black slum dwellers. In the South they were made aware of their status daily through the practice of rigid segregation, while outside the South the few black students could easily be absorbed into the life of the school or effectively isolated. Frequently their lives were such that they could forget that they were black while they remained on campus. The transition from school to work, difficult at best, became increasingly so for black college students. They were not being prepared for the reality of what they would face as professionals in a racist society.

The response of black students to this situation has been an attempt to organize themselves. The first of these organizations outside the South was the Student's Afro-American Society at Columbia Univeristy. It was followed by Harvard Univeristy's African and Afro-American Students group, Yale University's Black Students' Alliance, Princeton University's Association of Black Collegians, Dartmouth College's Afro-American Society, the University of California at Berkeley's Afro-American Student Union, Hunter College's Kubanbanya, City College's Onyx, and other similar organizations at colleges throughout the United States. In December 1966, a northeastern regional conference, attended by three hundred delegates from thirty schools, met at Columbia University. In 1985, this Conference was held at Cornell University.

One of the primary functions of these organizations is to stress black consciousness and black pride. Through them, students identify with each other and with their less fortunate fellow blacks. Frequently the students spend their free time working with black slum dwellers, especially in tutorial programs and other educational projects. This action provides a link between the politically sophisticated students and the powerless slum dwellers. Furthermore, these students are more likely than the others to understand the nature and functioning of the society in which they live. Consequently, they provide an important source of black leadership at a crucial time.

Another development in the black movement is the attempt among leaders of the more militant organizations to link the movement for black equality in the United States with the movements of other oppressed peoples throughout the world, especially those in Africa, Asia, and Latin America. One of the first black leaders in years to see the struggle of black Americans in international terms was Malcolm X, who traveled and consulted extensively in Africa and Asia.[45] An attempt to link the struggle of black people in the United States and that of Africans led Malcolm X to establish the Organization of Afro-American Unity. Since his death several other black leaders have made contacts with revolutionary individuals and organizations throughout the world.

These leaders see the struggle of black Americans as being similar to those of other oppressed peoples, and they increasingly turn to the Third World for support. In 1967 Stokely Carmichael was the guest of honor and a delegate at the meeting in Havana, Cuba, of the Organization of Latin American Solidarity, an organization of the leaders of revolutionary movements in Latin America. In his address to the conference he said:

> We greet you as comrades because it becomes increasingly clear to us each day that we share with you a common struggle; we have a common enemy. Our enemy is white Western imperialist society; and our struggle is to overthrow the system which feeds itself and expands itself through the economic and cultural exploitation of nonwhite, non-Western peoples. We speak to you, comrades, because we wish to make clear that we understand that our destinies are intertwined. We do not view our struggle as being contained within the boundaries of the United States, as they are defined by present-day maps. . . .[46]

At the first meeting of the National Conference for New Politics in Chicago in September 1967, black delegates insisted that the conference adopt a resolution pledging total and unquestionable support to all wars of national liberation in Africa, Latin America, and particularly Vietnam.

According to one reporter, "Negroes increasingly see Black Power as not confined to ghetto rebellions, but rather as part of a general fight of the oppressed against the oppressor all over the world."[47] He cited several instances in which black leaders in the United States had met with leaders of revolutionary movements around the world. Floyd McKissick of CORE joined a team of other Americans which traveled to Cambodia to investigate the claims by the U.S. Department of Defense that the area of Cambodia which borders on South Vietnam was used by the North Vietnamese forces as a sanctuary. While there, he reportedly conferred with the chief of state on "peace and racism." A black lawyer and other leaders went to North Vietnam to gather evidence for the International War Crimes Tribunal organized by Bertrand Russell, and representatives of SNCC served as judges on this tribunal. In addition, SNCC maintained an international affairs department through which contact was made with other revolutionary movements, principally in Africa. When the United Nations sponsored a seminar on racial discrimination and colonialism in South Africa in the summer of 1967, both CORE and SNCC were represented.

Increasingly, the more militant black leaders attempted to internationalize the movement for equality. Such events as the assassination of

Patrice Lumumba in the Congo and that of Malcolm X in New York at a time when he was establishing contacts with African leaders, and also the implication of the Central Intelligence Agency in counterrevolutionary acts outside the United States, forced some of the black leaders to see their fight for equality in global terms. More recently, the struggle against apartheid in South Africa has generated enormous support among blacks in the United States. By 1984 anti-apartheld demonstrations were commonplace, especially on college campuses.

By the end of 1972 the status of the black American remained a domestic problem of considerable magnitude. Although greater changes had occurred in the previous ten years than during the nearly one hundred years since Reconstruction, blacks remained a large underclass of citizens. The movement responsible for these changes appeared to have suffered an irreparable split over the introduction of the concept of Black Power. The militant leaders who favored the concept talked in terms of black liberation, while the more moderate leaders who opposed it clung to a belief in racial justice through the democratic process. In the meantime, black people throughout the United States were becoming increasingly politically aware of the society in which they lived.

This increasing political awareness was manifested by the widespread support in black communities throughout the United States for a black state legislator from Georgia who was denied his seat because of his outspoken opposition to the war in Vietnam; by the support accorded the world's heavyweight champion when he was stripped of his title for refusing to permit himself to be inducted into the armed forces (again because of opposition to the war in Vietnam); and by the nationwide solidarity expressed by black people when a congressman from New York, one of the most powerful elected black officials in American history, was denied his committee chairmanship and his seat in Congress. Such incidents as these were rather widely interpreted by blacks as a continuing refusal on the part of white Americans to permit blacks to share power in the society. That is, white persons in positions of power appeared willing to resort to whatever tactics were necessary to perpetuate the low status of black people in the society. The 1967 mayoral elections in Cleveland, Ohio, and Gary, Indiana, illustrated the point. In both these cities black mayors were elected, primarily because of the heavy turnout of black voters. In both cities at least 90 percent of the traditionally Democratic white voters switched parties and cast their ballots for the white Republican candidates rather than vote for blacks.[48]

In addition to increased political awareness, blacks in 1972 were more aware of their own history and of the history of the United States than at any previous time. A continuous series of past injustices and the refusal of white Americans to discontinue such practices had increased impatience and bitterness throughout the black community. For their part, white Americans generally appeared to be incapable of understanding this mood. Therefore, with few exceptions, there was little dialogue between the growing number of black militants and white Americans. Large numbers of black people were demanding control over the institutions in their communities as a means of dealing with the problems they faced. Although the Black Power militants were in a minority, an increasingly large number of blacks rejected integration as necessary for the achievement of equality. Integration, they felt, failed to solve these problems. White Americans, for the most part, rejected this notion and expressed satisfaction with the pace of civil rights in the United States. The result was that relations between black and white Americans reached a point of greater strain than at any other time in the twentieth century.

Finally, the strain in race relations in the United States was intensified by systematic attempts to curb black militancy. Black Americans had learned through the years that increased militance in pursuing their goal of liberation was likely to be met by attempts to preserve white supremacy at all costs. At no time had this been more evident. Attempts to control the pace of the movement frequently took the form of silencing the more militant leaders, either by assassinating them (e.g., Medgar Evers, Martin Luther King, Jr., Malcolm X) or by jailing them (e.g., H. Rap Brown, Eldridge Cleaver, LeRoi Jones). Black Americans saw such acts as further manifestations of the racism which pervaded the fabric of the society.

For the black community the murder of Martin Luther King, Jr., on April 4, 1968, clearly indicated the extent to which white bigots were willing to go to preserve the low status of the black man in the society. Although the bullet which killed King may have been fired by a single individual, that individual did not exist in isolation. His act must be understood within the larger context of the racism which has become institutionalized in American society.

Until his death, King remained the most widely respected leader in the black community. While many of the militants disapproved of his goals and tactics, his dedication and courage were unchallenged. He steadfastly maintained a faith in nonviolence as a means of achieving the liberation of black Americans. With his assassination many black people who shared his belief became disillusioned, as the widespread disorders which followed his murder showed.

In black communities throughout the United States the response to his assassination was immediate and angry. Altogether 125 cities were affected; serious outbursts occurred in Baltimore, Chicago, Kansas City, Missouri, Pittsburgh, and Washington, D.C. A total of 46 persons were killed, 2600 were injured, and nearly 22,000 arrested. The rage of these black people was manifested by rioting, looting, and destroying buildings and other property. After nearly ten days, 55,000 federal troops, working with local police, were able to restore order.

White Americans responded to the murder of Martin Luther King, Jr., with a massive outpouring of both genuine sentiment and sentimentality, and many of the individuals who had been the strongest opponents of his goals were among those most dramatic in their mourning. The results: one of the longest periods of mourning and one of the largest funerals in American history. For many in the black community the message of the assassination was clear: any serious attempt to fundamentally alter the existing pattern of race relations in the United States would be met with whatever measures were necessary to curb it.

The assassination of Martin Luther King, Jr., removed from the scene one of the great reformist leaders in the history of the United States. The "dream" he envisioned at the March on Washington in 1963 has continued to remain a dream for black people, although the administration of Lyndon B. Johnson attempted, through the "Great Society" programs, to alleviate some of the poverty of the black community and provide its inhabitants with some measure of control over their lives. Johnson's mistake, however, was the misguided notion that America's domestic problems could be solved while waging one of the most brutal wars of genocide in human history. Because of his stubborn insistence on accelerating the war of aggression in Indochina, he was finally hounded out of office by opposition to this war policy. In the meantime, Richard M. Nixon was elected president after campaigning on a platform which promised, in many subtle and not so subtle ways, to reverse whatever gains blacks had managed to make during the height of the civil rights movement.

•   •   •

Through the black revolt, which culminated in the civil rights movement, black people managed through intensive struggle to gain the rights of citizenship *in principle*. But they soon learned that legal equality in principle did not lead to justice in practice. Thus, the tactics of the black movement changed. The movement for Black Power served as a transition between the civil rights and black nationalist movements. It is to a discussion of black nationalism and then to affirmative action that attention is now turned.

SELECTED BIBLIOGRAPHY

BARBOUR, FLOYD B., ed. *The Black Power Revolt.* Boston: Porter Sargent, 1968.

BATES, DAISY. *The Long Shadow of Little Rock.* New York: David McKay Co., 1962.

BELFRAGE, SALLY. *Freedom Summer.* New York: Viking Press, 1965.

BENNETT, LERONE. *Before the Mayflower*, Baltimore: Penguin Books, 1966.

BURNS, W. HAYWOOD. *The Voices of Negro Protest in America.* New York: Oxford University Press, 1963.

CLARK, KENNETH. *Dark Ghetto.* New York: Harper & Row, Publishers, 1965.
COLES, ROBERT. *Children of Crisis: A Study of Courage and Fear.* Boston: Atlantic Monthly Press, 1967.
CONOT, ROBERT. *Rivers of Blood, Years of Darkness.* New York: Bantam Books, 1967.
CRUSE, HAROLD. *The Crisis of the Negro Intellectual.* New York: William Morrow & Co., 1967.
FAGER, CHARLES E. *White Reflections on Black Power.* Grand Rapids, Mich.: Wm. B. Erdmans Publishing Co., 1967.
FORMAN, JAMES. *The Making of Black Revolutionaries.* New York: Macmillan Co., 1972.
GRIER, WILLIAM H., and PRICE M. COBBS, *Black Rage.* New York: Basic Books, 1968.
HAYDEN, TOM. *Rebellion in Newark.* New York: Random House, 1967.
HERSEY, JOHN. *The Algiers Motel Incident.* New York: Bantam Books, 1968.
HOLT, LEN. *The Summer That Didn't End.* New York: William Morrow & Co., 1965.
HUGHES, LANGSTON. *Fight for Freedom: The Story of the NAACP.* New York: Berkley Publishing Corp., 1962.
HUIE, WILLIAM BRADFORD. *Three Lives for Mississippi.* New York: Trident Press, 1965.
JONES, LE ROI. *Home: Social Essays.* New York: William Morrow & Co., 1966.
KILLENS, JOHN O. *Black Man's Burden.* New York: Trident Press, 1965
KILLIAN, LEWIS M. *The Impossible Revolution? Black Power and the American Dream.* New York: Random House 1968.
———, and CHARLES GRIGG, *Racial Crisis in America: Leadership in Conflict.* Englewood Cliffs, N.J.: Prentice-Hall, 1964.
KING, MARTIN LUTHER, JR. *Stride toward Freedom.* New York: Harper & Brothers, 1958.
———. *Where Do We Go From Here: Chaos or Community?* New York: Harper & Row, Publishers, 1967.
KUGLER, RICHARD. *Simple Justice: The History of Brown v. Board of Education and Black America's Struggle for Equality.* New York: Random House, 1975.
LEWIS, ANTHONY. *Portrait of a Decade.* New York: Random House, 1965.
LOMAX, LOUIS. *The Negro Revolt.* New York: Harper & Row, Publishers, 1962.
MALCOLM X. *The Autobiography of Malcolm X.* New York: Grove Press, 1964.
MORGAN, CHARLES. *A Time to Speak.* New York: Harper & Row, Publishers, 1964.
MUHAMMAD, ELIJAH. *Message to the Black Man in America.* Chicago: Muhammad Mosque of Islam No. 2, 1965.
PINKNEY, ALPHONSO. *The Committed: White Activists in the Civil Rights Movement.* New Haven, Conn.: College and University Press, 1968.
———. *The American Way of Violence.* New York: Random House, 1972.
POWLEDGE, FRED. *Black Power, White Resistance: Notes on the New Civil War.* Cleveland: World Publishing Co., 1967.
Report of the National Advisory Commission on Civil Disorders. New York: Bantam Books, 1968.
THOMPSON, DANIEL C. *The Negro Leadership Class.* Englewood Cliffs, N.J.: Prentice-Hall, 1963.
WILKINSON, J. HARVIE III. *From Brown to Bakke: The Supreme Court and School Integration, 1954–1978.* New York: Oxford University Press, 1979.
WILLIAMS, ROBERT F. *Negroes with Guns.* New York: Marzani & Munzell, 1962.
WRIGHT, NATHAN, JR. *Black Power and Urban Unrest.* New York: Hawthorn Books, 1967.
ZINN, HOWARD. *SNCC: The New Abolitionists.* Boston: Beacon Press, 1964.

NOTES

[1] See Anthony Lewis, *Portrait of a Decade* (New York: Random House, 1965), chap. 3.
[2] See Martin Luther King, *Stride Toward Freedom* (New York: Harper, 1958).
[3] See Louis Lomax, *The Negro Revolt* (New York: Harper, 1962), pp. 81–100.
[4] King, *Stride Toward Freedom,* pp. 102–7.
[5] Charles Morgan, *A Time to Speak* (New York: Harper & Row, 1964), pp. 38–39.
[6] Lewis, *Portrait of a Decade,* pp. 46–69.
[7] See Daisy Bates, *The Long Shadow of Little Rock* (New York: McKay, 1962); Robert Coles, *Children of Crisis: A Study of Courage and Fear* (Boston: Atlantic Monthly, 1967).

[8]Lerone Bennett, Jr., *Before the Mayflower* (Baltimore: Penguin, 1966), p. 407.

[9]Lomax, *Negro Revolt*, pp. 132–46.

[10]See Alphonso Pinkney, *The Committed: White Activists in the Civil Rights Movement* (New Haven, Conn.: College and University Press, 1968): Howard Zinn, *SNCC: The New Abolitionists* (Boston: Beacon Press, 1964).

[11]Bennett, *Before the Mayflower*, pp. 329–40.

[12]See Sally Belfrage, *Freedom Summer* (New York: Viking, 1965); Pinkney, *The Committed;* Elizabeth Sutherland, *Letters from Mississippi* (New York: McGraw-Hill, 1965).

[13]See William Bradford Huie, *Three Lives for Mississipi* (New York: Trident Press, 1965).

[14]John Herbers, "Communique from the Mississippi Front," *New York Times Magazine,* November 8, 1964, p. 34.

[15]See Pinkney, *The Committed,* chap. 5.

[16]Robert Coles, "When the Southern Negro Moves North," *New York Times Magazine,* September 17, 1967, p. 25.

[17]Kenneth Clark, *Dark Ghetto* (New York: Harper & Row, 1965), p. 11.

[18]Malcolm X, *The Autobiography of Malcolm X* (New York: Grove Press, 1964).

[19]Martin Luther King. Jr., *Where Do We Go From Here?* (New York: Harper & Row, 1967), pp. 23–32.

[20]Quoted in Gordon Parks, "Stokely Carmichael: Young Man Behind an Angry Message," *Life,* May 19, 1967, p. 82.

[21]Stokely Carmichael and Charles V. Hamilton, *Black Power: The Politics of Liberation in America* (New York: Random House, Inc., copyright 1967), p. 44.

[22]See Fred C. Shapiro, "The Successor to Floyd McKissick May Not Be So Reasonable," *New York Times Magazine,* October 1, 1967, p. 102.

[23]King, *Where Do We Go From Here?,* pp. 32–34.

[24]Ibid., pp. 44–63.

[25]*New York Times,* October 14, 1966, p. 35.

[26]See " 'Black Power' and Coalition Politics," *Commentary,* September 1966, pp. 35–40.

[27]Carmichael and Hamilton, *Black Power,* chap. 3.

[28]David Danzig, "In Defense of 'Black Power,' " *Commentary,* September 1966, p. 46. Reprinted from *Commentary,* by permission; copyright © 1966, by the American Jewish Committee.

[29]Joyce Ladner, "What 'Black Power' Means to Negroes in Mississippi," *Transaction 5* (November 1967), 14.

[30]*New York Times,* November 2, 1967, p. 52.

[31]William Brink and Louis Harris, *Black and White* (New York: Simon & Schuster, 1967), p. 67.

[32]See Robert Conot, *Rivers of Blood, Years of Darkness* (New York: Bantam, 1967); R. J. Murphy and James Watson, *The Structure of Discontent* (Los Angeles: Institute of Government and Public Affairs, University of California, 1967); T. M. Tomlinson and D. L. TenHouten, *Los Angeles Riot Study Method: Negro Reaction Survey,* (Los Angeles: Institute of Government and Public Affairs, University of California, 1967).

[33]Tom Hayden, *Rebellion in Newark* (New York: Random House, 1967); report of the New Jersey Select Commission on Civil Disorder, *New York Times,* February 11, 1968, p. 1.

[34]See Tom Parmenter, "Breakdown of Law and Order," *Transaction 9* (September 1967), 13–22.

[35]Figures compiled from news reports in the *New York Times* during August 1967.

[36]*Violence in the City—An End or a Beginning?* (Los Angeles: Governor's Commission on the Los Angeles Riots, 1965).

[37]Hayden, *Rebellion in Newark,* p. 38; *New York Times,* February 11, 1968, p. 1.

[38]Parmenter, "Breakdown of Law and Order," pp. 15–16; John Hersey, *The Algiers Motel Incident* (New York: Bantam 1968); Alphonso Pinkney, *The American Way of Violence* (New York: Random House, 1972), pp. 126–30.

[39]See Stanley Lieberson and Arnold R. Silverman, "The Precipitants and Underlying Conditions of Race Riots," *American Sociological Review* 30 (December 1965), 887–98.

[40]*Report of the National Advisory Commission on Civil Disorders* (New York: Bantam, 1968), p. 1.

[41] Ibid., p. 203.

[42] Ibid., p. 2.

[43] James A. Geschwender, "Social Structure and the Negro Revolt: An Examination of Some Hypotheses," *Social Forces* 43 (December 1964), 248–56; Ruth Searles and J. Allen Williams, Jr., "Negro College Students' Participation in Sit-Ins," *Social Forces* 40 (March 1962), 215–20.

[44] Ernest Dunbar, "The Black Revolt Hits the White Campus," *Look,* October 1967, pp. 27–31.

[45] Malcolm X, *Autobiography of Malcolm X,* especially chaps. 17–19.

[46] Reported in John Gerassi, "Havana: A New International is Born," *Monthly Review* 19 (October 1967), 27.

[47] William Worthy, "The American Negro is Dead," *Esquire,* November 1967, p. 126.

[48] Jeffrey K. Hadden, Louis H. Masotti, and Victor Thiessen, "The Making of the Negro Mayors, 1967," *Transaction* 5 (January-February 1968), 21–30.

CHAPTER NINE
FROM BLACK NATIONALISM TO AFFIRMATIVE ACTION

By the end of the 1960s, white Americans had become exasperated with black rebellions, student demonstrations, and the constant stream of revolutionary rhetoric which had characterized much of the antiwar movement. Hence, in the election of 1968 Americans elected a staunchly conservative president, one who promised to deal effectively with such protest movements. The administration of Richard Nixon brought about massive repression not only of blacks but of all of those perceived as radicals. The election was a three-way race between Nixon, Hubert Humphrey of Minnesota, and George Wallace of Alabama, who campaigned as an independent candidate. Since the Wallace campaign was avowedly racist, Nixon attempted to attract voters in the South, who had long voted Democratic, with what he called his "southern strategy." "Law and order" became his key campaign slogan and was widely recognized as a code for curbing the ever-accelerating drive among blacks for liberation. Having won the election with the support of southern whites, he proceeded on a course of widespread repression.

At about the same time the Black Power movement had broadened its thrust into black nationalism, which many blacks had seen as the most viable means toward achieving black liberation. As a movement, black nationalism was not new in the United States, for some black leaders had advocated this ideology for centuries. However, black nationalist sentiment gained its widest expression and acceptance in the late 1960s and the early 1970s.

In this chapter it is only possible to describe briefly the general thrust of the black nationalist movement in the United States, and to discuss its manifestations, both individual and collective. Then attention is turned to the present situation, where the rise of conservatism in the society has had negative effects on black progress.

THE BLACK NATIONALIST TRADITION

Since the history of black people in the United States has been complex, in a discussion of black nationalism it is necessary to somehow contend with what appears to be a complex of contradictions, for conventional notions of the concept of nationalism frequently do not apply to America's black population. Yet the ideology of nationalism is widespread in the black community and has persisted for centuries. Unlike the more conveniently defined conception of nationalism, which usually applies to the movement of nation-states for political independence, black nationalism in the United States refers to the sentiments which characterize the aspirations and actions of national minorities within already existing states.

Like that of other oppressed peoples, Afro-American nationalism is an expression of a desire for some degree of political, social, cultural, and economic autonomy. It is a movement for self-determination brought about by centuries of oppression. The diversity of approaches stems from the peculiar status of black people in the United States historically and at the present time. As a movement black nationalism has evolved through various forms, depending upon conditions prevailing at the time. These forms have included colonization, emigration, internal statism, and cultural pluralism. However, throughout its long history the ideology of black nationalism has contained a common core of features.

Perhaps the most elementary component of black nationalist ideology is the notion of unity or solidarity. A second element is the feeling of pride in cultural heritage, and its component, black consciousness. Finally, black nationalist ideology holds that in order for Afro-Americans to liberate themselves from oppression, some degree of autonomy from the larger society is essential.

Such acts as slave revolts, petitions to state legislatures and to Congress for assistance to settle in Africa, the establishment of the black church, fraternal organizations, and mutual aid societies, may be seen as nationalist efforts by Afro-Americans prior to the Civil War. One of the leading figures in the early back-to-Africa movement for blacks was Paul Cuffee, a prosperous black sea captain who lived in Massachusetts at the turn of the nineteenth century. Cuffee was the first in a long line of blacks who felt that the only hope for equality and justice for Afro-Americans was for them to return to Africa.[1] Consequently, after traveling in Sierra Leone Cuffee returned and established branches of the African Institution, an organization dedicated to this goal, in several cities. Unable to receive financial support for his work, Cuffee, at his own expense, transported thirty-eight Afro-Americans to their homeland in 1815.

After the death of Cuffee in 1817, the Negro Convention Movement was organized in Philadelphia. The Convention Movement assisted in the emigration of blacks to Canada, but its main objective was opposition to the American Colonization Society, an organization established and financed by whites eager to see blacks relocated in Africa. One of the leaders of the Convention Movement for a short time was Martin R. Delany, a Harvard-trained physician, who was unquestionably the leading advocate of black nationalism in the two decades preceding the Civil War.[2] The grandson of slaves, Delany was born "free" in Charleston, Virginia, in 1812. Initially he opposed relocation to Africa, but later supported it. By the age of 40 Delany had pursued successful careers in journalism and medicine, but his interest remained in the resettlement of blacks outside the United States, first in the western hemisphere and later in Africa. He traveled throughout West Africa, negotiating treaties for the emigration of American blacks to that region. His travels convinced him that because of its wealth, blacks could establish a powerful nation in Africa.

Following Delany, the most prominent spokesman for emigration was Henry M. Turner, a bishop in the African Methodist Episcopal Church. Like Delany, Turner was born free, had also served as an officer in the Union army, and later worked in the Freedmen's Bureau. When Delany died, Turner became the leading spokesman for the resettlement of blacks in Africa.[3] The failure of Reconstruction and the virtual reenslavement of blacks toward the end of the nineteenth century generated widespread interest in black nationalism in general and in the emigration of blacks from the United States in particular.

In 1881 Turner organized the African Emigration Association. Through the A.M.E. Church he had built a large following among the poor blacks in the South, and the church sponsored several trips for him to visit Africa, during which time he became convinced that all Afro-Americans should relocate in Liberia. The efforts of the Emigration Association were not successful, but in 1884 Turner formed the International Migration Society, which ultimately transported five hundred blacks to Liberia in two years.

At the beginning of the twentieth century, when white supremacy had become firmly institutionalized in the South, Turner, continuing his emigration activities, met his most formidable critic, Booker T. Washington, who urged blacks to "stay at home." This opposition, along with that of the black middle class and the black press, led to the demise of Turner's emigration movement.

Both Henry M. Turner and Booker T. Washington died in 1915. When Marcus Garvey arrived in the United States from Jamaica the following year, he found a powerless and demoralized black population. Although W. E. B. Du Bois was active in intellectual circles, he did not have a mass following among poor blacks. Therefore, Garvey arrived at a time when there was no black leader of national prominence who commanded a following among the masses of black people. The second decade of the twentieth century was one of massive black migration from the rural South to the urban North. Blacks in the South had already been disfranchised, and southern whites, with the approval or at least the acquiescence of the federal government, were determined that blacks remain slaves in practice if not in name.

This mood of hopelessness that Marcus Garvey found among urban blacks in the North enabled him to ultimately build the largest black nationalist movement in history. Upon his arrival in Harlem he organized the Universal Negro Improvement Association (UNIA), a multifaceted organization with millions of members and nine hundred chapters throughout the world.[4] The UNIA developed multimillion-dollar business enterprises, including the Black Star Shipping Line, the Negro Factories Corporation, a chain of cooperative grocery stores and restaurants, and a publishing company. But the activities of the UNIA were much more than economic: its ideology combined territoriality—cultural and religious nationalism—with economic nationalism. In short, the UNIA became the first organization to embrace the complete spectrum of black nationalism, and its leader was the first black man to develop a comprehensive ideology of black nationalism.

One of the fundamental aims of the UNIA was "Africa for the Africans," but it was in cultural nationalism that Garvey made his most important contribution to black Americans. He taught pride in blackness, racial solidarity, and respect for the African heritage of black people. A combination of factors, including the racist nature of American society and Garvey's difficulty in working with others, militated against the success of his ideas and programs. He was bitterly opposed by the black middle class and the black press for many of his more outlandish practices, such as insisting upon distinguishing among blacks based on skin color and making a tacit alliance with the Ku Klux Klan. He was ultimately convicted on a charge of using mails to defraud, sentenced to five years in prison, pardoned, and deported from the United States in 1927. He died in London in 1940 at the age of 53, never having visited the Africa he worked so tirelessly to see liberated from colonial domination.

After Garvey's deportation, the black nationalist movement declined. During the depression of the 1930s American blacks were concerned mainly with economic survival, and during World War II they thought that conditions for blacks would improve once the war was over. After the war, the integration-oriented civil rights movement became the major thrust of the black movement. With the appearance of Malcolm X in the

1960's, black nationalist ideology again made its impact felt in the black community. Malcolm X did not command a broadly based organization like Marcus Garvey, nor was he a scholar in the tradition of W. E. B. DuBois. He did not command the respect of poor blacks in the rural South and white liberals throughout the country as did Martin Luther King, Jr. But the depth of his understanding, his keen intelligence, his leadership abilities, and his integrity were such that had he lived to develop his ideas and organizational skills, he could very well have become the most important black man in American history.

While Malcolm X's views on various subjects changed during his brief lifetime, such themes as black unity, pride, and self-respect remained central to his thinking.[5] His dream was to organize the one hundred million blacks in the western hemisphere and unite them with the three hundred million blacks in Africa. Therefore, he attempted to internationalize the black struggle. The essence of his philosophy can be summarized as pride in blackness, the necessity of knowing black history, black autonomy, black unity, and self-determination for the black community.

EXPRESSIONS OF BLACK NATIONALISM

While there was no single formal organization comparable in size and influence to Garvey's UNIA, elements of black nationalism penetrated the entire black community, cutting across age, educational, and regional lines. In addition to the proliferation of local, national, and international black nationalist organizations ranging anywhere from the Black Liberators of St. Louis, to the Nation of Islam, to the Congress of African Peoples, individual expressions of nationalist ideology could be discerned throughout the black community. Black people greeted one another as "brother" and "sister," and the colors of black liberation—red, black, green—were worn in many forms. Afro hair styles, for large segments of the black community, replaced conventional styles. In many communities individuals observed Black Solidarity Day by remaining at home rather than working or going to school. Even older blacks adjusted to being called "black" or "Afro-American," rather than "Negro" or "colored." Many prominent blacks publicly expressed their solidarity with the black nationalist movement—a new development, for historically middle- and upper-class blacks opposed black nationalism.

One of the most important changes was the diminishing of self-hate and the increase in self-esteem with the ascendancy of contemporary nationalism. Many studies conducted in the 1950s reported that in experimental situations black children usually expressed a preference for white dolls over brown dolls.[6] While some of these studies contained methodological flaws, the conclusion was clear: self-hate was widespread in the black community, and it was learned in early childhood. Later studies, however, showed that following the spread of nationalist ideology in the black community, black children expressed an overwhelming preference for brown dolls over white dolls.[7] This change in attitude among black children cannot be minimized, for its significance is crucial in the movement for black liberation.

On another level, black nationalist organizations and caucuses are found among high school and college students, in prisons, and in the military; among artists, politicians, law-enforcement personnel, and scholars; and in virtually all professional and lay organizations that have black members. One of the more significant developments was the creation of Afro-American studies programs and courses on the high school and college levels. These programs and courses have not only corrected distortions and omissions about Afro-Americans, but they have also humanized American higher education. Furthermore, they have led to the development of other ethnic-studies programs and women's studies.

In the arts, especially creative writing, the theater, and music, the contributions of black people have been the most notable and innovative, and at the same time the least recognized by the larger society. Recently black artists have attempted not only to entertain their audiences, but to educate them. Among black politicians at all levels caucuses have been formed to promote legislation aimed at advancing the cause of black liberation. These groups vary, from the National Organization of Black Elected Officials to the Congressional Black Caucus to the Alabama Conference of Black Mayors.

Law-enforcement personnel are subjected to many stresses and strains in American society, and the black policeofficer has historically been trapped in a network of contradictions that seemingly defy resolution. In the late 1960s and early 1970s, black police attempted to reconcile some of their role conflicts by organizing themselves into black nationalist organizations within police departments. The contemporary young black policeofficer sees himself or herself as black first and policeofficer second. Like police, black professionals have organized themselves into nationalist groups to promote the cause of black liberation. Such groups exist among lawyers, physicians, social workers, and in virtually all of the academic disciplines. Finally, black nationalist groups have been formed among religious leaders and lay personnel within predominantly white religious groups throughout the country. These groups encourage their parent organizations to serve the cause of black liberation through the empowerment of black members.

Perhaps the formally organized large nationwide black nationalist organizations attracted greatest attention. Three of these groups, representing different approaches to black nationalism, will be discussed briefly for purposes of illustration. The Black Panther party (revolutionary nationalism), the Congress of African peoples (cultural nationalism), and the Nation of Islam (a combination of religious, cultural, and economic nationalism), popularly known as the Black Muslims, made an impact not only on the black community, but on the nation as a whole.

The Black Panther party, founded by Huey P. Newton and Bobby Seale in Oakland, California in the fall of 1966, quickly became the leading revolutionary black nationalist group in the United States.[8] Originally organized as a self-defense group to curb police brutality in Oakland's black community, the party soon expanded its program and through the years developed a Marxist-Leninist ideology, openly advocating the overthrow of capitalism. The program of the party appealed to large numbers of poor blacks outside the labor force because of their inability to secure employment. At the same time, the party's insistence upon maintaining arms for self-defense, combined with its revolutionary program, caused its members to be constant targets of police departments throughout the country. In the two years between 1968 and 1970, dozens of Panthers were killed and thousands arrested on trumped-up charges. All evidence suggests that the police harassment of the Panthers was part of a nationwide campaign to destroy them. It had all the earmarks of a "search and destroy" mission, directed by the federal government.

Throughout its brief history, the Black Panther party had a powerful influence on youth the world over, especially the oppressed in the United States. Groups of Chinese-Americans, Mexican-Americans, Puerto Ricans, and poor whites organized themselves along the lines of the Black Panther party, adopted its tactics, and formed alliances and coalitions with the party.

The Black Panther party was opposed from the beginning by some black nationalists. Chief among its opponents in the black community were those who identified with cultural nationalism. The cultural nationalists and their leading spokesman, Imamu Baraka (formerly LeRoi Jones), opposed the revolutionary tactics of the Panthers on the grounds that a violent revolution in the United States was impossible without a cultural revolution to unify the black community. In addition, the cultural nationalists opposed alliances and coalitions with white revolutionary groups, a major part of Panther strategy. Although there were few broadly based cultural nationalist groups in the black community, this ideology attracted large numbers of college students and other black intellectuals. An essential element of cultural nationalism was the doctrine of Kawaida (traditional black values and customs), with its seven principles of a black value system: unity, self-determination, collective work and responsibility, cooperative economics, purpose, creativity, and faith.[9]

Attempts were made to create a new value system among blacks through the Congress of African Peoples, an organization founded in

1970.[10] An additional purpose of these organizations was instilling pride and self-confidence in Afro-Americans. The cultural nationalists were also active in conventional politics, for they maintained that one step toward black liberation was black political power wherever blacks predominated in the population. The Congress played a leading role in the National Black Political Convention, held in Gary, Indiana, in 1972. Finally, the Congress of African Peoples envisioned the formation of an international black political party composed of Africans and peoples of African descent wherever they were found. The purpose of this party was to create a vehicle for blacks the world over to attain self-determination, self-sufficiency, self-defense, and self-respect.

While individual expressions of cultural nationalism have persisted and gained acceptance in recent years, organizations committed to this ideology have been somewhat less successful. But one organization which combined religious, cultural, and economic nationalism appears to have thrived. Originally a religious group which rejected Christianity, the Nation of Islam was founded in Detroit in 1930. Through the years it developed into a powerful movement with temples in every major city in the country. Its theology was frequently at odds with orthodox Islam, but its appeal to poor blacks has been widespread. The Nation of Islam's appeal to the poor is manifold; it provides economic security, self-respect, and proof that black Americans can achieve a significant measure of autonomy from the larger society.[11]

The theology of the Nation of Islam holds that blacks were the original people, that because of recent origin whites are innately inferior, and that Allah is the supreme black man, who will reappear in America to free the blacks from oppression. It is believed that white people are incapable of such human emotions as love and compassion, and that because of this blacks must separate themselves in order to survive. Cultural nationalism is an important aspect of the Nation of Islam. Through its network of schools, blacks are taught self-pride and pride in cultural heritage.

AFFIRMATIVE ACTION AND ITS OPPONENTS

President John F. Kennedy was assassinated in 1963. His successor, Lyndon B. Johnson, vowed to rid the society of its remaining practices of segregation and discrimination. But America's war of aggression in Vietnam meant that Johnson was required to devote more time and money to this misguided venture. Johnson was seen by many blacks as the second Abraham Lincoln, for he vigorously pursued a policy of equal rights for all. But many Americans and people the world over failed to understand the vigor with which the world's most industrialized nation prosecuted a war against a divided poor Third World country. Johnson was soon to learn that it was impossible to maintain a humane domestic policy while pursuing a war abroad. Wholesale disenchantment with Johnson because of the Vietnam War forced him to decline to seek reelection in 1968.

Johnson's presidency proved to enhance the civil rights of blacks; he presided over the Civil Rights Acts of 1964 and the Voting Rights Act of 1965. But his successor, Richard Nixon, was not only unsympathetic to blacks, he was antagonistic. For example, one of his first acts as president was to attempt to slow the pace of school integration by announcing that his administration would rely less on fund cutoffs by the Department of Health, Education and Welfare to achieve integration in the schools and more on the courts.[12] Such an approach would have made the courts rather then the executive branch enforcers of the law. And as was demonstrated in the early days after the *Brown* decision, it would have placed the burden of bringing lawsuits on the victims themselves. A Supreme Court ruling was required to inform Nixon that his plan was unacceptable.

In the meantime Nixon selected John Mitchell as his attorney general. Mitchell recommended that the Voting Rights Act of 1965 not be renewed. He proposed a substitute bill that would have substantially weakened the enforcement provisions. Mitchell's proposal passed the House of Reprensentatives but failed in the Senate.[13]

Thus, the way was paved for a reversal of the trend toward equality for black Americans. The Watergate scandal, with all of the earmarks of fascism, brought the downfall of the Nixon administration. His vice president, Spiro Agnew, a strong opponent of black rights, had already been forced to resign after pleading *nolo contendre* to one count of income tax evasion in a case in which he was accused of accepting kickbacks from Baltimore contractors. In 1974 Nixon became the first American president to resign his office after the House Judiciary Committee voted to impeach him.

Nixon was replaced as president by Gerald Ford, a conservative Republican but much less vociferous than his predecessor. Ford's tenure in office was a brief one, for he was to face the electorate in two years. He retained most of the staff he inherited from Nixon, and although he did not have a record of active interest in civil rights, he did little to turn back the clock. But he also did little to enhance the rights of black people. In the election of 1976 he was opposed by a southerner, Jimmy Carter, who during the campaign had gained the support of most of the black leadership. Gerald Ford had angered the American voters when he abruptly pardoned Nixon for all crimes after having indicated that he would not. Ford lost the election to Carter.

The Carter administration, a moderate one, had promised to pursue the cause of civil rights for blacks. Black voters in key states strongly supported Carter, and with their assistance he became president. During his one term, the rights of black citizens became one of his major concerns, and from the outset he appointed more blacks, other minorities, and women to key positions than had any of his predecessors. Furthermore, through a variety of programs he attempted to reduce youth unemployment, a serious problem for minorities. But progress in civil rights was tempered with caution because the mood of the country was rapidly becoming more conservative. It is because of this resurgence of conservatism and the perception of many voters that Carter was a liberal that he lost the election of 1980 to Ronald Reagan, an old-line conservative. Indeed, a *New York Times*/CBS national poll found that white people voted Republican because, among other reasons, they believed that the Democratic party had been too concerned with blacks.[14]

Ronald Reagan had a long history of antagonism toward blacks and other minorities. Because the election of 1980 also produced a Republican majority in the Senate, Reagan and his right-wing supporters there made it clear early in his administration that on domestic matters (e.g., social welfare programs, busing, abortion, prayer in schools, and voting rights) they intended to return the country to what it was prior to the depression of the 1930s.[15] Before assuming the presidency, Reagan opposed the Civil Rights Act of 1964 on the grounds that it was an unconstitutional infringement on private property rights. The list of other antiblack measures supported by Reagan and his administration is a long one indeed. His negative stand on civil rights and his support of right-wing groups have brought the forces of reaction and bigotry to the forefront of American politics, and in some cases have encouraged the use of violence against blacks and other minorities.[16]

The Reagan administration has opposed every legislative initiative and judicial decree to advance black rights. He and his associates opposed the extension and strengthening of the Voting Rights Act of 1965, a piece of legislation considered by many to be one of the most important in many years. They have reversed the federal government's long-standing commitment to end segregation in education, housing, and employment. The Civil Rights Commission has been stacked with people opposed to civil rights. The Justice Department is no longer a major proponent of equal rights; indeed, the department has opposed some of the civil rights legislation supported and in some cases initiated by previous officials in the department. The administration supported a move to grant tax exemptions to schools that practice racial discrimination.

Many programs designed to assist the poor (especially minorities) have been drastically reduced or eliminated. These include food stamps, public housing, hot lunches for school children, job training, medical care for the poor and the aged, college loans, supplementary aid to pregnant women and infants, community services, and legal aid. Homelessness is a major problem in the United States, and the administration, rather than assisting in alleviating the problem, has elected to ignore it. It is estimated by a national advocacy group for the homeless that the number of people in this condition is probably as many as three million, and their numbers are growing.[17]

And now to the debate over affirmative action. The Reagan administration appears to be opposed to all forms of affirmative action, whether they involve government contractors, companies with no government contracts, or even municipal governments. It is its position (1) that racial and sexual discrimination no longer exist in the United States; (2) that affirmative action discriminates against white males, thereby violating the Constitution; and (3) that affirmative action is a form of racism.

The government's contract-compliance program began in 1941 as an effort to prevent job discrimination by defense contractors. Through the years it grew steadily, with bipartisan support. Then in 1965 Lyndon Johnson issued an executive order to ensure that all workers were hired and promoted without regard to race, color, religion, sex, or national origin. Furthermore, this order, still in effect, requires that government contractors hire and promote women and members of minority groups in ways that roughly reflect the composition of their labor markets. It has been supported by five presidents, Democrats and Republicans, in both houses of Congress, by the American Federation of Labor-Congress of Industrial Organizations, and the National Association of Manufacturers, a trade organization representing more than 13,600 corporations.

The secretary of labor has been at odds with the Department of Justice on the question of affirmative action. The Justice Department officials have advocated that the president repeal certain Labor Department rules issued under the executive order. "The rules provide that if a federal contractor is 'deficient in the utilization of minority groups and women' the contractor must set goals and timetables and make 'good faith efforts' to achieve them."[18] The Labor Department rules affect 15,000 companies employing twenty-three million workers at 73,000 installations.

But members of the Reagan administration continue to oppose affirmative action. Indeed, in 1985 the administration served notice on some fifty cities, counties, and states that it would sue them in order to overturn their affirmative action programs. The government uses the *Memphis Firefighters v. Stotts* case, in which the Supreme Court ruled (with government support) in 1984 that a court cannot order an employer to undertake an affirmative-action remedy if it conflicts with the vested seniority rights of current employees. The court ruled that in laying off workers cities may not give preference to minorities over white workers with greater seniority.

The Reagan administration maintains that this decision also struck down preferential quotas in hiring and promotion. But the court did not address affirmative-action remedies in situations where there is no conflict with seniority rights.[19] In its decision the Court did not refer to its past decisions approving of affirmative-action remedies in general. In the

Regents of the University of California vs. *Allan Bakke* case, race-conscious remedies were upheld as constitutional, and in the *United Steel Workers of America* vs. *Weber* case, voluntary goals and timetables were upheld as lawful.

Representatives of states, counties, and municipalities have vowed to maintain their affirmative-action programs regardless of the wishes of the Department of Justice. The city of Indianapolis, Indiana, provides an interesting and instructive case. The Department of Justice announced on April 30, 1985, that a motion had been filed to modify the affirmative-action programs in the police and fire departments in that city. It was the first time that the Justice Department had ever taken a city to court to overturn its existing quotas for hiring women, blacks, and Hispanic workers.[20] This move was part of the Reagan administration's strategy to bring affirmative-action plans around the country in line with its interpretation of the *Stotts* case in Memphis. The administration maintains that the court's decision in this case also struck down preferential quotas in hiring and promotion.

The program that the Justice Department is attempting to overturn in Indianapolis resulted from a lawsuit that the department brought against the city in 1978. A court-approved agreement settled the suit against the city. In other words, the Department of Justice is suing Indianapolis for abiding by an agreement that it (the Department of Justice) demanded and approved under a previous administration. The mayor of the city, William Hudnut, a Republican, has pointed out that the plan has had a "positive effect" and had increased black representation in the fire department from 8 percent to 13 percent. The Indianapolis plan calls for the city to fill 25 percent of its training clases for police officers and firefighters with black applicants. The city also appoints women to at least twenty percent of openings for officers.[21] The mayor said the citizens of Indianapolis are satisfied with the plan as it is now structured, and that "there is a subtle tendency for people to say it's not required and to go back to business as usual. Well, Indianapolis won't go back to business as usual."[22]

It is significant that Reagan's plans to dismantle affirmative action have met with strong opposition in several states and cities throughout the country. New York state officials announced that they would not change their programs and invited the Department of Justice to sue them. Similar replies came from New Jersey and other states as well as the cities of Chicago, Boston, and Miami. Even white-owned newspapers in Mississippi that had long supported segregation and discrimination denounced Reagan's plans and announced that they supported goals and timetables.[23]

In addition to opposing affirmative action in employment, the Reagan administration has long opposed the transportation of students to eradicate segregated schools. Indeed, the Department of Justice, through its civil rights division, filed a friend-of-the-court brief in support of the Norfolk, Virginia, school board in 1984 in an effort to overturn the city's thirteen-year-old busing program for elementary-school students. This represented the first time the department argued that a school board could return to a neighborhood school system even if the result was segregated schools.

It should be clear by now that blacks and other minorities in the United States are in the midst of a serious crisis. For many years minorities have depended on the federal government to protect them from the racism practiced by states and municipalities, but now they have virtually no allies in Washington. Under previous administrations, the Civil Rights Commission was one of the agencies to which they could turn. The commission, established in 1957 as the federal government's independent watchdog over civil rights matters, especially the monitoring of federal laws and policies with respect to discrimination or other denials of equal protection of the laws, has been rendered completely ineffective by Ronald Reagan. In 1983 he fired commisioners who criticized his lack of enforcement of civil rights laws. His appointments to the commission have been people who are openly opposed to civil rights. Since it was reconstituted there has not been a monitoring report or statement on civil rights enforcement published.[24] Because of inaction by the commission, the chairman of the House Judiciary Subcommittee on Civil and Constitutional Rights maintains that the commission has moved "from watchdog to lap dog."

The debate over affirmative action and other civil rights programs is hardly new; it is just that the blatancy of the Reagan administration's antiminority position on virtually every issue has caused considerable alarm among civil rights advocates. Furthermore, in recent years there has emerged a group of black and white neoconservatives who support the president's position. The black neoconservatives support the president on several issues crucial to black people: they oppose affirmative action; they support the move to lower the minimum wage for young employees; they oppose the busing of students to promote quality education; they oppose federal programs designed to assist disadvantaged people. In short, their positions are opposed to the best interests of black people.[25] These people serve as informal advisers to the president, are welcomed at the White House, and since their views correspond with those of the president, they assist in the formulation of public policy.

The black neoconservatives are clearly not without their white counterparts. There are those who maintain that social programs, especially social welfare, have been detrimental to the poor. Some advocate the abolition of all welfare and urge that it be replaced by private charity. They criticize all federal antipoverty programs as counterproductive, and some champion what is call the "minimal state."[26] The books these people write and the views they espouse have had and continue to have a growing impact on public policy.

Needless to say, in this conservative era the scholars who oppose the Reagan administration's antiblack policies rarely have their voices heard. They are largely ignored by the media, but many of them have written important books, works that call for greater civil rights for minorities and maintain that it is the obligation of the government to make amends for past and present injustices inflicted upon Afro-Americans.[27]

Even if one assumes that the forces receptive to progressive change in the status of Afro-Americans outnumber the conservatives in the general population, it is certainly not true for those in government and other policy-making institutions. Conservatism appears to be the dominant ethos in the United States today, and it will no doubt maintain its sphere of influence even after Ronald Reagan's second term as president ends in 1988. But the widespread spirit of meanness brought about by conservatives in positions of power cannot last forever.

It should be noted here that on July 2, 1986, the Supreme Court, in two decisions, rebuffed the Reagan administration's stand on affirmative action. These decisions involved a union in New York City and the Fire Department in Cleveland. In both *Local 28 of the Sheet Metal Workers* vs. *Equal Employment Opportunity Commission* and *Local 93 of the International Association of Firefighters* vs. *City of Cleveland,* the court firmly endorsed the use of affirmative action in the workplace to cure past discrimination against minority groups, a position that the Department of Justice has long opposed. The Court held that existing civil rights law "does not prohibit a court from ordering, in appropriate circumstances, affirmative raceconscious relief as a remedy for past discrimination." Officials of the Reagan administration called these rulings "disappointing."[28]

The United States is basically a reformist society. Social change comes slowly, especially when it involves changes in black-white relations. It is a society more concerned with order and stability than with human rights. Hence problems involving black people were permitted to compound themselves throughout the long period between Reconstruction and World War II. Rather than move to alleviate the problems of segregation and discrimination, the federal government either supported white supremacy or remained aloof while states and other political subdivisions perpetuated these practices. Hence the present crisis is a result of problems compounded through the decades. That the status of black people represents a major social problem in the United States is a result of long-standing indifference on the part of public officials, at all levels, to blacks' status as citizens. The problem of the status of black people is, then, social in origin. It is a product of segregation and discrimination fostered by the ideology of white supremacy. This ideology permits whites to maintain dominance over blacks, thereby continuing to enjoy their position of privilege in the society. Otherwise they would be forced to share power with blacks in all social institutions, thereby weakening and ultimately eliminating white dominance and privilege.

A typical American approach to social problems is to permit them to go unattended in the hope that they will somehow disappear. Once the problems have reached crisis proportions, attempts are made to deal with them without changing the basic institutions which are responsible for creating them. Again, this is especially true of problems stemming from black-white relations. Whether the racial crisis in the United States deteriorates or improves depends on the willingness of white Americans, especially those in positions of power, to face the problems with candor and to deal with them boldly. The demand by black Americans for equality is in no sense unreasonable; indeed, it is long overdue. And this demand will likely intensify with time. The mood and power of black Americans at the present time are such that this demand cannot long be ignored. The longer the delay, the greater the physical and social destruction which is likely to result; domestic tranquility depends on racial justice. Afro-Americans are aware of the nature of their oppression, and it is unlikely that an aroused black community will long permit its inhabitants to remain an oppressed colony in a rich nation.

Black Americans have never been an integral part of society. They have been excluded from the major institutions of the society, and as a result, they view society from a vantage point different from that of white Americans. Because of this rejection, they have maintained a detachment from society which is difficult for those who have been accepted by society and who identify with it to understand. This detachment has led to greater insight into society's contradictions and a greater receptivity to social change. Few of them have any vested interest in maintaining the status quo. Consequently, black Americans are likely to view the racial crisis in the United States with greater urgency than are white Americans. The extent to which the society is able to avoid increased racial conflict depends upon the willingness of white Americans to come to terms with the reality of the status of Afro-Americans and the requirements for improving this status. The reality is that, as the society is presently structured, the dominant whites maintain the oppression of black people because of the privileges they enjoy in all institutions. The existing inequalities are not the result of an aberration; they have been firmly rooted in the social structure for centuries. And the requirements for improvement include, above all, greater sharing of the power in the society by members of America's internal colony. Past experience indicates that the prognosis is not favorable.

SELECTED BIBLIOGRAPHY

ALLEN, ROBERT. *Black Awakening in Capitalist America.* New York: Doubleday & Co., 1970.
BARBOUR, FLOYD, ed. *The Black Power Revolt.* Boston: Porter Sargent, 1968.
BITTKER, BORIS I. *The Case For Black Reparations.* New York: Random House, 1973.

BLAUNER, ROBERT. *Racial Oppression in America.* New York: Harper & Row, Publishers, 1972.

BRACEY, JOHN, et al., eds. *Black Nationalism in America.* Indianapolis and New York: Bobbs-Merrill Co., 1970.

BREITMAN, GEORGE, ed. *By Any Means Necessary.* New York: Pathfinder Press, 1970.

———. *The Last Year of Malcolm X.* New York: Schocken Books, 1968.

———, ed. *Malcolm X: The Man and His Ideas.* New York: Pioneer Publishers, 1965.

———, ed. *Malcolm X Speaks.* New York: Grove Press, 1966.

BROWN, H. RAP. *Die Nigger Die!* New York: Dial Press, 1969.

CARMICHAEL, STOKELY. *Stokely Speaks.* New York: Random House, 1971.

———, and CHARLES HAMILTON, *Black Power: The Politics of Liberation in America.* New York: Random House, 1967.

CLARKE, JOHN H., ed. *Malcolm X: The Man and His Times.* New York: Collier Books, 1969.

CLEAGE, ALBERT. *Black Christian Nationalism.* New York: William Morrow and Co., 1972.

———. *The Black Messiah.* New York: Sheed and Ward, 1969.

CONE, JAMES H. *A Black Theology of Liberation.* Philadelphia: J. B. Lippincott Co., 1970.

CRONON, EDMUND. *Black Moses: The Story of Marcus Garvey and the Universal Negro Improvement Association.* Madison: University of Wisconsin Press, 1964.

CRUSE, HAROLD. *The Crisis of the Negro Intellectual.* New York: William Morrow and Co., 1967.

———. *Rebellion or Revolution?* New York: William Morrow and Co., 1968.

DRAPER, THEODORE. *The Rediscovery of Black Nationalism.* New York: Viking Press, 1970.

EDWARDS, HARRY. *Black Students.* New York: Free Press, 1970.

EPPS, ARCHIE. *The Speeches of Malcolm X at Harvard.* New York: William Morrow and Co., 1968.

ESSIEN-UDOM, E. U. *Black Nationalism: A Search for an Identity in America.* Chicago: University of Chicago Press, 1962.

FAGER, CHARLES E. *White Reflections on Black Power.* Grand Rapids, Mich: Wm. B. Erdmans Publishing Co., 1967.

FANON, FRANTZ. *Black Skins, White Masks.* New York: Grove Press. 1967.

———. *The Wretched of the Earth.* New York: Grove Press. 1963.

FAX, ELTON. *Garvey: The Story of a Pioneer Black Nationalist.* New York: Dodd, Mead and Co., 1972.

FLEMMING, JOHN, et al. *The Case for Affirmative Action for Blacks in Higher Education.* Washington, D.C.: Howard University Press, 1978.

FONER. PHILIP, ed. *The Black Panthers Speak.* Philadelphia: J. B. Lippincott Co., 1970.

———. ed, *W. E. B. Du Bois Speaks.* New York: Pathfinder Press, 1970.

FOREMAN, JAMES. *The Making of Black Revolutionaries.* New York: Macmillan Co., 1972.

FULLINWIDER, S. P. *The Mind and Mood of Black America.* Homewood, Ill.: Dorsey Press, 1969.

GARTNER, ALAN, et al., eds. *What Reagan Is Doing to Us.* New York: Harper Row, Publishers, 1982.

GARVEY, AMY-JACQUES. *Garvey and Garveyism.* New York: Collier Books, 1970.

———, ed. *Philosophy and Opinions of Marcus Garvey.* New York: Arno Press, 1967.

GLAZER, NATHAN. *Affirmative Discrimination: Ethnic Inequality and Public Policy.* New York: Basic Books, 1975.

GOLDMAN, PETER. *The Death and Life of Malcolm X.* New York: Harper & Row, Publishers, 1973.

GOLDSTEIN, RHODA, ed. *Black Life and Culture in the United States.* New York: Thomas Y. Crowell Co., 1971.

HARRIS, SHELDON. *Paul Cufee: Black America and the African Return.* New York: Simon & Schuster, 1972.

HILL, ADELIDE, and MARTIN KILSON, eds. *Apropos of Africa.* New York: Doubleday and Co., 1971.

HOUGH, JOSEPH. *Black Power and White Christians.* New York: Oxford University Press, 1968.

JACKSON, GEORGE. *The Blood in My Eye.* New York: Random House 1972.

———. *Soledad Brother.* New York: Bantam Books, 1970.

JONES, FAUSTINE. *The Changing Mood in America: Eroding Commitment?* Washington, D.C.: Howard University Press, 1977.

JONES, LEROI (Imamu Baraka). *African Congress.* New York: William Morrow and Co., 1972.

———. *Raise, Race, Rays, Raze.* New York: Random House, 1971.

————, and LARRY NEAL, eds. *Black Fire: An Anthology of Afro-American Writing.* New York: William Morrow and Co., 1968.

LECKEY, R., and H. E. WRIGHT, eds. *The Black Manifesto.* New York: Sheed & Ward, 1969.

LINCOLN, C. ERIC. *The Black Muslims in America.* Boston: Beacon Press, 1961.

MALCOLM X. *The Autobiography of Malcolm X.* New York: Grove Press, 1965.

————. *Malcolm X on Afro-American History.* New York: Pathfinder Press, 1970.

MARINE, GENE. *The Black Panthers.* New York: New American Library, 1969.

MEAD, LAWRENCE. *Beyond Entitlement: The Social Obligations of Citizenship.* New York: Free Press, 1985.

MEMMI, ALBERT. *The Colonizer and the Colonized.* Boston: Beacon Press, 1967.

MOORE, GILBERT. *A Special Rage.* New York: Harper & Row, Publishers, 1971.

MUHAMMAD, ELIJAH. *Message to the Blackman in America.* Chicago: Muhammad Mosque No. 2, 1965.

MURRAY, CHARLES. *Losing Ground: American Social Policy, 1950–1980.* New York: Basic Books, 1984.

NEWTON, HUEY P. *To Die for the People.* New York: Random House, 1972.

————. *Revolutionary Suicide.* New York: Harcourt Brace Jovanovich, 1973.

PADMORE, GEORGE. *Pan-Africanism or Communism.* New York: Doubleday & Co., 1972.

PINKNEY, ALPHONSO. *The Myth of Black Progress.* New York: Cambridge University Press, 1984.

————. *Red, Black and Green: Black Nationalism in the United States.* New York: Cambridge University Press, 1976.

REDKEY, EDWIN. *Black Exodus: Black Nationalist and Back to Africa Movements, 1890–1910.* New Haven, Conn.: Yale University Press, 1969.

ROBINSON, ARMSTEAD, ed. *Black Studies in the University.* New York: Bantam Books, 1969.

RUDWICK, ELLIOTT. *W. E. B. Du Bois: Propagandist of the Negro Protest.* New York: Atheneum, 1968.

SEALE, BOBBY. *Seize the Time: The Story of the Black Panther Party and Huey P. Newton.* New York: Random House, 1970.

SOWELL, THOMAS. *Affirmative Action Reconsidered.* Washington, D.C.: American Enterprise Institute for Public Policy Research, 1975.

ULLMAN, VICTOR. *Martin R. Delaney: The Beginnings of Black Nationalism.* Boston: Beacon Press, 1972.

VINCENT, THEODORE. *Black Power and the Garvey Movement.* Berkeley, Calif: *Ramparts* Press, 1971.

WEINBERG, MEYER, ed. *W. E. B. Du Bois: A Reader.* New York: Harper & Row, Publishers, 1970.

WILLIAMS, WALTER. *Youth and Minority Unemployment.* Stanford, Calif: Hoover Institution, 1977.

WILMORE, GAYRAND. *Black Religion and Black Radicalism.* New York: Doubleday & Co., 1972.

WILSON, WILLIAM. *The Declining Significance of Race.* Chicago: University of Chicago Press, 1978.

YETTE, SAMUEL. *The Choice: The Issue of Black Survival in America.* New York: G. P. Putnam's Sons, 1971.

NOTES

[1]William Alexander, *Memoir of Captain Paul Cuffee, A Man of Colour* (London: published by the author, 1811); Sheldon Harris, *Paul Cuffee: Black America and the African Return* (New York: Simon & Schuster, 1972).

[2]Frank A. Rollin, *Life and Public Services of Martin R. Delany* (Boston: Lee and Shepard, 1868); Victor Ullman, *Martin R. Delany: The Beginnings of Black Nationalism* (Boston: Beacon Press, 1972).

[3]Edwin S. Redkey, *Black Exodus* (New Haven, Conn.: Yale University Press, 1969).

[4]Edmund D. Cronin, *Black Moses* (Madison: University of Wisconsin Press, 1964); Elton C. Fax, *Garvey: The Story of a Pioneer Black Nationalist* (New York: Dodd, Mead, 1972); Amy-Jacques Garvey, *Garvey and Garveyism* (New York: Collier Books, 1970); Amy-Jacques Garvey, ed., *Philosophy and Opinions of Marcus Garvey* (New York: Arno 1968); Theodore G. Vincent, *Black Power and the Garvey Movement* (Berkeley: Ramparts Press, 1971).

[5]George Breitman, ed., *Malcolm X: The Man and His Ideas* (New York: Pioneer Publishers 1965); George Breitman, *The Last Year of Malcolm X* (New York: Shocken Books, 1968); George Breitman, ed., *By Any Means Necessary* (New York: Pathfinder, 1970); George Breitman, ed., *Malcolm X Speaks* (New York: Grove Press, 1966); John H. Clark, ed., *Malcolm X: The Man and His Times* (New York: Collier, 1969); Archie Epps, ed., *The Speeches of Malcolm X at Harvard* (New York: William Morrow, 1969); Peter Goldman, *The Death and Life of Malcolm X* (New York: Harper & Row, 1973); Malcolm X, *The Autobiography of Malcolm X* (New York: Grove Press, 1965); Malcolm X, *Malcolm X on Afro-American History* (New York: Pathfinder, 1970).

[6]These studies are summarized in Kenneth B. Clark, *Prejudice and Your Child* (Boston: Beacon Press, 1963).

[7]J. Hraba and J. Grant, "Black is Beautiful: A Reexamination of Racial Preference and Identification," *Journal of Personality and Social Psychology* 16 (1970), 398–402; S. H. Ward and J. Braun, "Self-Esteem and Racial Preference in Black Children," *American Journal of Orthopsychiatry* 42 (July 1972), 371–78.

[8]Philip S. Foner, ed., *The Black Panthers Speak* (Philadelphia, Lippincott 1970); Gene Marine, *The Black Panthers* (New York: New American Library, 1969); Gilbert Moore, *A Special Rage* (New York: Harper & Row, 1971); Huey P. Newton, *To Die for the People* (New York: Random House, 1972); Huey P. Newton, *Revolutionary Suicide* (New York: Harcourt Brace Jovanovich, 1973); Bobby Seale, *Seize the Time: The Story of the Black Panther Party and Huey P. Newton* (New York: Random House, 1970).

[9]Imamu Baraka (LeRoi Jones), *Raise, Race, Rays, Raze* (New York: Random House, 1971), pp. 133–46.

[10]Imamu Baraka, *African Congress* (New York: Morrow, 1972).

[11]E. U. Essien-Udom, *Black Nationalism* (Chicago: University of Chicago Press, 1962); C. Eric Lincoln, *The Black Muslims in America* (Boston: Beacon Press, 1961); Elijah Muhammad, *Message to the Blackman in America* (Chicago: Muhammad Mosque of Islam No. 2, 1965).

[12]Michael W. Miles, *The Odyssey of the American Right* (New York: Oxford University Press, 1980), pp. 518–19.

[13]Ibid., pp. 319–20.

[14]*New York Times,* December 3, 1983, p. 1.

[15]See Alphonso Pinkney, *The Myth of Black Progress* (New York: Cambridge University Press, 1984).

[16]Ibid., pp. 171–73.

[17]*The New York Times,* February 16, 1986, p. 31.

[18]*New York Times,* January 30, 1986, p. B9.

[19]*New York Times,* June 19, 1985, p. A22.

[20]*New York Times,* April 30, 1985, p. 1.

[21]Ibid., p. 23.

[22]*New York Times,* May 1, 1985, p. B28.

[23]*New York Times,* May 4, 1985, p. 1.

[24]*New York Times,* October 30, 1985, p. A26.

[25]See, for example, Walter Williams, *Youth and Minority Unemployment* (Stanford, Calif: Hoover Institution, 1977); William Wilson, *The Declining Significance of Race* (Chicago: University of Chicago Press, 1978); Thomas Sowell, *Affirmative Action Reconsidered* (Washington, D.C.: American Enterprise Institute for Public Policy Research, 1975).

[26]See, for example, Nathan Glazer, *Affirmative Discrimination: Ethnic Inequality and Public Policy* (New York: Basic Books, 1975); Lawrence Mead, *Beyond Entitlement: The Social Obligations of Citizenship* (New York: Free Press, 1985); Charles Murray, *Losing Ground: American Social Policy, 1950–1980* (New York: Basic Books, 1984).

[27]See, for example, Carol C. Collins, ed., *Black Progress: Reality or Illusion* (New York: Facts on File Publications, 1984); John Flemming et al., *The Case for Affirmative Action for Blacks in Higher Education* (Washington, D.C.: Howard University Press, 1978); Alan Gartner et al., eds., *What Reagan Is Doing to Us* (New York: Harper & Row, 1982); Faustine C. Jones, *The Changing Mood in America: Eroding Commitment?* (Washington, D.C.: Howard University Press, 1977); Alphonso Pinkney, *The Myth of Black Progress* (New York: Cambridge University Press, 1984); Stephen Steinberg, *The Ethnic Myth* (Boston: Beacon Press, 1981).

[28]*New York Times,* July 3, 1986, p. 1.

INDEXES

NAME INDEX

Agnew, Spiro, 213
Ali, Muhammad, 189

Baldwin, James, 130
Baraka, Imamu (formerly LeRoi Jones), 200, 211
Bernard, Jessie, 101
Blauner, Robert, 155
Brown, H. Rap, 200
Brown, John, 11

Carmichael, Claude P., 139, 140–41
Carmichael, Stokely, 160, 169, 186, 187, 198
Carter, Jimmy, 213–14
Cayton, Horace, 61–63, 120
Clark, Kenneth, 52, 63
Clausen, John A., 145
Cleaver, Eldridge, 200
Cuffee, Paul, 206–7

Davis, Allison, 61, 105
Delany, Martin R., 207
Dollard, John, 60
Douglass, Frederick, 8
Drake, St. Clair, 61–63, 120
Du Bois, William E.B., 16, 20, 24, 26, 208

Elkins, Stanley, 12
Evers, Medgar, 200

Ford, Gerald, 213
Franklin, John H., 6, 8, 9, 14, 23
Frazier, E. Franklin, 3, 6, 25, 61, 62, 116, 121

Gardner, Burleigh, 61
Gardner, Mary, 61
Garvey, Marcus, 28, 155, 207–8
Gordon, Milton, 154, 155
Grace, Charles Emanuel, 122
Grant, Ulysses S., 19

Hamilton, Charles, 187
Harris, Louis, 161, 163
Havighurst, Robert J., 105
Hayes, Rutherford B., 22
Hill, Robert, 106
Hollingshead, August B., 139–40
Hudnut, William, 216
Humphrey, Hubert, 205
Hunter, Floyd, 110

Ickes, Harold L., 29

Jackson, Jesse, 123
Johnson, Andrew, 19–20
Johnson, Charles S., 54, 55, 60
Johnson, Lyndon B., 100, 201, 212–13, 215
Jones, LeRoi, 200, 211
Julian, Percy, 164

Kardiner, Abram, 141, 143
Kemble, Frances, 6
Kennedy, John F., 212
King, Martin Luther, Jr., 55, 122, 123–24, 160, 181, 186, 188, 200–201

Lee, Robert E., 19
Lincoln, Abraham, 15–16, 17, 19, 212
Lumumba, Patrice, 199

Malcolm X, 185–86, 197, 199, 200, 208–9
Malzberg, Benjamin, 138, 140
McKissick, Floyd, 187–88, 198
Meredith, James, 186
Mitchell, John, 213
Moynihan, Daniel P., 88, 99–100, 101, 103
Muhammad, Elijah, 155, 160
Muhammad, Marith Deen, 155
Myrdal, Gunnar, 116, 117, 120, 134, 156

Newton, Huey P., 211
Nixon, Richard M., 88, 201, 205, 213

Ovesey, Lionel, 141, 143

Parks, Rosa, 176–77
Pasamanick, Benjamin, 139, 140
Pettigrew, Thomas F., 140
Phillips, Ulrich B., 13
Prosser, Gabriel, 123

Reagan, Ronald, 214, 216, 217
Redlich, Frederick C., 139–40
Roosevelt, Eleanor, 29
Roosevelt, Franklin D., 29
Roosevelt, Theodore, 25
Russell, Bertrand, 198

Scammon, Richard, 65
Srole, Leo, 139–40
Stampp, Kenneth M., 3–5, 8, 12
Steale, Bobby, 211

Taeuber, Alma, 57
Taeuber, Karl E., 57
Taft, William H., 25
Tannenbaum, Frank, 7
Tilden, Samuel, 22
Till, Emmett, 176
Truman, Harry S, 30–31
Turner, Henry M., 207
Turner, Nat, 11, 116, 123

Vesey, Denmark, 11, 123

Wallace, George, 205
Washington, Booker T., 5, 24–25, 26, 207
Wattenberg, Ben, 65
Wilkins, Roy, 160
Williams, Ernest Y., 139, 140–41
Woodson, Carter G., 16

SUBJECT INDEX

A. Philip Randolph Institute, 169, 188
Abolitionists, 12, 15, 18
Abortion, 101, 104
Abuse, substance, 143–47
Achievement, debate over educational, 76–77

Addiction, drug, 143–47
AFDC, 103
Affiliation, religious, 118–19
Affirmative action, 212–19
Africa
    efforts to return to, 206–8
    independence of colonies in, 176
African Emigration Association, 207
African Institution, 206
African Methodist Episcopal Church, 118–19, 207
African Methodist Episcopal Zion Church, 119
Afro-American studies programs, 210
Age
    composition of population, 41–43
    differential income between blacks and whites
        by, 87, 88
    mental illness rate by, 141–42
    unemployment rate by, 82–83
Agricultural Adjustment Administration, 29
Aid to Families with Dependent Children (AFDC),
    103
Alabama, University of, 177, 179
Alabama Conference of Black Mayors, 210
Alan Guttmacher Institute of New York, 104
Alcohol abuse, 146, 147
Alcoholic psychoses, 140
Amendments. See U.S. Constitution
American Baptist Convention, 119
American Colonization Society, 207
American Federation of Labor-Congress of In-
    dustrial Organizations, 191, 215
Antebellum period. See Slavery
Antimiscegenation laws, 158
Apartheid in South Africa, 199
Arrest rate for blacks, 132–34
Arts, contributions of blacks to, 28, 210
Assimilation into American society, 153–75
    attitude-receptional, 161–63
    behavior-receptional, 163–68
    civil, 168–70
    cultural, 154–56
    identificational, 159–61
    marital, 158–59
    primary vs. secondary, 158
    stages and subprocesses in, 154
    structural, 156–58
Assistance
    conflict over government responsibilities, 168,
        169–70
    dependency on, family stability and, 103
    during New Deal, 29
    under Reagan administration, 214–15
    See also Affirmative action
Atlanta, Georgia, destruction during Civil War, 19
"Atlanta Compromise" speech, 24
Attendance, school, 71, 72
Attitude-receptional assimilation, 161–63
Attitudes of white people
    black uprisings of 1963–67 and, 196
    identificational assimilation and, 160
    New Deal as turning point in, 29
    toward slaves, 7–9
    See also Assimilation into American society; Dis-
        crimination; White supremacy, institutional-
        ized
Awareness
    of history, 199–200
    political, 196–99

Baltimore, Maryland, mental illness among blacks in, 139
Banks, black, 85
Baptist church, 116, 118, 120
Behavior-receptional assimilation, 163–68
Birmingham, Alabama, civil rights demonstration in, 181–82
Birth rate, 37–39, 100–101, 104–5
Black Cabinet, 29
Black Codes, 20
Black Enterprise, 84
Black Liberators, 209
Black Muslims, 119, 122, 155, 211
Black norm, 143
Black Panther party, 210–11
Black Power movement, 168, 169, 186–92, 205
Black Solidarity Day, 209
Black Star Shipping Line, 208
Boycotts
  bus, 122, 123, 176–77
  economic, 179
Brown v. *Board of Education,* 71–73, 213
Bureau of Refugees Freedmen, and Abandoned Lands, 20, 97, 116
Bus boycott, 122, 123, 176–77
Business
  ceiling on black advancement in, 80
  enterprises, 83–86
  See also Occupations

Cambridge, Maryland, demonstrations in, 182
Cancer, incidence of, 40, 41
Catholic schools, 121
Census Bureau, 48, 88, 111, 158, 159
Censuses, population, 37
Central Intelligence Agency, 199
Charleston, South Carolina, planned slave revolt in, 11
Chattel slavery. *See* Slavery
Chicago, Illinois
  black population density in, 57
  interracial marriages in, 159
  social stratification in, 61–63
  study of police practices in, 137
Chicago, University of, 162
Child-rearing practices, 105–6
Children
  effects of family disorganization on, 102–3
  infant mortality rates, 40, 41
  out-of-wedlock, 100–101, 104
  slavery and, 3, 4, 96
  See also Family
Christian Methodist Episcopal Church, 119
Christ's Sanctified Holy Church, 119
Church, the. *See* Religion
Church of God, 122
Church of God in Christ, 119
Cincinnati, Ohio, mental illness among blacks in, 139
CIO, 29–30
Citizenship, 160
Civil assimilation, 168–70
Civil Rights, Office for, 74, 75
Civil Rights Acts
  of 1866, 21, 109
  of 1870, 109
  of 1875, 23, 109

of 1957, 109
of 1960, 109, 181
of 1964, 74, 80, 108, 109, 164, 165, 167, 168, 182, 183, 186, 192, 213, 214
of 1968, 80
Civil Rights Commission, 214, 217
Civil rights movement, 179–83
  the church and, 55, 118, 122–24, 181
  deadlock in, 192–93
  reformist orientation of, 191
Civil War, 15–19
  destruction caused by, 18–19
  emancipation, 17–18, 96
  family life and, 96
  nationalist efforts by blacks prior to, 206–7
  participation by blacks in, 16–17
Class, social. *See* Social stratification
Coalition politics, 188–89
Cocaine, 147
College
  black student organizations at, 197
  desegregation, 178–79
  enrollment, 75–76
  income and attendance of, 88, 89
  quality of black education in, 75–76
  students, increasing political awareness of, 196–97
  unemployment rate for graduates of, 83
Colonialism, internal, 195
Columbia University, 197
Commerce, Department of, 89
Community, black, 51–68
  control of schools, 77
  growth and development of, 51–53
  influence of politics on, 110–11
  internal colonialism of, 185
  rural, 53–56, 60–61
  social stratification of, 59–65
  urban, 56–59, 61–64
  See also Assimilation into American society; Institutions, social
Compromise of 1877, 22–23
Confederate armies, 17, 18
Conflict
  power, 168–69
  value, 168, 169–70
Congregational church, 119, 121
Congressional Black Caucus, 112, 114, 210
Congress of African Peoples, 209, 211–12
Congress of Industrial Organizations (CIO), 29–30
Congress of Racial Equality (CORE), 180, 186, 187, 189, 198
Conservatism, resurgence of, 214–19
Contract-compliance program, 215
Cornell Studies in Intergroup Relations, 162
Cornell University, 197
Cosmetics business, 84
Cotton States Exposition (1895), 24
County government officials, 113
Crime, 131–35. *See also* Juvenile delinquency
Cults, religious, 119, 122
Cultural assimilation, 154–56
Cultural nationalism, 208, 211–12
Cultural paranoia, 143
Culture
  distinctive black, 156

Culture (*cont.*)
  native
    in religion, 115
    slavery and loss of, 6–7, 153, 154
    survivals of, 155

Danville, Virginia, demonstrations in, 182
Death rate, 5–6, 39–41
De facto segregation, 166–67, 180
Deinstitutionalization of mental patients, 138
Delinquency, juvenile, 131, 135–38. *See also*
    Crime
Democratic Party, 29, 112, 188
Demonstrations, civil rights, 179–83
Dependency, welfare, 103
Depressants, 144, 145
Deprivation, relative, 195–96. *See also* Socioeco-
    nomic status
Desegregation in education, 73–77, 167, 175–76
  attitudes of whites toward, 162–63
  resistance in South to, 176–79
  violence over, 177–79
Despair in slums, 183–86, 193
Destruction caused by Civil War, 18–19
Detroit, Michigan, uprising in, 195
Developing nations
  comparisons to, 48, 59, 185, 196
  linking black movement to, 198
Deviance, social, 130–52
  crime and delinquency, 131–38
  drug addiction (substance abuse), 143–47
  environment and, 130, 140, 141, 143, 147
  mental illness, 138–43
Discrimination
  in administration of justice, 131–32, 134, 135,
    167–68
  against voting rights, 168
  behavior of, 163–68
  in education, 166–67
  in employment, 89, 165–66
  in housing, 164–65
  New Deal and, 29
  "racial succession," 52–53
  See also Attitudes of white people; Civil rights
    movement; Revolt, black
Disfranchisement, 25, 26, 107, 108
Distribution, regional. *See* Regional distribution
Distribution of power, civil conflicts over, 168–69
Divorce rate, 100, 103
Drug addiction, 143–47

Earnings. *See* Income
Economic boycott, 179
Economic Opportunity Act of 1964, 184–85
Economics of rural black community, 55–56
Economic status. *See* Socioeconomic status
Education, 69–77
  Afro-American studies programs, 210
  desegregation of, 73–77, 167, 175–76
    resistance in South to, 176–79
    violence over, 177–79
  discrimination in, 166–67
  for free blacks, 15
  officials, black, 113–14
  poverty and, 89
  quality of, 71–77

quantity of, 70–71, 72
  during Reconstruction, 21–22
  in rural communities, 55
  during slavery, 70
  social stratification and, 60–65
  in urban black community, 59
Education, Department of, 75
Emancipation, 17–18, 96
Emancipation Proclamation, 17
Emigration, efforts at, 206–7
Employment
  discrimination in, 165–66
  opportunities, 78, 80, 165
  See also Occupations
Enlistment Act of 1862, 16
Environment, social deviance and, 130, 140, 141,
    143, 147
Episcopal church, 116, 121
Equal employment opportunities, 165
Ethnic power, concept of, 190. *See also* Black ̇
    Power movement
Extended-family pattern, 98

Fair Employment Practices Law (1945), 30
Fair Housing Act of 1968, 165
"Falling Behind" (Center on Budget and Policy
    Priorities), 90
Family, 95–106
  developmental process, 95–97
  juvenile delinquency and, 136
  of lower-class urban blacks, 63
  in 1980, deomgraphics of, 97–99
  patterns of family life, 105–6
  under slavery, 3, 6, 95–96
  stability of, 96, 97, 99–105
  strengths of, 106
Father Divine Peace Mission Movement, 122
Fathers, families without, 96, 97–98, 101–3, 104,
    105, 136
Federal Bureau of Investigation (FBI), 132, 137,
    167
Federal Bureau of Narcotics, 144, 145
Federal Housing Administration, 29
Female headed households, 96, 97–98, 101–3,
    104, 105, 136
Females, mental illness among black, 142
Fertility rate, 37–39, 100–101,
    104–5
Field slaves, 5
Fifteenth Amendment, 21, 26, 108–9
Financial institutions, black, 85
Ford Foundation study on drug addiction, 144–
    45
Fortune magazine, 84
Fourteenth Amendment, 21, 24, 26, 108–9
Free blacks, 2, 13–15
  aid to runaway slaves, 12
  attitudes toward, 7–8
  family relations of, 96
  religion of, 116
  social stratification of, 59
Freedmen's Bureau, 20, 97, 116
Freedom Budget, 169, 188
Freedom riders, 180
Fugitive Slave Law (1793), 12
Functional psychoses, 140

Gabriel (slave), insurrection plan of, 10
Ghettos, 52, 183–86, 193. *See also* Urban areas
Government
  affirmative action and, 212–19
  assistance to black business sector, 84
  black public officials, 112–15
  employment, 81
  responsibilities, conflicts over, 168, 169–70
Grandfather clauses, 109
Great Depression of 1930s, 28–29
"Great Society" programs, 201
Greenwood, Mississippi, 181

Hall v. *deCeur*, 24
Harlem, 53, 58, 120, 135, 145, 208
Harpers Ferry, attack on, 11
Health, 5–6, 39–41, 138–43
Health, Education and Welfare (HEW), Department of, 74, 101, 213
Health and Human Services, Department of, 40
Heroin, use of, 144, 145, 147
Higher education. *See* College; Education
Historical background, 1–35
  Civil War, 15–19
    destruction caused by, 18–19
    emancipation, 17–18, 96
    family life and, 96
    nationalist efforts by blacks prior to, 206–7
    participation by blacks in, 16–17
  institutionalized white supremacy, 23–31
    black response to, 25–26
    Great Depression, 28–29
    Jim Crow, emergence of, 23–25, 97
    New Deal, 29
    religion and, 117
    World War I and aftermath, 26–28, 44
    World War II, 30, 44
  politics, trends in, 107–8
  Reconstruction, 19–23
    black church during, 116–17
    Compromise of 1877, 22–23
    Radical Reconstruction, 20–22, 107, 108
  slavery. *See* Slavery
History, awareness of, 199–200
Home ownership, 62, 98
Hopelessness, feelings of, 193–94
House churches, 120
House slaves, 5, 12
Housing, 184
  developments, 52–53
  discrimination in, 164–65
  in 1980s, 98–99
  in urban black community, 58

Identificational assimilation, 159–61
Illiteracy rate, 70–71. *See also* Education
Illness, mental, 138–43. *See also* Health
Income, 86–90, 166, 184
  dissolution of marriage and, 100
  in government employment, 81
  in 1980, 98
  poverty among blacks, 89–90, 103, 169–70, 183–86, 193
  in professional jobs, 80
  in rural black communities, 54
Indentured servants, 2

Indianapolis, Indiana, affirmative action case in, 216
Infant mortality rate, 40, 41
Inferiority, claims of racial, 7–8, 13–15, 26, 27. *See also* Discrimination; White supremacy, institutionalized
Institutions, social, 95–129
  family, 95–106
    developmental process, 95–97
    juvenile delinquency and, 136
    of lower-class urban blacks, 63
    in 1980, demographics of, 97–99
    patterns of family life, 105–6
    under slavery, 3, 6, 95–96
    stability of, 96, 97, 99–105
    strengths of, 106
  politics, 106–15
    black participation in, 21, 25
    coalition, 188–89
    historical trends, 107–8
    organization and behavior, 110–12
    public officials, 112–15
    voting rights, 14, 21, 25, 26, 29, 107, 108–10, 168, 181, 183
    racism in, 163
  religion, 115–24, 212
    affiliation, 118–19
    civil rights and the church, 55, 118, 122–24, 181
    developmental history, 9, 115–18
    of lower-class urban blacks, 64
    of middle-class urban blacks, 62
    in rural black communities of South, 54–55
    structure and patterns, 120–22
    structural assimilation and, 156
    See also White supremacy, institutionalized
Integration. *See* Assimilation into American society; Desegregation
Integrationists, 76
Internal colonialism, 185
Internationalization of movement for equality, 197–99, 209
International Migration Society, 207
International War Crimes Tribunal, 198
Interracial marriages, 158–59, 163
Interstate Commerce Commission, 180
Islamic groups in black community, 119, 209, 212

Jim Crow laws, 23–25, 97
Joint Committee on National Recovery, 29
Justice, Department of, 132, 181, 182, 214, 215, 216
Justice, discrimination in administration of, 131–32, 134, 135, 167–68
Juvenile delinquency, 131, 135–38. *See also* Crime

Kawaida, doctrine of, 211
Kinship relations, 106. *See also* Family
Knights of the White Camelia, 22
Knowledge, health and, 40–41
Ku Klux Klan, 22, 182, 208

Labor, Department of, 99
Labor, division of slave, 4–5. *See also* Occupations
Labor Department, 215

Law-enforcement positions, blacks in, 113, 210. *See also* Crime; Police
Laws
  on free blacks, 13, 14–15
  of slavery, 3–4, 7
  See also U.S. Constitution; U.S. Supreme Court; specific laws
Leadership, black, 110, 111–12, 197. *See also* Politics; Religion
Legal system, lack of respect for, 167–68
Liberation, black. *See* Nationalism, black
Liberation, black theology of, 124
Liberia, 207
Life expectancy, 40, 43
Life insurance companies, black, 85–86
Lifestyle
  health and, 40–41
  social stratification and, 62–63
  See also Rural areas; Urban areas; Socioeconomic status
Lincoln University, 15
Literary activity of Negro renaissance, 28
Little Rock, Arkansas, mob violence in, 178
Living standards. *See* Standard of living
Looting, 194, 195
Los Angeles, California
  black population density in, 57–58
  interracial marriages in, 159
Louisiana, mental illness among blacks in, 139
Louisville, New Orleans, and Texas Railroad v. *Mississippi*, 24
Lower class
  cultural assimilation of, 155
  political behavior in, 110–11
  in rural black community, 60
  in urban black community, 61, 63–64
Lynching, 27

Males, black
  frustrations as head of household, 103–4
  mental illness among, 141–42
March on Washington (1963), 182, 201
Marijuana, use of, 144, 146, 147
Marriage
  age of, 43
  assimilation through, 158–59, 163
  after out-of-wedlock childbirth, 101
  rate, 100
  slavery and, 3, 96
Matricentric family, 96, 97–98, 101–3, 104, 105, 136
Median age, 41–42
Memphis Firefighters v. *Stotts*, 215–16
Mental illness, 138–43. *See also* Health
Methodist church, 116, 118–19, 120
Metropolitan government, movement toward, 114–15
Mexican-Americans, drug addiction among, 145
Michigan, University of, 163
Middle class
  cultural assimilation and, 155
  defining, 65
  family patterns in, 105–6
  political behavior of, 111
  in rural black community, 60
  in urban black community, 61, 62–63

Midwest, the
  black public officials in, 112
  desegregation of schools in, 74
Migration
  institutionalized white supremacy and, 25
  from South, 27, 44, 184, 208
  urbanization, 46–48, 51–52, 97, 117–18, 167
Militancy, black. *See* Revolt, black
Military service of blacks
  ban on segregation in, 31
  during Civil War, 16–17
  during World War I, 27
  during World War II, 30
Ministers, black, 116–17, 118, 123
Minority group, blacks as largest visible U.S., 36
Mississippi, University of, 178–79
Mississippi Summer Project, 182–83
Montgomery Bus Boycott, 122, 123, 176–77
Moorish Science Temple of America, 122
Morphine, use of, 145
Mortality rates, 5–6, 39–41
Mothers for Adequate Welfare, 169
Moynihan Report, 99–100
Municipal officials, 113
Muslim Mission, 119, 122, 155, 211

Narcotics addiction, 143–47
National Advisory Commission on Civil Disorders, 160, 196
National Association for the Advancement of Colored People (NAACP), 26, 28, 62, 180, 187–89
National Association of Manufacturers, 215
National Baptist Convention, U.S.A., 118
National Baptists Convention of America, 118
National Black Political Convention (1972), 212
National Commission on Marihuana and Drug Abuse, 143–44, 145
National Conference for New Politics (1967), 190, 198
National Conference on Black Power (1967), 189
National Council of Churches, 191
National Guardsmen in Little Rock, Arkansas, 178
National Institute on Drug Abuse, 146
Nationalism, black, 64, 76, 124, 137–38, 155, 205–12
  components of, 206
  cultural, 208, 211–12
  expressions of, 209–12
  tradition, 206–9
National Opinion Research Center, 162
National Organization of Black Elected Officials, 210
National Student Association, 189–90
National Urban League, 62, 104, 143, 187–89
National Welfare Rights Organization, 169
Nation of Islam, 119, 209, 212
Native culture, 6–7, 115, 153, 154
Negro American Labor Council, 191
Negro Convention Movement, 207
Negro Factories Corporation, 208
Negro Family: The Case for National Action, The (Moynihan), 99–100
Negro renaissance, 28
Neoconservatives, 217–18
Newark, New Jersey, uprising in, 194–95

New Deal policies, 29
New York City
  black population density in, 58
  community control of schools in, 77
  drug addiction in, 145
  Harlem, 53, 58, 120, 135, 145, 208
  residential discrimination in, 53
New York Citywide Coordinating Committee of
  Welfare Recipients, 169
New York State, study of mental illness in, 138–
  39
New York Times (newspaper), 65, 90
Niagara Movement, 26
Nonopiates, use of, 147
Nonviolence, philosophy of, 177, 179, 180
Norm, black, 143
Northeast and North Central states, the
  desegregation of schools in, 74
  distribution of blacks in, 44, 45
  historical trends in black political life in, 108
  income in, 87
  religion in, 117
  residential segregation in, 57
  rural black communities in, 53

Oberlin Colleges, 189
Occupations, 77–86
  business employment, 83–86
  of free blacks, 14
  gains from 1940–1980, 78–80
  gap between blacks and whites, 77–78
  government employment, 81
  income and, 88–89
  of slaves, 4–5
  social stratification and, 60–65
  unemployment, 42, 81–83, 103, 166, 184
Officials, public, 112–15
Organic psychoses, 140
Organization, political, 110–12
Organization of Afro-American Unity, 198
Organization of Latin American Solidarity, 198
Out-of-wedlock births, 100–101, 104
Overseers of slaves, 8, 9

Paranoia, cultural, 143
Pennsylvania, mental illness among blacks in, 139
Philadelphia, Pennsylvania, study of juvenile de-
  linquency in, 137
Plessy v. *Ferguson*, 24
Police
  black, 210
  relations with, 130, 131, 136, 137, 167, 194, 195
Policy Planning and Research of Department of
  Labor, Office of, 99
Political awareness, 196–99
Politics, 106–15
  black participation in, 21, 25
  coalition, 188–89
  historical trends in, 107–8
  organization and behavior, 110–12
  public officials, 112–15
  voting rights, 14, 21, 25, 26, 29, 107, 108–10,
    168, 181, 183
Poor People's Campaign, 169–70
Population, characteristics of, 36–50
  age and sex composition, 41–43

density in urban black community, 57
family system in 1980s, 97–99
fertility, 37–39
of free blacks, 13–14
health and mortality, 5–6, 39–41, 138–43
size and growth, 36–37
See also Regional distribution
Populist movement, 108
Poverty among blacks, 89–90
  despair in the slums, 183–86, 193
  family stability and, 103
  Poor People's Campaign, 169–70
Power
  civil conflicts over distribution of, 168–69
  ethnic, concept of, 190
  See also Black Power movement
Pregnancy, teenage, 104–5. *See also* Birth rate
Prejudice
  attitude-receptional assimilation and, 161–63
  behavior-receptional assimilation and, 163–68
  of police, 136
  See also Discrimination; White supremacy, institu-
    tionalized
Presbyterian church, 121
President's Commission on Mental Health (1978),
  141
Prestige criteria, 61, 64–65. *See also* Social stratifi-
  cation; Socioeconomic status
Primary assimilation, 158
Primary elections, 109
Prisons, 131, 134, 137–38
Professional occupations, employment in, 78–80
Progressive National Baptist Convention, Incorpo-
  rated, 118
Protest movement. *See* Civil rights movement
Psychoses, 138–43
Public behavior, social stratification and, 62–63
Public education. *See* Education
Public officials, 112–15
Puerto Ricans, drug addiction among, 145, 146
Punishment of slaves, 4, 8–9

Race relations
  Compromise of 1877 and, 22–23
  Jim Crow laws, 23–25, 97
  recent alterations in, 196–201
  rise of unions and, 29–30
  transformation into urban problems, 46–47
  See also Violence, racial; White supremacy, insti-
    tutionalized
"Racial succession," 52–53
Racial violence. *See* Violence, racial
Racism, 91
  family stability and, 103–4
  growth of black community and, 51
  mental illness and, 141, 143
  social deviance and, 130
  in social institutions, 163
Radical Reconstruction, 20–22, 107, 108
Reagan administration, 90, 103, 214–18
Reconstruction, 19–23
  black church during, 116–17
  Compromise of 1877, 22–23
  Radical Reconstruction, 20–22, 107, 108
Red Shirts, 22
Red Summer (1919), 27
Reformist society, United States as, 218

Regents of the University of California v. *Allan Bakke*, 216
Regional distribution, 43–48
  age according to, 42
  behavior-receptional assimilation by, 164
  desegregation of schools by, 74
  income according to, 86–87
  in 1980s, 98
  residential segregation by, 57
  rural-urban, 42, 45–48, 53
  South-nonSouth, 43–45
  structural assimilation by, 156, 157
  See also South, the
Regional government, movement toward, 114–15
Regional officials, 113
Relative deprivation, 195–96
Religion, 115–24, 212
  affiliations, 118–19
  civil rights and the church, 55, 118, 122–24, 181
  developmental history, 9, 115–18
  of lower-class urban blacks, 64
  of middle-class urban blacks, 62
  in rural black communities of South, 54–55
  structure and patterns, 120–22
Renaissance, Negro, 28
Republican Party, 22
Resettlement of blacks in Africa, 207–8
Residence, differential income between blacks and whites by, 87, 88
Residential segregation, 52–53, 54, 57, 157
Resilience, 105
Resistance. *See* Revolt, black
Respectability, social stratification and, 60, 62, 63, 65
Responsibilities, government, 168, 169–70
Revolt, black, 175–204
  beginnings of, 175–79
  Black Power movement, 168, 169, 186–92, 205
  civil rights movement, 55, 118, 122–24, 179–83, 191, 192–93
  consequences of, 192–201
  despair in slums and, 183–86
  of slaves, 10–13
Richmond, Virginia
  destruction during Civil War, 18
  planned slave revolt in, 10
Riots, race, 15, 27, 194–95, 196
Roman Catholic Church, 119, 121
Runaway slaves, 12–13
Rural areas
  birth rate in, 38–39
  black communities in, 53–56, 60–61
  churches in, 121–22
  distribution of blacks in, 42, 46–47
  social stratification in, 60–61

Savings and loan associations, black, 85
Schizophrenia, 140
School
  attendance, 71, 72
  Catholic, 121
  de facto, segregation in, 166–67
  facilities, 73–74
  See also Education
Schoolteachers, status of, 64
SCLC, 169, 180, 186, 189, 269

Secondary assimilation, 158
Segregation
  de facto 166–67, 180
  in education, 71–74
  growth of black community and, 51
  index, 57
  Jim Crow laws, 23–25, 97
  residential, 52–53, 54, 57, 157
  in the military, 16–17, 27, 30, 31
Self-esteem, increase in, 209–10
Selma-to-Montgomery march, 183
Services, religious, 120–21
Sex
  composition of population by, 42–43
  differential income between blacks and whites by, 87, 88
  drug addiction by, 146
  mental illness rate by, 141–42
  occupational status by, 80
  public officials by, 114
  unemployment rate by, 82–83
Sexual promiscuity, 96–97
Single-parent families, 96, 97–98, 101–3, 104, 105, 136
Sit-in movement, 179–89
Size of black population, 36–37
Size of family, 98
Slavery, 1, 2–15
  attitudes of white people toward, 7–9
  black ownership of slaves, 14
  Civil War and, 15–19
  Compromise of 1877 and, 22–23
  education during, 70
  evolution of, 2, 7
  family system in, 95–96
  free blacks and, 2, 7, 12, 13–15
  general characteristics of, 2–6
  laws on, 3–4, 7
  legacy of, 164
  loss of native culture in, 6–7, 153, 154
  reactions of slaves, 9–13
  religion during, 115–16
  social stratification during, 5, 59
Slave traders, 10
Slums
  despair in, 183–86, 193
  uprisings in, 194–95
Small-business enterprises, decrease in, 84
SNCC, 179, 181, 186, 189
Social contacts, interracial, 156–58
Social deviance. *See* Deviance, social
Social institutions. *See* Institutions, social
Socialization, 105–6. *See also* Assimilation into American society
Social stratification
  of black community, 59–65
    black v. white, differences in, 64–65
    rural, 60–61
    urban, 61–64
  crime and, 135
  cultural assimilation and, 155
  family patterns and stability and, 99, 105
  mental illness and, 139–40
  political behavior and, 110–11
  in slavery, 5, 59
Social welfare. *See* Assistance
Society for the Propagation of the Gospel in Foreign Parts, 115

Socioeconomic status, 65, 69–94
  birth rate and, 38–39
  crime and, 134, 135
  education and. *See* Education
  income and, 86–90, 166, 184
    dissolution of marriage and, 100
    in government employment, 81
    in 1980, 98
    poverty among blacks, 89–90, 103, 169–70,
      183–86, 193
    in professional jobs, 80
    in rural black communities, 54
  in 1986, 193
  occupational status, 77–86
    in business, 83–86
    of free blacks, 14
    gains from 1940–1980, 78–80
    gap between blacks and whites, 77–78
    government employment, 81
    income and, 88–89
    of slaves, 4–5
    social stratification and, 60–65
    unemployment, 42, 81–83, 103, 166, 184
  redistribution of blacks to improve, 44
  relative deprivation, 196–97
South, the
  black public officials in, 112, 114
  desegregation of schools in, 74, 75
    resistance to, 176–79
  disfranchisement of blacks in, 25, 26, 107, 108
  distribution of blacks in, 43–45
    by age, 42
  income in, 86–87, 89
  migration from, 27, 44, 184, 208
  politics in, 107, 108
  religion in, 117
  residential segregation in, 57
  rural black communities in, 53–55
  structural assimilation in, 156, 157
South Africa, apartheid in, 199
Southampton County, Virginia, Nat Turner's revolt in, 11
South Carolina, mental illness among blacks in,
  139
Southern Christian Leadership Conference
  (SCLC), 169, 180, 186, 189, 269
Southern Manifesto, 177
Stability, family, 96, 97, 99–105
Standard of living
  demands for satisfactory, 169
  of slaves, 5–6
  See also Socioeconomic status
State legislators, black, 113
Status
  juvenile delinquency and, 136
  of slaves, 3, 5
  See also Socioeconomic Status; Social stratification
Stereotypes, 63
Stimulants, 144
Store-front churches, 120, 122
Stratification, social. *See* Social stratification
Structural assimilation, 156–58
Student Nonviolent Coordinating Committee
  (SNCC), 179, 181, 186, 189
Subculture, drug, 146
Subfamily, 98
Substance abuse, 143–47
Succession, "racial," 52–53

Survey Research Center of University of Michigan, 163

Teenage pregnancy, 104–5. *See also* Birth rate
Tenderloin section of New York City, 53
Thirteenth Amendment, 21, 24
Title VI of Civil Rights Act, 74

Underemployment, 103
Underground Railroad, 12
Unemployment among blacks, 42, 81–83, 103,
  166, 184
Unified House of Prayer for All People, 122
Union Army, 16
Unionism, 29–30
Unitarian Church, 121
United Nations, 198
United States Colored Troops, 16
United States Commission on Civil Rights, 58, 74,
  167
U.S. Congress, blacks in, 107, 112, 114, 210
U.S. Constitution
  Thirteenth Amendment, 21, 24
  Fourteenth Amendment, 21, 24, 26, 108–9
  Fifteenth Amendment, 21, 26, 108–9
U.S. Supreme Court, 213
  on affirmative action, 215–16
  antisegregation decisions by, 31, 55, 71–73,
    167, 175–76
  on housing discrimination, 165
  institutionalization of white supremacy and, 23–
    24
  on interracial marriage, 158
  on voting rights, 109
United Steel Workers of America v. *Weber*, 216
Universal Negro Improvement Association
  (UNIA), 28, 155, 208
Upper class
  cultural assimilation and, 155
  in rural black community, 60
  in urban black community, 61–62
Uprisings. *See* Riots, race
Urban areas
  age distribution in, 42
  birth rate in, 38–39
  black community in, 56–59, 61–64
  churches in, 120, 121
  distribution of blacks in, 46–47
  drug addiction in, 145, 146
  social stratification in, 61–64
Urbanization, 46–48, 51–52, 97, 117–18, 167

Value conflict, 168, 169–70
Value system, 211–12
Veterans, unemployment of, 83
Vietnam War, 83, 137
Violence, racial
  against churches, 123
  during civil rights demonstrations, 182
  over desegregation of schools, 177–79
  after King's assassination, 200–201
  residential segregation and, 53
  riots of summers of 1963–67, 194–95, 196
  during World War I, 27
Voting behavior, 111

Voting rights, 107, 108–10, 181, 183
    after Civil War, 21
    discrimination against, 168
    disfranchisement, 25, 26, 107, 108
    of free blacks, 14
    during New Deal, 29
Voting Rights Act of 1965, 108, 110, 183, 192, 213, 214

Washington, D.C.
    black population density in, 58
    black upper class in, 62
    interracial marriages in, 159
Watergate scandal, 213
Watts, uprising in, 194
Welfare dependency, 103

West, the
    black public officials in, 112
    distribution of blacks in, 44, 45
    income in, 87
    residential segregation in, 57
White Citizens' Councils, 176
White-collar occupations, employment in, 78
White primary, 109
White supremacy, institutionalized, 23–31, 218
    black response to, 25–26
    Great Depression, 28–29
    Jim Crow, emergence of, 23–25, 97
    New Deal, 29
    religion and, 117
    during World War I and aftermath, 26–28
    during World War II, 30
Wilberforce University, 15
World War I, 26–28, 44
World War II, 30, 44